DEREK

Marian K. Aiken

Edited by Susan Little
Manuscript formatted by Cathi Bouton
Photos edited by John Dewing
Name sign model – Miles R. Nelson
Photo of Marian on back cover by Kaitlin Esaw
All other photos submitted by Marian Aiken
Pen and ink portrait by Mary Burkhardt

Printed in the United States of America

ISBN 9781502768520

"This is a success story! A young woman, single and with a severe hearing loss, who decides to fight the system by adopting an infant with three strikes against him from the get-go. She makes a home for Derek and fronts for him with the medical profession as he progresses from infant to teenage boy." ~ *Bob Simon*

"Readers of this book will get a glimpse into the perfect communication between a mother and her son that most people would not think possible given the physical circumstances. Should the reader doubt the value in disabled or special needs people or not respect them for the unique, valued and cherished individuals they were born to be, I promise that would change after reading **DEREK**." ~ *Steve Lagna*

"This story opens the reader to the idea of considering that every life is precious, and if a child is disabled they still have immeasurable gifts to offer to the world.

~ *Sue La Fetra*

"In giving herself away and loving unconditionally, the author finds joy, peace, and contentment while caring for her son. This is an uplifting and inspirational story." ~ *Annette Simon*

"Any person who reads this story will certainly live an experience and gain valuable insight into understanding the real needs of special needs children and the unconditional love they can give. I just wanted to hold the pages close to my heart." ~ *Donna Barkley*

In honor of my sons ~

for without your presence in my life,

I would never have experienced the

incredible journey which I have lived the past 37 years.

May each of you continue to strive and

make the best of your individual situation,

to overcome the extremely unique

challenges placed upon you.

With love,

Mom

Introduction

I was twenty-one and in my senior year at Salem College in West Virginia, majoring in elementary education, when I began living and working with people who were deaf and used American Sign Language as their primary mode of communication. The student teaching requirement was coming up and I knew I would have great difficulty working in a regular elementary school because of my own severe hearing loss. I spoke with my advisor to see if I might do my student teaching with deaf children. Yes, it was possible! Arrangements were made for me to live in an apartment in the administration building on the campus of the West Virginia School for the Deaf (WVSD) in Romney, West Virginia.

There was one major problem: I knew almost no sign language!

I was born hard of hearing, and since my hearing loss was progressive, I had little usable hearing by the time I was in college. Still, because I could speechread well, I had never learned American Sign Language (ASL), the native language of the American Deaf community. Where the spoken language utilizes auditory (hearing) and vocal (speaking) features, ASL uses visual (seeing) and spatial (physical movement) properties. ASL is a complete, complex language and the third most-used language in the United States.

Not only did I not know ASL, I hadn't socialized with people of the Deaf culture. Anxiety overtook me as the time approached to leave the small college town of Salem, West Virginia, and venture almost one hundred miles over scenic Route 50 to Romney in my brother's old Chevy Nova, which I was permitted to use during my senior year. Just driving the old Nova through the mountains of West Virginia was scary enough without thinking of what I had gotten myself into. What on earth made me suggest going to WVSD to student teach? Why didn't I think before offering to enter a world that would be so different from what I knew? My college advisor and I had visited the school a month earlier, but my doubts didn't register until I was on the road in the old car loaded up with my clothes, typewriter, and books. I so much wanted to turn back! I was in a state of panic and my stomach felt queasy, but I drove on.

I finally reached Romney and found my way to the school's administration building, where I was shown to my apartment and began to unpack my things. It was a weekend and I had until Monday morning before meeting the staff I would be working with in the elementary department. I didn't know anyone and I was too frightened to go to the dining room for meals because I couldn't communicate with the people there. It was like being in a foreign country without knowing the language or the culture. I was petrified!

I quickly fell in love with that welcoming community. I felt safe walking down the street. The people were friendly and would wave, say hello, and introduce themselves like they did in my even smaller hometown in Pennsylvania.

I soon began to interact with the students more and more freely, learning sign language from daily interaction with them and with the Deaf adults who worked at the school. I'd point to food selections in the dining room or objects in the environment and gesture "what?" Students would compete to see who could show me the sign first. They'd laugh at my clumsy attempts to get my fingers and hands to do the right thing. What seemed like a game to the students was a serious survival skill for me. Since I had depended on speechreading since childhood, my eyes and brain were already trained to catch small, quick movements. I am certain this helped me learn the signs more quickly than if I had been an auditory learner. After three or four weeks, my initial fear of completing that long drive from Salem seemed absurd.

Romney is nestled in the northeastern panhandle of West Virginia and was the largest community I had ever lived in. I finished my student teaching, received my degree in Elementary Education, and was hired to return to WVSD as a teacher in the fall of 1972. I was excited to continue to live in Romney and even more excited about teaching. WVSD was the state-run residential school that educated and met the unique needs of deaf children in West Virginia. Although some families moved into the area to allow their deaf child to live at home and attend the school, the majority of students were housed in large dormitories. Each fall brought children who were deaf from every corner of the state into peaceful, quaint Romney.

The buildings on campus were large brick structures. Enormous columns bordered the steps into the elementary building. The classrooms were located in the center of the building; large wings on either side served as the dormitory living quarters. Girls from pre-kindergarten through sixth grade lived in one wing, boys in the other. Each side had a large playroom with a TV and study area. The dining room was in the basement. Also in the basement was a small bowling alley that could be used on weekends or when the weather prohibited the children from playing outside on the spacious, well-kept grounds. The sleeping areas were just large rooms with beds lined up in rows, so there was virtually no privacy. Each child had a closet and storage area for clothes and personal items. The children became friends quickly and many friendships continued on into adulthood.

Other parts of the campus served the middle and high school deaf students, who had dormitories and a dining room of their own along with classrooms and various vocational training shops. The large gym and indoor swimming pool were shared by all students who attended the School for the Deaf, as well as the students from the School for the Blind, which was located on the lower part of the campus.

The children were happy to be together and among others who used the same language. Their hands would move fluidly as they shared their thoughts, made jokes among themselves, and became friends. Most of the students were excited when it came time for them to return to their families for holidays and vacations, but there were a few who did not look forward to these visits home. For some children, the school had become their family; it was a place where they could socialize, interact, understand each other, feel secure and cared for.

For all of us, communication was key. To this day, many parents of deaf children neglect to learn and use ASL with their child, and the child feels a certain degree of isolation. When these kids arrived at WVSD, they moved into a community where their peers "spoke" the same language. Finally, they were on equal footing and completely engaged as part of a real community.

Some of our students were in foster care. Some of these children did well, but most of them didn't have the parental love and security that every child needs. One was Joey. He was a beautiful child with blonde hair and hazel eyes. His parents hadn't learned how to communicate with their deaf child and used corporal punishment to make him obey even when he had no idea what was expected of him. He had been passed from one home to another with foster parents who also couldn't communicate with him. By the age of fourteen, he had lived in a total of eleven different foster homes.

Another child in foster care (who was eventually adopted) was Terry. Terry had been born with hearing but had been deafened at a young age by meningitis (inflammation of the brain). He had an impish look with eyes that were magnified by his thick-lensed glasses. His deafness shattered his parents' dreams for their child, and they didn't know how to communicate with him or how to care for him. He developed emotional difficulties and was placed in foster care. Although his foster mother loved him and cared for him, she never learned his language. Other children had been removed from their parents due to neglect or for other reasons that were kept confidential.

I was concerned for children like Joey and Terry who had experienced little stability in their short lifetimes. I decided to take action.

And now my story truly begins ~

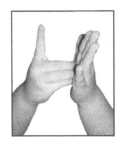

Chapter One
Home study - 6 months old

*T*hree times I drove to the welfare office and turned around without even going into the building. On my fourth attempt, I didn't drive. I walked from my home. I was determined to enter that front door and apply for a license to adopt a child. I was sweating, my hands were clammy, and my stomach was full of the jitters as I opened the door of the West Virginia Department of Welfare, Romney office on September 16, 1976.

The idea of adopting a child had been on my mind for more than a year. I had gotten to know students at the West Virginia School for the Deaf who were in the foster care system and it was clear they would have benefitted from a secure home. As a residential school, WVSD provided the only sense of stability for some of these children. Maybe I could take in one of them!

I was pretty sure that foster and adoption placements were handled by the Department of Welfare, and I was suspicious of the agency. My concept of the Department was that it helped poor, nonworking people with finances, and I did not like that concept. Why I had developed such a negative concept about that department is still beyond me. I was not certain I wanted to be involved with them.

The friendly receptionist invited me to take a seat. I didn't know how the communication would go. *Will I be able to understand the social worker's speech? Does she have false teeth that slip around when she talks? Maybe she knows some ASL?* I hoped she was not chewing gum because I had a tough time understanding people who were. Soon, the receptionist returned to inform me that a social worker named Sandy would be with me in a few minutes.

Panic flowed through my body and had me looking for the women's restroom. I hadn't even filled out any papers and here I was, meeting with a social worker! Shortly, a well-dressed, slender lady with blonde hair in a French twist entered the waiting area. She smiled pleasantly as she introduced herself as Sandy and invited me to a smaller room where we could talk in private. She was friendly, warm, spoke clearly, and was not chewing gum. After introductions, she told me how the adoption program operated in West Virginia. I was overwhelmed with information. She was talking about many things I had never experienced, and I was wishing I had brought a notepad. Sandy handed me several forms to complete and return, and I hoped she felt positive about me after our first meeting.

I completed the lengthy application forms as soon as I got home. I was so excited to begin the process of adopting that the next day I drove straight to the Department of Welfare as soon as school was finished and submitted my application. Within a couple of days, I received a letter from Sandy stating that she would make a home visit sometime during the next week. *Wow,* I thought, *things are moving quickly! Is my home clean enough to present to a social worker or should I get busy and scrub every little corner? What will she be looking for and discussing with me?* My emotions were running so high I could hardly focus on my job.

Before an adoption can take place, the agency completes a "home study" that puts prospective parents through a thorough evaluation with a social worker and staff. Sandy came to my home and seemed to think my place was acceptable. Then we sat at my kitchen table, me fidgety but trying to create the impression that I was calm, and Sandy all business with her note pad and pen. *Should I offer her a glass of water or a cup of coffee?* It was too late. The question and answer period had already started. She liked to write a lot during our meetings.

"Marian, why do you wish to adopt a child?" Sandy asked with a smile.

"Um... Uh... Well, I've seen some of the deaf children at school who are in foster care who could benefit from a more stable home environment. Um...let's see.... (*My mind is tossing* around the reasons...*if only I can get the right words out of my mouth!*) Also, I feel I spend too much time on my schoolwork and would really enjoy using my after-school time in a different way," I stammered.

Sandy nodded and went on, asking, "Marian, how will your family accept a deaf child? Will they be supportive of your desire to adopt as a single parent?"

"I'm certain they would be," I responded, shifting a little in my seat. Actually, I hadn't yet mentioned my idea of adoption to my family.

"Okay, great." Sandy said.

Then she focused on my hearing loss. I felt a little uncomfortable about sharing some of my personal history, especially about being deaf. At this time, people with disabilities still faced discrimination in society: in the workplace, in obtaining higher degrees in education, even in being approved for home and car loans. *Will my loss of hearing become an obstacle in adopting?*

It wasn't always obvious that I was deaf. Since I had some residual hearing as a child and into my teenage years, my speech was mostly clear. However, it wasn't perfect, and people who didn't know me would sometimes ask what country I was from. My ability to understand conversations by speechreading and watching the speaker's face to help make sense of what was being said was still fair in quiet settings and if I knew the topic of discussion. I had relied heavily on vowels to understand what people were saying, and when I could no longer hear vowel sounds I had to question how much conversation I understood correctly with speechreading alone. I also couldn't hear most environmental sounds. Most people who knew me weren't aware I had lost what low-frequency residual hearing I had as a child. Still, I could no longer fake hearing on the phone, comprehend TV dialogue, or even follow lectures in college classes without an interpreter. In fact, I didn't even have a phone in my home. All of these changes affected how I perceived myself. Where did I fit? With people who had hearing and couldn't sign or with deaf people who used ASL and little speech?

I had spent the first twenty-one years of my life in the hearing community with people who knew no ASL. Now, I was finally settling into a different community where people could sign, and I very much wanted to be comfortable among this group of people. I was still adjusting.

I decided to get directly to the point. "Sandy, do you think my deafness will hinder my ability to parent a child?" I asked.

"Marian, I have high respect for the deaf members in our community and those who work at WVSD," she replied.

I was hugely relieved; her outlook on deaf people was a big plus for me.

Next, the inevitable topic of finances came up. I got very tense when Sandy asked if I would be able to support a child on my income and afford medical insurance as well. To me, this was private information, but for the adoption process it needed to be recorded for all to see. I also had to provide names of six people to serve as references, confirm that I would be able to provide appropriate childcare when I was working, pass a physical, and go through a process that confirmed I wasn't a criminal. Finally, we talked about what type of child I wanted to adopt. Did I prefer a little girl or a boy? Would I accept a child who was a different ethnicity than I? Sandy continued to ask questions, while I continued to respond. Sandy continued to record information, and I continued to wonder what she was writing.

We met several more times over a two-month period. Eventually, my interviews and medical exam were done, my references were submitted, and my background check was completed. On my application I requested a preschool-age deaf child, possibly one with one other minor disability. And the waiting began.

Sandy remembers: **The West Virginia Department of Welfare was looking hard for families that would adopt special needs children. We had a long list of young couples that wanted normal, healthy, white infants. These children, as they became available, would be placed immediately with families that had been waiting, in many cases, for several years. The State decided to review the lists of children waiting for placement, many of whom were considered hard-to-place children. These were children who were over the age of five, had different ethnic backgrounds, were sibling groups, or were handicapped children who had many different needs. The State decided to**

4

look for families that would accept special needs children and prioritize completing adoption studies on these families over the families that wanted normal, healthy white infants. This was about the time Marian decided to explore the possibility of providing a home for a child.

Sandy would sometimes show up unannounced on her way home from the office since she lived a short way from me. My heart always skipped a beat when I saw her at my front door. *Has she found a deaf child for me?* I couldn't wait to hear what she had to say.

For months, there was no good news and it seemed that the waiting would never end. There was only one deaf child listed for adoption in the state and he had already been placed in a foster-adopt home. I had told only a few close friends of my plans. After a time, they understood that asking if I had heard anything yet was not a welcomed part of our conversation.

Then, one day Sandy dropped by to tell me that the Department of Welfare could not find a new foster home for a student at WVSD who was in foster care. "Can Rossie stay with you temporarily until another foster family can be located?" she asked.

My mind flashed back to the day a couple of years earlier when Rossie came into my classroom and begged me to take him home for the winter break. I held back tears, as I had to tell him it wasn't possible. I didn't have permission to take him home at that time and there wasn't adequate time to get permission. Besides, he had a foster home to go to then. Still, Rossie had frequently spent weekends at my home and even had traveled with me to my hometown in Pennsylvania one year for Christmas vacation. Sandy was Rossie's social worker; she knew our history together, and she knew I could communicate with him. Also, my home had now been approved for adoption.

I liked the permanence of adoption and hadn't planned to be a foster parent. However, "Yes, I can do this for a couple of weeks," I stammered. Last-minute paperwork was done, a bedroom cleared of my junk, and Rossie moved in.

Rossie was not the kind of child I had planned to adopt. He was deaf but he was not a preschool-aged child. He was twelve and had been in foster care for more than seven years.

He was bright, handsome, strong, but troubled. Rossie had been influential in my decision to adopt, but I didn't foresee him living under my roof. His temporary stay stretched on. He'd stay in the dormitory during the school year and with me during vacations. I deeply loved Rossie and his sense of humor when he was relaxed and calm, but he was quick to anger. In general we got along and enjoyed each other's company. I encouraged him to do his best in school and tried to support him emotionally as best as I could.

Meanwhile, Sandy and I continued to look for a younger child for me to adopt. We had heard of a few children in different states who needed a permanent home. One little girl who lived in New York was deaf from meningitis and had a slight limp. She appeared to be a happy five-year-old, and I was certain she would be the perfect child for me. However, she found a home with a married couple. Same story for other deaf children I thought were a good match. My hopes for adopting began to falter. *Will I ever find a child to be my daughter or son? Why is this taking so long? It's been more than two years!*

Then one day in early spring of 1979, Sandy dashed in late for a foster parent meeting I was attending. She found a chair across from me, sat down, and mouthed the words, "A baby boy in Morgantown (West Virginia)."

I was stunned. I became restless and unable to focus on the meeting. According to the agenda we wouldn't have a break for another hour. Every few minutes my eyes shifted from the speaker to my watch to Sandy, hoping she'd mouth a few more words.

At last there was a break in the meeting.

"The information I have to share is not extensive," Sandy said as we huddled in the corner. "The baby was born January 3, 1979, over two months premature," she continued. "He is deaf and delayed in all areas. He has been in the hospital almost all of his life. Would you be interested in checking into this?"

I was not even certain I correctly understood the information Sandy was giving me. I was trying to focus on her speech. I just couldn't be sure of everything she said. Before I had an opportunity to ask any questions, it was time to return to our meeting.

I paid no attention to what was going on in the room. *My application is for a deaf, preschool-age child, not a baby! A deaf baby! How will I manage a baby?* I had no intention of adopting a baby, particularly one that was severely disabled. *What on earth will I do with a baby? A deaf baby boy—what will I do with a deaf baby boy?* Oh, I was beside myself. *Can I possibly care for an infant and continue my work at school and be a foster mom for Rossie?*

We didn't know the extent of the baby's additional disabilities even though Sandy had spoken with Janet, his social worker in Morgantown, a couple of times. Janet used terms we just didn't understand: asphyxia, hypoglycemia, hypocalcemia, hyperbilirubinemia, staph sepsis, disseminated intravascular coagulation and intra-cranial hemorrhage, apnea and bradycardia spells, respiratory distress syndrome, just to name a few! *How will I ever learn to cope with these conditions? I can't even pronounce many of them!* Sandy and I discussed what might happen to this child if I should decide to become his mom. The more we talked, the more depressed I became. At times, I felt I should just forget about this child and continue to look for one who fit the description in my adoption home study.

Yet I could not forget this baby. He was so close to home, only about 100 miles away, not in New York or Texas or Oregon. He was born in West Virginia and needed a home. The trial period could determine whether I felt competent caring for him. Not being able to use the phone, I drove to Sandy's office. She was out, but I left a note asking her to make an appointment for us to go to Morgantown to speak in person with Janet and meet the infant.

About two weeks later Sandy and I made our first visit to Morgantown. I was glad she was driving. I wouldn't have been able to focus on the road had I been behind the wheel. Sandy attempted to carry on a conversation as she drove, but my mind was not focusing clearly and I didn't want to talk. We met with Janet before going to the foster home where the infant had been placed.

"Marian, do you have any questions you'd like me to answer before we go to the foster home?" Janet asked.

"I can't think of any right this moment," I responded and glanced toward Sandy for some suggestions. I just wanted to meet the baby. I hadn't seen any pictures of him and had only a vague idea of what he might look like. Finally, Janet drove Sandy and me to the foster home.

We pulled up in front of an enormous house. I didn't recall ever having seen such a big home. There were several steps to the front door where a couple of children and a big black dog met us. Ruth, the foster mother, was feeding the baby in the kitchen. After she finished, she held him for a while—a long while. *Is she ever going to share him with me? I didn't come all this way to watch her hold him.* I kept quiet because I didn't want to be pushy, and finally Ruth placed him in my arms.

I felt his body rattle with each rise and fall of his tiny chest. Suddenly his body stiffened as he arched his back. *Dear Lord, don't let me drop him. Why did Ruth lead me to this uncomfortable chair where my feet can't even reach the floor and expect me to hold this infant?* I stroked his misshapen head; it was turned strongly up and back to the right into my left shoulder. I rubbed his small chest as it rattled with each breath hoping that would relax him. His little hands were drawn into fists and his thumbs wouldn't move. His eyes were blue. The left one could hardly be seen and the right one was in constant movement. I followed his eyes with mine to see if he could focus on anything at all. I couldn't figure it out. I held him, but it wasn't easy. I had never seen a baby like him. My left arm began to ache.

I could tell that Sandy, Janet, and the foster mother were discussing his birth history, hospitalizations, medical issues, feeding difficulties, and prognosis, but I was barely paying attention. I couldn't focus on the conversation by speechreading and take care of this baby in my arms! I just wanted to cuddle him and see if I could get a response from him.

I really needed to change position. Before I moved, I wanted to have a plan for shifting the baby into my right arm. *How do I do this? What do I do with his floppy head? I sure wish this chair was more comfortable!* I finally put my right hand behind his very floppy head and somehow safely shifted him around so I could cradle him in my right arm. This was a much better position and I could now see his right eye better. He had relaxed. I could still feel his chest rattle with each breath, but I loved his cute turned up nose and the tiny toes that stuck out at the foot of his pale blue sleeper. He had pretty hair—fine, wispy, and strawberry-blond. *I think you've already won my heart little one.*

Once I became accustomed to his movements, I felt more comfortable holding him.

Sandy looks back: **I remember traveling to Morgantown, West Virginia, to meet this little boy, his foster parents, and his social worker. We entered the kitchen area where the foster mother was sitting at the table feeding this infant. At the time, he was several months old but had been born premature. He was born from a diabetic young mother who was a student at West Virginia University at the time of his birth. Due to the fact that he was born premature, his lungs were still underdeveloped and he had difficulty breathing. The foster mother explained that at times he would choke or forget to breathe because he was so young. The child was very thin and tiny, considering his age. His birth weight had been low and he had not gained much weight due to the fact that he had been extremely ill, off and on, since he was born. The child also experienced frequent ear infections and respiratory problems. He sounded very congested and did not seem to have much life about him. He looked frail to me and I hoped that Marian was not disappointed in her first meeting with him.**

The foster mother explained that she would need to flick the bottom of his feet sometimes in order to make him continue breathing. She said he would often stop breathing and there were many times when he was rushed to the emergency room at West Virginia University Hospital because of his respiratory problems. She said he was on various medications and that he was thriving, though slowly. I kept thinking how fragile this little fellow was and that most of his life he had spent in the Neonatal Intensive Care Unit. I was surprised that Marian appeared to feel very much at ease in handling this small child. The foster mother also seemed to appreciate the fact that Marian was so interested in this child to whom she herself had devoted so much time.

"Marian, it's time we head back to Romney," Sandy said. I would have given anything to sit in that uncomfortable chair for another hour. My heart sank as I stood to give the baby back to the foster mother.

"Just put him in the bassinet, Marian."

With a gentle squeeze, I reluctantly laid him in his bassinet.

Then, with my back toward the others in the kitchen, I signed to him, "I love you!" I didn't use the one-handed 'I love you' symbol that is made up of three fingerspelling handshapes for "I," "L," and "Y." In my opinion, it really doesn't convey much feeling. It's almost equivalent to simply waving goodbye. I leaned slightly forward and looked him straight in the eye as I signed "I LOVE YOU!" As I signed this to him there was a pause in the movement of his right eye, and he made actual eye contact with me. *Will this critically ill child join me permanently in a life and home where he will truly realize the meaning of these three signs I'm giving him today?* I hesitated as I turned to leave. *Will I ever see him again?*

I felt a lump in my throat, and my legs felt heavy as we walked to the car. I could still feel his warm body and labored breathing on my chest.

"Marian, what do you think?" asked Sandy as she turned around in the front seat so I could speechread her from the back seat. I don't recall if I answered or not.

"Marian, did you like him?" Janet asked.

Once again I am not certain if I responded with words or only a blank look and a nod. They looked at me, puzzled. I just couldn't express myself to them. I was feeling sort of numb. I was overcome with a mixture of sadness and joy. I wanted to cry more than anything else. And I was scared. I don't remember ever having such intense feelings before. I was glad I was sitting in the back seat alone because a zillion thoughts were running through my mind: *A baby, a very sick baby, can I care for him? Do I really think I can do this? He is not like any baby I have ever known. What can I expect from adopting such an infant? Who will take care of him while I work? He will need so much love and that I can provide. However, with my limited knowledge is it fair to bring such a child into my life?* Over and over again these thoughts ran through my mind. I needed time to think.

I had told my parents of my plans to adopt a child, and they knew that I was making the initial visit that day. They would be expecting a phone call with an update about the baby. Since I had no phone, I drove to my friend Donna's house, told her about my day with the baby, and sought her help in calling my parents. I would speak for myself, and she would sign whatever my parents said.

"Hello, this is the Aiken residence," Donna signed to me when my father answered the phone.

She handed me the phone: "Hi Dad. Is Mom around too? Can I talk to both of you at the same time?" I shifted from one foot to the other.

I passed the phone back to Donna. "Sure, let me get her on the other phone," Donna signed to me while my Dad spoke. "Hold on a second, Marian."

"Hello, Marian. This is Mom. I am here now," Donna signed.

Donna passed the phone back to me so I could once again speak, and my parents could hear my voice. "Mom, Dad, I met the baby today in Morgantown," I began. "Umm..." I stammered and hesitated trying to think of what to say. "He is very small for his age, and he has lots of medical problems," I continued. "He is not like any baby I have ever seen before in my life, but he is rather cute in his own way." I tried to think of positive things to say. It was really hard to know what my parents were feeling on the other end of the line. "I really need to give this a lot of thought and consideration before I make any decisions about this baby," I said, choking back tears.

Donna signed for my father: "Marian, we know this must be a difficult decision for you, but we will love any child you bring into our lives."

Mom added: "Marian, we will support you in whatever decision you make."

Soon after my first visit with that tiny infant, I began to have morning sickness. It was just something that went along with having a baby, I guess.

I so much wanted to give this child a chance. However, I knew almost nothing about how I could care for him. *How will my family and friends react to all of this?* They said they would be supportive, but they had yet to see the child. *Can I actually take on such a responsibility and do what is needed in the correct way?* My thoughts went back and forth between 'Yes, I can' and 'No I can't make this commitment.' However, something deep inside kept urging me to go ahead and give it a chance. And that is what I did. Once again I went off to Sandy's office to request that she keep me updated on the baby's medical condition, and to tell her to inform Janet that I definitely was planning to bring this child into my life.

During that waiting period, I was not able to concentrate much of the time. When a woman is expecting a child, she knows the wait is usually nine months. For an adoptive parent the wait can be an eternity, especially when you know the child is so close and yet so far. I decided that I should begin gathering some necessary supplies and set up a room for the baby. I also felt comfortable discussing the adoption with my friends and began to include Rossie in my plans. I needed to help him to feel important and not neglected, which was no easy task with a teen who had been passed around from house to house for most of his life. For a rough and tough sixteen-year-old, the concept of having a baby enter his life was almost incomprehensible. Rossie didn't like the idea at first, but with time, and having him help me fix up a bedroom for the baby, he warmed up to the idea.

One day my friend Sue came over. We walked up the street to see my garden, which was on a neighbor's property. When we were walking back to my place I noticed some cars parked in front. "Sue, why are Donna's, Nancy's, and Claudia's cars here?" I asked.

"I don't know," answered Sue with a straight face.

I began to think something was wrong and quickened my step as we headed toward the house. I never locked my doors when I went to the garden since I lived in a safe neighborhood where people watched out for each other. I ran up the steps and nervously opened the front door fully expecting something was wrong. Instead, "SURPRISE!" A surprise baby shower for me, complete with gifts of blankets, toys, clothing, shampoo, and diapers.

I would be able to buy most supplies for the baby from a local store. However, because of my deafness, I would need some special equipment that wasn't as easily available. I was able to locate a Deaf couple in town who no longer needed their baby-cry signal, which I could borrow until I got one of my own. A baby-cry signal is a device that parents who are deaf use to alert them when their child needs attention during the night. A microphone and transmitter are placed near the child's bed and a receiver goes in the parents' room. When the child makes a noise, the receiver sets off a signal light that awakens the parents. I felt relieved to have this piece of equipment that would allow me to sleep instead of worrying that I would not be able to hear the baby.

I waited and waited for a definite go-ahead from Morgantown. *Will they actually permit me to become this child's mom? How much longer will it take to make a decision?* While I waited, I decided on a name for the baby. Since he was an infant and deaf, he probably didn't even know he had a name. I had a couple of names I especially liked. I decided on "Derek," which meant 'ruler of the people.' *Will my Derek become a ruler of people or a ruler of his own life? Or a ruler of my life!* I would retain his given name, Michael, for his middle name.

Rossie and I created a name sign for Derek. In the Deaf community people are given personal "sign names" to identify and refer to a specific person. When used, this eliminates the need to fingerspell the name each time a person is referred to. Rossie wanted the name sign to be almost like his. You can see Derek's name sign in the chapter headings with his initial (fingerspelled) "D" on the palm of the left hand. This became Derek's name sign and only his, not every person who has the name Derek.

The waiting continued. I became impatient and edgy. *When will I be able to see him again and hold him?* In my spare time I worked in the garden and started to make a quilt for Derek. Since I was not sure about his vision, I appliquéd large animals out of many different fabrics, colors, and textures. This helped me pass the time and focus on something other than the delay. One day, I had a strange feeling that Derek would not be coming to live with me, or at least not soon. I could not stand being alone with these thoughts. I walked next door and confided in my neighbor, Jenny.

"I have this strange feeling something is wrong with Derek," I said with a lump in my throat.

"You're too excited!" she replied. "Just continue to be patient and you'll be a mom before you know it."

A couple of hours later, Sandy was at my front door. She had received a call that Derek was back in the hospital with possible seizures.

About two weeks later I returned to Morgantown to learn more about Derek. Apparently, having a prospective adoptive parent visit with the foster family was unusual. Of course, not many special needs adoptions had taken place in our area and none with a prospective parent who was deaf. Although I now had a phone and TTY in my home, at the time I did not have access to operator relay services for my TTY machine. (A TTY or TDD is a special piece of equipment that allows a deaf person to type messages and receive phone calls by reading on the TTY machine what the other person wants to communicate. In the 1970s, it was the only way for a deaf person to make phone calls independently.) However, I could only call people who had a machine in their home. Therefore, I couldn't call the foster home to ask specific questions as they came to mind. I could only communicate in person or through Sandy. If I wanted some confidential information I was out of luck. I was frustrated and felt trapped. It was important that I learn as much as possible about caring for Derek. How could I do this if I could not communicate directly with Ruth, the foster mother? I needed to learn his "norm" in life. Fortunately, Sandy took on the responsibility of arranging more visits for me.

Sandy recalls: **Marian wanted to be able to learn the child's body rhythms and vibrations so that she would know that these were either normal for the child or that the child was needing medical attention. Marian, being deaf herself, had to go more by vibrations rather than hearing the child's noises, such as the congestion in his lungs and bronchial tubes. She also needed to be able to feel when he was crying because the child did not make many sounds when he cried. If you were not looking at him, you might not realize that he was crying. I felt that she needed a much better idea of what she was considering in taking this special child into her home.**

I made two or three informal visits alone with the foster family. Then, Sandy and I traveled once again to Morgantown for a day full of doctor appointments at West Virginia University Hospital Medical Center where Derek had been born. There was a large group of people present: Ruth, nurses, social workers, residents, doctors, and a sign language interpreter. I almost never jitter my feet but I did that day. Every time I'd glance at a different person, their eyes were on me. I'd try to give a pleasant smile, but my face always felt stiff and my body rigid. *Will everything I do be criticized? Will these people determine my ability to care for this infant today?* These thoughts kept running through my mind. We waited for what seemed like hours until Ruth had me hold and feed Derek. Surprisingly I felt relaxed and at peace when I focused on him and mentally blocked out the people surrounding us. Then suddenly, we were called into a small examination room, and Ruth asked me to undress him. As I began to unsnap the sleeper, Derek's body immediately stiffened. I stood there puzzled and wondered where to begin. Although the sleeper was rather stretchy, Derek's body was not! His arms became stiff, his head rotated strongly to the right, his legs were fixed at the knees. Derek was not smiling either. In fact, there was an expression of fear on his face. *Does my face show fear as well? Why did Ruth have to pick this specific outfit for the day?* After much struggling and tugging, I finally managed to get the sleeper off. I felt like a fool and had worked up a good sweat!

I had made arrangements for an interpreter to be present for all of these hospital appointments (hospitals didn't provide them at all in those days). Obviously, it was critical that I understood what the doctors were saying. Most of the time I felt comfortable speechreading in small groups or with people I knew, but a hectic day of rapid speech and unfamiliar words was really taxing. My nerves were stressed beyond my ability to depend on speechreading only.

Among the group was a physical therapist. When I realized who this person was, I became self-conscious about the way I was holding Derek. Still, I pulled a book out of my bag that a friend had given me about baby massage and infant exercises and showed it to her.

"What do you think about using ideas from this book with Derek?" I asked.

"I think several of the ideas would be of benefit to him," she responded after flipping quickly through the book. "How would you reward him if he did something that was correct during therapy time?" she asked politely.

"The reward would be visual and tactile in nature, a touch

or a pat," I said. "When some receptive language begins, then the reward can be more of a visual/sign response," I continued. I think they were kind of shocked that I would even attempt to use sign language with such a young baby. To me, it was just common sense that vocal/auditory rewards wouldn't benefit a deaf child.

While we waited to be seen by the next doctor, the therapists, hospital social workers, and nurses expressed an interest in learning about my work with the deaf children at the school. Sometimes I felt more like a public relations person than a prospective parent.

The neurologist arrived and had a great deal of depressing news to share. I definitely was not prepared to hear things he was about to say. "He will most likely die before his first birthday," the doctor said, looking me straight in the eye. "If he does survive, he would be better off in an institution. It's questionable whether he will ever be able to bond and interact with those in his environment," he continued. "We suspect his vision is very poor and with his profound deafness, he may respond as a deaf/blind child as well as profoundly mentally retarded. He may be a toe walker but most likely will never walk at all." The neurologist continued to speak without much facial expression. He went on to talk about the possibility of seizures developing and said that Derek could possibly have hydrocephalus (excessive fluids on the brain). The list continued to grow with more negatives than positives. I was saddened and shocked to the point where I literally could not respond as I snuggled Derek in my arms. *How can anyone predict the life of a four-month-old child?* It was far beyond my comprehension.

We saw many more specialists that day, so many that I honestly do not remember most of what they said. Did they say anything positive? I'm not sure since my mind had been shocked into numbness during the meeting with the first doctor. However, I do remember it was much easier to put the sleeper on than it was to take it off.

Derek was exhausted from all the waiting, poking, and all the people. He finally went to sleep in my arms before it was time for me to return home. *Have I proven to these people that I am capable of caring for this child?* I felt insecure for the next couple of days trying to figure out what they would make of all the questions I asked, or didn't ask. Again Sandy and I discussed with hope the idea of my bringing this infant into my home on a trial basis.

I worked on Derek's quilt and readied a room for him. I traveled to my brother's in Ohio and brought back the family bassinet.

Paula was a friend from church who lived across the street from my workplace with her husband and children. I always enjoyed watching her interact with her kids, so I asked her if she would consider caring for Derek while I taught. I tried my best to make clear his health issues so that if she agreed to care for him she would know what to expect. Having Derek close during the day was the safest situation I could arrange other than to hire a nurse to come into my home, which was a couple of miles from school. With Paula I'd be able to run across the street to feed him at lunchtime.

The waiting continued. My friends continued to support me emotionally, and other supports began to solidify. In a small town like Romney people get to know each other. One of my neighbors was on the rescue squad. I contacted the squad and let them know of my plans to care for Derek. Since they didn't have a TTY, making a phone call would be tricky if I needed to contact them in an emergency. So, I asked them if it would be okay to call and say several times, "This is Marian Aiken. This is Marian Aiken. This is Marian Aiken on Potomac Avenue and I need help immediately!" They agreed to keep our address posted.

Another arrangement I made was with my personal doctor to accept Derek as a patient. Once again, I explained what I knew about what might happen and what care he might need. I tried to relate his medical history and reasons he had been hospitalized. To my relief, she agreed to give it a try.

Sandy remembers: **I was very apprehensive about Marian accepting this child into her care due to the fact that his needs were so extensive and he appeared so frail. I thought about Marian and her devotion to her career as a teacher in the Elementary Department at the School for the Deaf. She worked with preschoolers and kindergarten-aged children. I know she spent many long hours developing workbooks: drawing,** coloring, as well as developing new strategies to assist the children in learning new concepts. I wondered how she would have time to continue this devotion as well as remain able to care for a multi-handicapped special needs child. I was afraid that she would be overwhelmed eventually by the demands that would be placed on her.

I also was very concerned over the fact that Marian was deaf and might not be able to be made aware of this child not breathing in the middle of the night or know when he was crying or choking. Of course, I discussed this with Marian as to what her plan of action would be in caring for this child. She explained all the preparations that she had made with the rescue squad, her physician, locating a babysitter, and finding a cry signal. Marian convinced me that she definitely was ready to accept this child into her home and that this was a very well thought-out and explored commitment on her part. I then had to convince my supervisor that Marian was capable of caring for the infant. After several meetings with the supervisor, he agreed that our agency should not stand in her way in accepting this child into her home. Arrangements were then made for Marian to have Derek placed with her as soon as he was well enough to make the trip to Romney.

Days turned into weeks and the waiting period lingered on. I continued to feel excited but concerned about my ability to care for Derek, especially when and how much of his medications to administer. I made arrangements for several more short visits to the foster home before Derek's health would permit him to join me in Romney. To my surprise, I was asked to stay in Morgantown one weekend while the foster family was on vacation. I was so anxious and excited that I practically skipped everywhere and my jaws ached from constantly smiling. I made arrangements for Rossie to stay with friends and found someone to take care of my dogs.

Ruth had charted all the information about his medications and had color-coded them as well. For example, those with red dots on the bottles were given three times a day. Those with yellow dots were given twice a day. Those with red and blue dots were given three times a day and stored in the refrigerator! I felt as if my hands would shake off my wrists as I learned how to measure correctly all the liquid medications Derek had to have, even though he had such a hard time swallowing. *Can*

I do this? What if I make a mistake? Please God, let me learn all these important things and not blow it!

Ruth also had complete instructions about his feeding schedule and when and how much formula he should have. She showed me how to mix it and what the best temperature was for him. Thank heavens she had written everything down so I could reread all the information. Otherwise I don't think I could have remembered everything. She had even talked to her local rescue squad about keeping information on Derek for the weekend, but she hadn't gotten the immediate support that I'd gotten from the squad in Romney. It made me happy and proud to know that my smaller community was more willing to commit to helping me, even before Derek was a resident of Romney. But I was still nervous and insecure. *Is the foster family, especially Ruth, reluctant to leave me in their home for the weekend knowing that I can not use the phone?* I know I would have been! However, they packed up their car and drove away.

Their house was extremely large in comparison to my place, and it came with a huge black dog. Fortunately I loved animals, especially dogs, but I was accustomed to littler dogs, either with smaller tails or no tails at all. Thump, thump, thump went the dog's tail on the hardwood floor. More than once the vibrations of the thumping spooked me. To add to the eeriness, the electricity went off the first evening. Panic! *My gosh, what am I going to do now? How will I ever find my way around this huge house? I wish it were my place in Romney where at least I can walk around without getting lost in the dark.* Thankfully I knew where Derek was: resting contentedly in my arms. I snuggled him close and a fearful tear or two trickled down my cheeks in the darkness of this strange house. Luckily, Derek's social worker, Janet, happened to come by shortly after the power had gone off to check on us. Between the two of us, we managed to find a flashlight. I was able to give Derek his medications. She stayed with us for more than an hour until the power came back on.

According to the schedule, it was time for Derek to have a bottle and go to bed. *Do I really want to put him in his bassinet? How will I know if he is awake? Will he sense that Ruth is not nearby?* Oh, decisions! Eventually I put Derek in his own bed to fall asleep, but as soon as he was sleeping soundly I gently transferred him to the double bed where I was to sleep. I was restless but dozed off for a couple of hours.

The next morning Derek was rather startled when he awoke to find himself on this big bed next to me. A little grin was on his face. Soon after we had awakened, a public health nurse came to demonstrate CPR for infants. It was hard for me to speechread her and concentrate while holding Derek and feeling his body vibrate with his labored breathing. However, I think being there alone and having the nurse and Janet see how I handled Derek was worthwhile. That had not been the point of my being there, but I'm convinced it helped ease their doubts about the ability of a single person who happened to be deaf to care for such a child.

It took Derek more than an hour to drink five to six ounces of formula. At five months old, his sucking skills were worse than a newborn's. I would place the nipple gently in his mouth as I positioned a couple fingers under his chin and rubbed his cheeks to try to stimulate his oral responses. He had poor lip closure around the nipple of the bottle. *How will I ever have time to feed Derek when I need to go to work?* Well, we had all the time in the world that weekend to get it right. I felt like I was making progress when I finally realized one trick to feeding him, work left-handed. Because of his head position he needed to be held in my right arm while being fed, which encouraged him to turn his head more midline. I'm thankful I had fairly good use of my left hand.

I was giving him medications every two hours or so. This was the beginning of my clock-watching habit. I now checked the clock frequently to make certain all medications were given on time. *How will I ever get anything done if I need to keep measuring medications so frequently?* I certainly had a great deal to learn!

When not dressing, feeding, or giving Derek medications, I held him and held him and held him some more. I played with him as much as you can play with a five-month-old with severe cerebral palsy. I would sit with my legs stretched out on the sofa and Derek on my lap with his head at my knees. I would take a bright-colored toy and move it slowly near my face to encourage eye contact. Then I would slowly, very slowly, hold the toy a foot from his eyes to see if he could visually follow it. I would massage his right hand gently and extend his arm to stimulate him to reach out and attempt to hold what I had in my hand. All this time, I maintained eye contact with him. His body would relax, and he would begin to smile spontaneously with a cockeyed, toothless smile.

With the freedom of not having everyone's eyes on me that weekend, I also signed to Derek. I just signed everything I was thinking. I signed about his little white bunny. I signed silly things and serious ideas. I signed songs and stories. He focused on me. He watched and seemed to try to keep his head in position so he could see. Yet he had been labeled as not being able to attend, bond, or survive. I took a couple of photographs, and my first picture showed him wearing the new yellow and white sweater and booties my mother had knitted and sent our way.

By the time the foster family returned, I was ready to leave their enormous house and return to my home, Rossie, and my dogs. I was not emotionally prepared to leave Derek behind. I hugged everyone good-bye and signed, "I love you" (all three signs!) to Derek. I walked slowly to my car, shuffling my feet all the way. With a lump in my throat I got into my

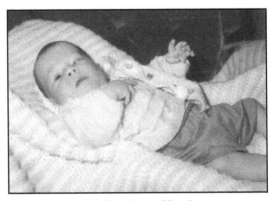

My first photo of Derek

car and drove three or four blocks, which was enough to get out of sight of the foster family's home, before I pulled over to shed some tears and whisper a prayer. *Derek, hurry up and become strong enough so you can join me in Romney. Derek, you are going to be a special son and we will have much happiness together. Thoughts of you fill my heart all the time.* I wiped my eyes, took a deep breath, and started the drive home a few hours away.

In the end, it turned out that this waiting period had a purpose: Derek grew somewhat stronger physically and was more able to break away from Ruth. One day she said, "I love this child and feel God has put him here for a purpose. Whatever happens with Derek is God's will." As he grew stronger, it appeared he learned that my touch was different from Ruth's. I noticed he relaxed more and his eye contact was better with me when I signed to him. He smiled a lot. I hoped this would help make the transition a bit easier for him.

Derek had fought hard to stay alive and continued to fight, one breath at a time. He needed unconditional love and stimulation if he was to survive. *Am I smart enough to learn about his disabilities and care for Derek?*

I knew very little about congenital cerebral palsy (CP). Cerebral palsy refers to motor impairment that appears in infancy or early childhood as a result of abnormalities in parts of the brain that control muscle movements. The diagnosis of cerebral palsy is not always made at birth and even after a child has been diagnosed, the extent and severity of involvement cannot be determined immediately. One could only speculate what caused Derek to have a malformation of the brain: premature and low birth weight, a lack of oxygen at delivery, circulation problems, internal bleeding in the brain, or severe physical trauma to the birth mother. Derek's CP could have resulted from one or more causes. It made no difference to me what caused his CP, I desperately wanted to give him the best chance possible to develop and survive.

July 27, 1979, fifty-nine days from when I first learned about him, Derek made his transition into his new home with me in Romney. Sandy and I left Romney early in the morning as we made one last trip together to Morgantown. Ruth told me not to bring anything and that she would have all Derek's things ready for him. I was excited and was a much more pleasant travel companion on this trip than I had been on previous trips. Close to seven months old now and weighing about twelve pounds, Derek was at last strong enough to make the trip to his new home. Ruth dressed Derek in a light blue tux suit with soft blue shoes. As I lifted him gently from Ruth's arms, that fantastic smile beamed at me. *Does he actually remember who I am? Can he possibly understand how overjoyed I feel?*

The temperature was close to 100° that day and the

humidity was unbearable. A combination of nervous sweat and the weather made my clothes stick uncomfortably to my back. My forehead perspired and my glasses kept sliding down my nose. I could see I needed to learn a new skill: how to hold this spastic infant and push my glasses up at the same time. *Come on, let's get our good-byes over with and get into the car.* All I wanted to do was to hit the road as soon as possible.

Various members of the foster family loaded Derek's supplies into the trunk and everyone came to the car to say good-bye again. I handed Derek back to Ruth for one last hug before placing him in his car seat. She handled things well, but I secretly cried. My tears were of happiness for me and of sadness for her. She knew she could always have contact with Derek. She had cared for him well in the short time she'd had him.

At long last, Sandy started the car, and we were en route to Romney.

As Sandy focused on the road, I focused on Derek strapped into his car seat behind us. I must have turned to check on him every five seconds or so. If his pacifier fell out, I put it back in his mouth. If he woke from his catnaps, I stretched my arms across the back of the front seat and shook a toy for him to look at.

Sandy knew of a nice restaurant along the way, and we pulled over there to rest and eat. It was my first time to be seen in public with Derek as my son. Once we were seated in the restaurant, I tenderly lifted Derek out of his car seat. Sandy helped prepare his bottle. "How old is the baby?" the waitress asked as we ordered our meals.

"Almost seven months," Sandy responded.

"Oh, he is so small," the waitress continued. "Is he your child?" she asked as she turned to me.

"Yes, he is now **my** son!" I exclaimed.

Sandy looks back: **The day Marian and I traveled to Morgantown, West Virginia, to bring Derek home was a very special day. Marian had waited a long time for this day. She had been very patient with our agency and with her adoption workers in helping all of us get used to the idea of Derek being placed in her home. She was also convincing as to the support system that she had developed in the Romney community. She** helped us to see that she was very ready for this placement to occur. It was hard for all of us to understand why Marian wanted to give up her independence of being a single lady to being tied down with an infant that was going to require a lot of her time and energy due to his tremendous needs. Still, Marian was very determined to make this happen.

I know it was hard for the foster mother to let Derek go. She had grown so attached to him because of all the time that she had devoted in caring for him. But, I also felt that she knew that Marian would keep in touch with her and she would be able to continue to see Derek grow. I remember that when we returned to Marian's place, she placed him in his bassinet in the living room. Derek looked up at her smiling, and I felt he knew that he had found his mother and his home.

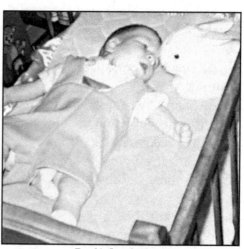

Derek's first day home

Almost the minute we arrived in Romney, neighbors and friends started coming to the front door, happy for me and excited that Derek had finally arrived. Even my dogs had to check the baby out. I called my parents.

As my friend Donna once again held the receiver, I dialed the number.

"Hello, hello," Donna signed to me as my parents answered the phone in unison.

I glanced across the room to catch a glimpse of Derek in the family bassinet as I burst out with pride, "Mom, Dad...your new grandson has arrived!"

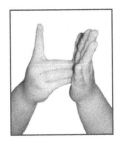

Chapter Two
6 months -
9 months old

I was overjoyed to have my new son, Derek, home. As is the case with most new parents, I was greatly excited. However, I was also insecure for the first week or so and couldn't get enough sleep. Derek, adjusting to his new surroundings, could be restless at bedtime. My concerns that he would stop breathing and that I would not catch him in time kept me awake at night. The social workers and I discussed a respiratory monitor for us to use at home, but at that time I felt a person should be able to live with his body as it was and not use machines just to stay alive. So, I woke up frequently to check on him.

One morning I had put Derek down for a nap on the sofa while I ate my breakfast. When I got up to put my dishes in the sink, I glanced over to see if he had woken up yet. He lay still and quiet and his lips were *blue*. I dropped my dishes on the floor as I ran to him, trembling and screaming, "Derek, wake up. Derek, breathe! Derek, Derek, please breathe. Breathe!" Fear had me screaming to my son who could not hear my voice.

I picked him up with shaking hands, gave him a pat on the back, a flick on the bottom of his foot, and a gentle shake. Tears ran down my cheeks. Thank God I had gotten there in time. Derek began to breathe and the color returned to his lips. I trembled as I plopped into the rocking chair, my tears wetting his fine hair while I held him tightly. I did not want to put him down for fear he'd stop breathing again. Once I lifted him away from my chest and looked him in the eye, he looked at me with a peaceful face and an impish smile as if to say, "What's going on here, Mom?"

For every parent, the early days are full of firsts in his or her child's life. Some of those firsts are more pleasant or relaxing than others. For example, when I was a high school babysitter, I had bathed lots of kids and it never seemed like a big deal. However, I was in for a great surprise the first time I attempted to bathe Derek! He may have been small, but because of his cerebral palsy, bathing him was a task that could leave anybody sweating!

Still, it became clear that Derek loved the water and being in the bathtub. I put several folded towels on the bottom of the tub to make it a bit softer for him. I had to be careful not to lose my balance as I knelt down to place him in the water. He'd become so excited that his entire body would arch and stiffen, making it difficult to hold him securely. Aside from the stiffness there was his extremely strong tonic neck reflex, which made him turn his head rigidly to the right side. He would not be able to turn it straight again on his own. His right arm would stiffen and rotate back while his left arm would do the opposite.

I had to use one hand to keep his face out of the water so he wouldn't drown and the other hand to get him clean. The muscles in my shoulders and back would cramp and ache. He loved to play in the warm water, and I'd let him until my knees were in severe pain. When I'd try to return to a standing position it was obvious that Derek thought it funny to watch Mom strain and struggle. He'd then become even more spastic, and I'd try with all my might to give him a "serious" look, which I could rarely do.

I quickly discovered I would never be dry by the time bath time was over, so I learned to put some towels or a rolled up rug on the floor for me too. Tiny as he was, bathing Derek was a tough task. I can hear the therapists now, saying, "Buy a special bathtub seat." Well, that would not have been to Derek's liking. He wanted to be in the water where he could kick and splash.

It was interesting to see how people would respond when meeting Derek for the first time. Rossie had been staying with friends the day I brought Derek home. He was a macho, six-foot teenager with mixed feelings about my bringing home a "not-so-perfect" kid. Nonetheless, there was a huge soft spot in his heart as well. He just melted when he first saw Derek, and they seemed to enjoy a special connection. Rossie would hold and rock Derek and try to feed him. He'd lie on the floor to be close by. What impressed me the most was that Rossie would sign everything to Derek, always getting some sort of response, and not feel embarrassed by how others felt about him signing to this little baby. Their love for each other was immediate.

Rossie feeding Derek

Neighbors, my colleagues, and my first babysitter had interesting first reactions to Derek:

He was so cute and adorable and a lot of work.

Derek always seemed so petite and fragile, but he had such a winning smile.

I was thrilled for Marian. However, when I first saw Derek, I'm not sure that I was prepared for the experience. He appeared to be a limp rag doll. I was shocked as I had never seen an infant quite like Derek before.

He seemed so helpless.

I loved his red hair!

I liked his smile. He physically moved very little but his smile said a lot.

I felt sorry for him in one way because of his condition and because his birth mother would abandon him, but I also felt he was lucky to be with someone like Marian.

He seemed so fragile and I just kept my eyes on him the entire time.

It was really exciting seeing Derek for the first time and thinking of all the exciting days ahead for Marian with him.

If it was interesting to see how people reacted when first meeting Derek, it was fascinating to see how he responded. You must remember that he spent most of the first six months of his life in a hospital, much of it in intensive care with little holding or hugging. Most premature infants have parents and other family members to visit them for feedings, rocking, and changing. Derek's experience with human contact in the NICU was mainly for purposes of medical treatment. As a result, when someone reached out to touch him, he frequently withdrew or became stiff and tense with the assumption that some kind of medical procedure would take place: blood drawn, medications administered, nasogastric tubes inserted for feeding (plastic tubes inserted through the nose which pass through the throat, down the esophagus and into the stomach), respiratory treatments, etc.

In the last couple of decades, the medical field has improved in the care of premature infants. Parents are encouraged to touch and hold their babies. Programs have been set-up for volunteers to cuddle and rock the infants when family members aren't able to be present. Infants who have positive physical contact seem to improve physically, have better weight gain, and respond more positively in general to overall medical treatment. It is extremely important that infants are nurtured physically and emotionally from birth.

Many of my friends were hesitant to hold Derek at first. Some just stood around and looked. Others were more courageous. They would pick him up and interact with him. As time went on, he learned who was most comfortable handling him and became more relaxed with these people. Likewise, I felt he was becoming more comfortable with my touch. He would not startle as much when I reached out to touch him. He would relax when I approached. Of course, I still needed to administer all his medications, but he also learned that he liked a variety of foods and that not everything that went into his mouth was medicine. It was clear to me he knew a medicine dropper from a spoon.

"Derek," I would sign, "You need medicine. Finish your medicine then you can eat bananas," followed by 'yum, yum' movements and lots of facial expressions. Each day led to more recognition of who I was. He would smile when I was in his line of vision. He made eye contact and relaxed. I was confident he knew I would handle him and care for him with love. Without a doubt, a mutual, loving relationship was developing.

Sandy recalls: **In the days that followed Derek's arrival in**

Romney, I knew that there was a special bonding occurring between Marian and Derek. Derek was very responsive to her visually. He would smile at her often. I also remember Derek smiling at Marian's two dogs. He would sometimes lie on the couch and the dogs would jump up on the couch and look at Derek. They were very protective and accepting of him. I felt that Derek also knew this. Derek appeared comfortable in Marian's care and she also was comfortable in caring for Derek. She appeared to be much at ease and not nervous at all when Derek would appear to be crying excessively or feeling uncomfortable in any way. Marian handled all of this very naturally and extremely well for a new parent. I could see that Derek was thriving in her care.

However, we didn't have a lot of time to adjust as a twosome after Derek got home. For various reasons, people were constantly coming and going. Some came to check if I needed anything, others came to bring a gift for Derek, some came out of curiosity, others came hoping to receive some fresh vegetables from the garden. Just three days after Derek arrived, we were expecting my parents and a family friend, Gift, to visit. I planned to feed Derek breakfast and give him a bath before our company arrived. While we were in the middle of breakfast my neighbor stepped through the back door and walked down the hall to where Derek and I were at the table.

"Marian, your parents just called me and said their motor home has broken down in Bedford, Pennsylvania," Jenny said.

"Bedford! Gosh, that's...what...two and a half hours from here!"

Jenny continued, "They'd like for you to maybe drive up and bring your mother and Gift back here while your Dad waits for the motor home to be repaired. Here's the location where you can find them," she said as she handed me a piece of paper with an address. "If you don't show up by one o'clock this afternoon, they'll just assume you and Derek could not make the trip and they'll come as soon as they can."

My parents had visited my brother in Ohio and then driven through northern Pennsylvania to visit relatives and friends. They stopped to bring Gift along to my place to meet Derek before returning to their home in Arizona.

"Jenny, what do you think I should do?" I asked. "Should I

try to make the trip up there alone with Derek?"

"Your Mom sounded pretty disappointed about the motor home and anxious to meet Derek. Why not give it a try?" Jenny encouraged.

While Jenny and I were having this conversation, Derek was waiting patiently for his next bite of breakfast. I signed to him, "Hurry, eat. We will go in the car meet Grandma, Granddad and friend." I gobbled down the rest of my breakfast and tried to wait patiently for Derek to eat a bit more without choking. I glanced at the clock and decided to forget the bath part of our schedule. Instead, I quickly shoved a few diapers, a change of clothes, and a couple of bottles into his diaper bag. I rushed out the door with Derek in his car seat, his diaper bag and my purse slung over my shoulder.

This was the first time I'd put Derek in my car. I fumbled with the seat belts before I figured out how to strap him in safely. As I absent-mindedly asked myself questions, "Where does this part go? I can't reach that part over there!", he would smile as if to say: "You'll get it one of these days, Mom." I finally got him buckled in and hoped the next time it would not take me more than five minutes.

I walked around the car to climb in and realized I wasn't really ready! *Oh gosh, I forgot his pacifier and the paper with the garage information Jenny gave me. Thank heavens I remembered before I pulled out. Marian, take a deep breath and slow down and think!*

I had never driven with a baby in my car. *Do I need to take curves a bit more gently? Will the motion of the car make Derek nauseated? If I need to brake quickly, will he startle and become more rigid?* Lots of questions ran through my mind. I used my peripheral vision to the max: eyes ahead, eyes on my speedometer, eyes on my rearview mirrors, and eyes on Derek. I drove a bit more slowly than usual with my precious son perched next to me. Another 90° day was predicted, but my car's air conditioner was in good shape. So began Derek's travels, sitting "shotgun" in front of the air conditioner!

Both my parents were retired teachers and their love for children and young people shone wherever they went. They could make the fussiest baby smile and parents glow with pride.

30

I was nervous about what their reaction would be to Derek. He was so different from what they were used to. They had very much enjoyed the deaf children I taught when they visited, and they welcomed Rossie and John, another student of mine, into their home. I had tried my best to describe Derek to them, explaining that although he was deaf, his other issues made him very different from my students. They already had one grandson who was a perfectly healthy baby. Would it be difficult for them to love Derek, who was only six months younger but so small and frail compared to my robust nephew? My nephew weighed twenty-five or so pounds in comparison to Derek's twelve and could already crawl, stand, and climb.

I was getting more and more anxious as I got close to Bedford. About a mile into the town I spotted the large sign of the garage where my parents waited and their disabled motor home was parked.

I stopped my car and got out slowly, stiff and shaky from tension. I took a minute to stretch then walked around the car to get Derek out of his car seat. His head turned strongly to the right as his body stretched and extended. However, he relaxed when I cuddled him and pulled away the back of his sleeper from his sweaty body. I opened the door of the motor home and climbed up the steps. Within minutes, Derek was in my father's arms, and my mother was taking pictures!

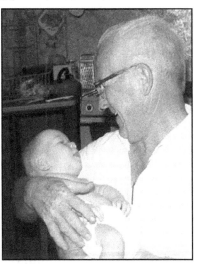

Derek meets Granddad

"What I remember most is that he looked up at me and smiled as I held him. I did not have any idea or feeling as to his disability." Granddad

"The very first time we saw him, he had this great smile; that was always a characteristic of Derek." Grandma

After an initial pass around, Derek to Granddad, Derek to Grandma, Derek to Gift, Derek back to Mom for some formula and a diaper change, I got a much-needed

Derek with Grandma

bathroom break. (It took a while before I learned how to take care of my own needs when I was traveling alone with Derek.) Dad was going to stay in Bedford until the motor home was repaired. The rest of us got into the car for the return trip to Romney. Mom and Gift sat in the back while Derek was in his car seat next to me, right in front of the air conditioner again. They would lean forward periodically so Derek could see them sharing smiles. Memories of that first meeting make me swell with pride knowing my parents immediately loved this fragile child I had brought into our family.

Like any grandchild, Derek received lots of attention that week from his visiting grandparents. Most of the time, he was in someone's arms being rocked or entertained. It was rather difficult to find appropriate toys to stimulate Derek with his limited physical ability. For instance, his profound hearing loss eliminated musical toys. However, Grandma was creative in what she would make for him. She began knitting small, brightly colored blocks that she stuffed with very lightweight material. She sewed a nylon ring on the corner of each block and then slipped the ring over one of his fingers or even his cortical thumbs (the thumbs are folded in the palm under the fingers), which could not be straightened out. Derek would try with all his might to lift that block into his field of vision and study it intently. If he was not in the mood to actually play with the block, Grandma would simply place it where he could look at the bright colors and letters. She began to sign with him and tell him the colors or the letters that she had knit onto the sides. This was just the first of many things Grandma and Granddad would make for this special grandson of theirs. They hit it off from the first minute. I can only say that I received much pleasure and joy because they accepted Derek as he was and shared their love with him just as they did with their other grandchildren.

I enjoyed traveling and had been doing so for several years. I would just pick up and go as the spirit moved me, sometimes traveling long distances to many states to visit friends and relatives. However, now I needed to prepare in a different way. Since Derek was under the care of the state when he arrived at my home, I was required to have written permission to leave the area with him. I had a difficult time comprehending the logic of this. If I were supposedly capable enough to care for him in my home, why would anyone question my ability to take him on trips? Fortunately, Sandy was able to get permission for me on the spur of the moment on many occasions.

It was not long after my parents left that I loaded up my car and took off to visit my friends on Long Island. Instead of being a single traveler with two dogs, I was now a traveling mom with one baby and two dogs. Just packing the car was a big change. In went diapers, formula, toys, stroller, baby clothes, blankets, car seat, bottles, medications, and, of course, Derek. His spot in front of the air conditioning also allowed him to see everything. I was certain that he would sleep while I drove such long distances. But to my surprise, he was observant of what he could see out the window from his car seat. He slept very little on that trip. When we arrived at my friends' home, Derek was the center of attention. I must admit, I was exhausted from the drive but Derek was not about to let me sleep that night. He was excited and wanted to play and have fun. It was like a slumber party for him.

It was wonderful to see my friends and be able to spend time with them. They did not shy away from holding or communicating with Derek in signs. However, I did sense their concern about his health issues. Questions kept popping into our conversations such as, "Are you sure he should be out here on the windy beach?" But at the time I was inspired to take Derek's socks off and move his feet around in the sand. To my surprise, he began to wiggle his toes and seemed to enjoy the activity. If I worried about every little thing concerning his health, he would live an extremely sheltered life. Where is a person to draw the line between a safe life and an enriched life?

After we returned to West Virginia, I noticed that my priorities were changing in my daily life. For example, instead of spending as much time as I usually did in my garden, I would simply pick the vegetables that were ready and not bother with the weeds. I'd put Derek in his stroller, and he'd come along while I harvested the vegetables. It turned out that he was crazy about squash, especially the butternut variety, baked in the oven and served with a bit of butter! That fall my garden yielded more than seventy-five large butternut squash and the two of us ate almost all of them. Of course, we shared a few here and there with various friends.

Instead of swimming laps, I would now do water exercises with Derek. They really didn't amount to much, just common sense play that included bending his arms and legs, turning his body from back to part way on one side and then rolling him the other way, turning his head from side to side, encouraging him to reach out for a simple toy and follow moving objects with his eyes. Instead of running at the track, I would go for pleasant walks with Derek in the stroller or an infant sling. Naturally, Rocca and Snooge, the dogs, would join us on our outings. Instead of reading biographies and other materials of interest to me, I signed picture baby books to Derek. Soon we both needed to make one more great change in our routine: I had to return to work.

School began and I took Derek to the babysitter I had made arrangements with. She seemed ready to care for him, but I would still run across the street to help feed him during my lunch hour. He spent much of his day sleeping or watching the sitter's children run around and play. I am not sure he was aware of what was really going on at that time. I did know that I was anxious for the school day to end so I could pick him up and go home to spend time together. My love for him just seemed to blossom more with each day.

We had been to see Dr. Giron, his new doctor in Romney, to meet each other and get refills for his medications. I might mention that speaking with Dr. Giron was most difficult even under the best of circumstances. She had a heavy accent, which makes speechreading harder. However, she would take extra time to repeat things for me and make sure I understood what she had said. If I presented her with a list of questions, she took time to answer them in a vocabulary that I could comprehend. Our second trip to Dr. Giron wasn't so casual. Derek was running a temperature of 103°F and was having an extremely difficult time breathing. Also, he was arching his body, clenching his fists, and stiffening his limbs. Feeding him was almost impossible when he was like this. The first time I saw him this way, I was terrified. Dr. Giron sent us to the small, local hospital so Derek could have his chest x-rayed, blood drawn, and then be admitted. I was not prepared for what was ahead of me, though I had known there would be times Derek would need to be hospitalized. The poor baby was petrified of the x-ray equipment and his stiffness made it extremely difficult to draw blood. Once again, the touch of humans was like that of his first several months of life—for medical needs rather than for comfort. Derek would try with all his might to cry, but there were no tears. Only very faint sounds coming from his already-damaged vocal cords could be heard above his raspy and labored breathing. I did my best to hold him and assist in whatever way was possible. After such stressful episodes, he would become like a limp, clammy rag doll and fall asleep in my arms.

I shed the tears he could not shed. I was certain he felt secure when I held him, and surely he knew that I did not want him to experience this pain. If only I could have held him in my arms until he was well again, it would have been comforting to me. Sadly, he needed to be placed in a croup tent for several days, and the time I could hold him was limited. Respiratory therapy began and he had to inhale medications followed by percussioning. Percussioning involves the use of soft rubber cups for patting on his chest and back to clear the mucus and fluids from his bronchial tubes and lungs.

Sometimes Derek would need to have his mouth cleared of secretions with a suctioning machine. IV's gave him fluids, antibiotics and other medications. I would sit nearby in a rocking chair hoping he would awaken and recognize me. I so much wanted to take him out of the croup tent to hold him for a few minutes. It was painful to sit by and watch his little body struggle for each breath. He was again the pale lifeless child I had met just months before. *Is the prediction of the doctors correct? Will he not see his first birthday?* At least he had been out of the hospital for a little over two and a half months. This was the longest period of time he had been well since his birth. It was also long enough to allow me to bond with Derek and see that he could enjoy life when he was at his best health.

After sleeping all night in that hard rocking chair, I would rush home, take a shower and head off to school. At lunchtime, I'd jump in my car and drive to the hospital to check on Derek. Then, back to school until the end of the day. Soon, it would be time to go home, take care of the dogs, grab a bite to eat, and go back to the hospital. Luckily, Romney is a small town. The drive from the hospital to my home took only three minutes. From school to the hospital was just over a five-minute drive. I would bring my schoolwork with me to help pass the time. It seemed like Derek might never get out of that oxygen tent! It was the old kind that needed to have ice placed in a large container at the head of the crib. A rather large orderly would come in and just dump the buckets of ice into the container. The entire crib would shake and often needed to be moved away from the wall. Predictably, every time this happened Derek would be sound asleep, and the process would scare the living daylights out of him. I tried my best to remind people to work a bit slower around Derek or to let him see them before doing something like that if he was awake. Often, however, my suggestions were forgotten or ignored.

Meanwhile, on top of my worries was the stress of speechreading all the medical staff and the need to learn new terminology related to the medical treatments Derek received. Also, while he was in the oxygen tent I had tried to sleep with one hearing aid on hoping that I would hear if Derek awoke at night. Of course it was unrealistic to think I would hear him through the oxygen tent. I just had forgotten I could not hear much any more.

After nine days, Dr. Giron felt Derek was well enough to breathe room air again. Oh, how thankful I was this time had come! We both were totally exhausted from this first hospital experience together, and I was really afraid. *Is it reasonable to hope that Derek's health will improve?* I clearly remember the day when Dr. Giron came into the room as I slept in the rocking chair with Derek snuggled in my arms. The past several nights I had rarely slept, so sleeping, especially with Derek in my arms, was a blessing. Dr. Giron awakened me to check on Derek and then gave orders to leave us in the rocker.

I began to see how much I was going to be dependent on her expertise in order to keep Derek in the best health possible. Those twelve days may have been the longest of my life. When Derek was released from the hospital, we returned home to start strengthening his body all over again.

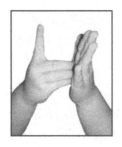

Chapter Three

9 months - 1 year old

*D*r. Giron discharged Derek on a Friday afternoon to allow us the weekend to begin recuperating from his hospitalization. We were so happy to be home in our own peaceful environment. We could sleep when and where we wanted to, either in our individual beds or with Derek in my arms and the dogs at our feet. There was no constant intrusion of nurses coming to take his temperature and blood pressure or bumping his bed while checking the IV pump. No more cleaning people screeching chairs on the floor as they mopped or the vibrations of the wastebaskets being dropped on the floor after being emptied. No more being startled awake with ice being dumped into the container at the head of his crib for the oxygen tent. Oh peace, blessed peace! I could actually walk around barefoot, get a cup of coffee when I wanted one, and sit with my feet up in a comfortable chair. We spent the weekend with me giving Derek respiratory treatments in between sleeping, playing, and just being together. I could hold him as much as my heart desired.

Then, before I knew it, the weekend was over. I needed to go back to work, and Derek needed to go back to the babysitter. Getting back into the school week was surprisingly smooth after that first experience in the hospital. Derek was glad to be with people he knew and in a more relaxed setting than the hospital.

Sandy had contacted Crippled Children's Services in our county so we would be able to receive physical therapy for Derek. Fortunately, the therapist worked at the local elementary school, which was not far from our home. The therapy space was filled with bright-colored mats, therapy balls, hammocks, special positioning chairs for children with physical disabilities, standing positioners, and wedges. Derek was only about nine months old when he began working with the therapist, John, who was a former Mr. USA. This very muscular man worked gently, yet firmly, with Derek, who was remarkably small. I took Derek once a week for therapy. John showed me various exercises to do with Derek as often as I was able. He showed me how to position Derek's body to see if he could learn to roll over and other exercises to strengthen his neck so that he could lift his head off the floor when placed on his stomach. I showed the babysitter how to do the exercises, and she would try to do some with him during the day. Derek enjoyed physical therapy. I was incredibly thankful for this because it certainly made our time together meaningful. He worked hard to improve and perform his best. After many of the sessions Derek would be totally exhausted, so exhausted that he would fall asleep before we ever left the parking lot to go home.

My class of deaf children was curious about what was going on in my life and how Derek was doing. They were most concerned during his hospitalization. When Derek was feeling better, we took a field trip to his therapy one day, and everyone was excited. Derek just smiled the entire time knowing he was showing off for them. He had also begun his career as "teacher." After going to his therapy, my eight-year-old students were asked to write about their experience that day. Recently, I found I'd kept their papers all these years.

Here's what they noticed:

> **Derek can't walk or sit or roll over on the mat.**
> **I was sad but Derek is not mentally retarded.**
> **He has C.P. Derek is deaf and cannot talk.**
> **Derek needs to practice everyday on his therapy.**
> **Miss Marian blows on his face so he will hold his head up.**
> **God will help Derek at physical therapy.**
> **I am sorry that Derek can't sign and needs to learn so
>   many things.**
> **I saw Carrie and Derek and felt really awful because they
>   cannot hold their heads up.**
> **Derek has friends at his school.**
> **Derek and his friends are happy like I am with my friends.**

With a hearing child, a therapist uses verbal commands. However, Derek's deafness made this impossible, and sometimes it was equally impossible to sign directions. So we had to devise a code that could be consistent with everyone who worked with him. I'd lie him on his stomach to practice lifting his head, hold his body with both my hands, then blow lightly on the back of his neck or hair instead of trying to give a signed command. We also worked in front of a mirror to allow for eye contact between us. Some other codes I came up with were two light squeezes on a limb, tickling the bottom of his foot with my toe, or blowing him a "hurricane" kiss if he was facing me.

Derek showed slight improvement with regular therapy, as he could sit up on the corner of the sofa for short periods of time and sit a bit more upright to be fed. His arms and legs were moving more and his ability to hold small toys in his right hand improved a little. He began to reach out for objects that were placed in front of him by grasping for lightweight, simple things like a big orange jack-o'-lantern card he had received from Grandma and Granddad. His lack of head control was a great concern to everyone. He had almost no ability to hold his head up or turn it from side to side, which infants much younger than he could do. If not given proper support, his head would flop back, and he could not pull it forward. He constantly kept it rotated to the right. Nevertheless, I was able to move and turn his head from side to side when he was relaxed. The therapist gave me a special pillow to help keep his head straight. I attached a colorful mobile to the kitchen counter and would lower it just within Derek's reach. I'd place him on the floor beneath the mobile, and he'd lie there happily and comfortable on his head pillow while I'd prepare dinner or wash dishes. He was busily entertaining himself while doing therapy. He'd bat that mobile and then smile in delight at what he

Playing with his mobile

had done. I think the biggest improvement was his eye control. Derek was able to visually follow objects, the dogs, and people. This inspired me because as a deaf child he would certainly benefit from having control of his eyes.

A couple weekends after our episode in the hospital, when Derek was feeling better, we had more company. My brother, Ronn, his wife, Jeanann, and my nephew, Geoff, made their first visit to West Virginia. They had heard of Derek through letters and phone calls. I was not sure what kind of picture they had formed from the information they had received. Geoff was only six months older than Derek and was a perfectly normal, healthy child. I was excited about their arrival but still concerned about how they would relate to Derek.

Jeanann recalls: **We first learned about Derek from Mildred, Ronn and Marian's mother, and were excited for Marian. We understood that the baby had problems that were life-threatening and knew that Marian would be hurt if something happened to the baby. We were enjoying our own son and knew what an investment in time, energy, and love a baby was, not to mention a baby with so many complications.**

We bought a huge green frog as a baby gift and took off for Romney. Derek was blond and cute and limp. I felt incredibly lucky to have a strong baby, but Derek wasn't so lucky because Geoff managed to tramp on him two or three times in the playpen. He was very curious about this new person.

I was sad and happy for Marian. Sad because I knew her experiences with Derek would be different than mine with Geoff. Happy because she was happy with her new son. If this was what she wanted out of life, we wished her the best.

Jeanann and Ronn also brought an inflatable plastic roller for Derek. It was one of the best baby gifts he received. I clearly remember blowing it up while he observed me, red-faced and struggling for breath. I placed him over the roller with his elbows tucked under his chest and before we knew it, he was attempting to lift his head to see what was going on in front of him. Derek struggled for several minutes to raise his head. Then, his efforts were rewarded when he actually held it up high, looking all around the room and beaming.

Thanksgiving was coming, and I wanted to fly to Arizona to visit my parents. Sandy made arrangements, once again, for me to take Derek out of the state. I had the feeling that the doctors thought it was too risky for Derek to fly. However, I packed up all the medications, a stack of medical background information, names and phone numbers of his doctor and social worker, and boarded a plane for Arizona with Derek snuggled in my arms.

This was his first airplane adventure. I was certain that he would sleep as we flew cross-country to Arizona. Maybe some other baby, but not mine! I was shocked at how aware Derek was of his surroundings. He seemed to take in everything that was in his visual range. He kept gazing at the window. I finally held him up to look out. He smiled with joy as he saw the clouds below us. Airplane seats are always uncomfortable for me, mostly because I am short, so my feet cannot reach the floor. I kept wanting to change position as holding Derek for hours and hours and trying to keep his body flexed added to my discomfort and aching muscles. However, Derek was having a great time. He smiled at everyone who went by. We were going to change planes in Dallas, and of course he fell asleep just before we landed. I carefully walked him around the airport so he wouldn't wake up but he did, just as we were boarding our plane to Phoenix. On the flight to Phoenix, his curiosity gave way to exhaustion and he fell asleep for the remainder of the trip. As I stood to get off the plane, a lady I had never met handed me a piece of paper and went on her way.

This is what she had written:

> Little one - your pale, wispy hair
> Splays out in every direction,
> And I can see only a curve of cheek
> As you bury your head in her shoulder...
>
> We walk behind you to our places,
> Seat belts attended, carry-on stashed,
> I glance across the narrow aisle that separates us...
>
> The back of your head was only a prologue
> To the joy of an upturned rose set in a field of pink...
> Eyes closed, your mouth is capped with a bright orange plug
> That somehow connects to safety...
> Your small, round self is enfolded by the woman
> Who somehow connects you to life.
>
> Jane Sackert

Grandma and Granddad were waiting for us at the gate when we arrived. They were eager to see Derek's precious smile, but he didn't wake up until we arrived at their place. That first smile was only the beginning of an infinite number they would receive during the next several days. Derek was the center of attention during our visit. He was always on someone's lap, folded in someone's arms, or being entertained in some way. There were walks around the park in the stroller and various sights to absorb. In fact, I was able to take some naps while Mom and Dad entertained their grandson. Grandma even made some attempts to feed him, something that he would demand during future visits, he would eye his plate and then shift his gaze to Grandma.

For Thanksgiving dinner, we went to the clubhouse of the retirement community where my parents lived and Derek even had turkey, potatoes, squash, and pumpkin pie for his first Thanksgiving. We ground the food in a blender, and he loved it, especially the whipped cream on the pumpkin pie. Granddad could not stop talking about how Derek loved his meals.

Soon it was time to say good-bye to Arizona and return to West Virginia. I so wanted my parents to be closer to us. Having had my grandmother live with us off and on for several years, I knew the value of having grandparents in one's life. However, after years of teaching, Mom and Dad had made their new home in Arizona and were beginning to enjoy their retirement. Derek loved his grandparents, and it was obvious they loved him.

Shortly after I returned from Arizona, this letter arrived in the mail:

What a special person is a grandchild!

When we heard that our single, deaf daughter planned to adopt a deaf child, we felt great pride in her purpose and compassion. Since she is trained in deaf education, we felt there could be no better parent for a deaf child. When we first saw Derek, it was love at first sight. Such a sweet smile and disposition for a baby with so many strikes against him! He has already fought so hard just to stay alive. We are proud of Derek and his mother. Our only concern is for the burden of a future with a multi-handicapped child. We believe that love and therapy and prayer can make a difference. We earnestly

pray that Derek may be able to get himself around by walking, crutches or wheelchair, and that he can learn enough to be a useful member of society. Whatever is in the future, we will love Derek for the person he is.

Can you love one child or grandchild more than another? When our adopted son and his wife presented us with a 100% normal, beautiful grandchild, we felt we could never love any child more, and that is so. But a special child with special problems calls for a special kind of love. This is our love for Derek.

Grandma and Granddad

Derek had another bout of ear infections and almost another trip to the hospital. Frequently it was touch-and-go. He managed to swallow enough antibiotics to help clear up many infections, so he didn't have to be admitted to the hospital for IV treatments. In fact, my obsession was to keep Derek out of the hospital!

Before too long, it was the Christmas season. I was not a big fan of giving a lot of gifts, but we did decorate our place with a tree and plenty of lights. I had a difficult time deciding which sparkle was brighter, between the lights on the tree and the twinkle of Derek's eyes. He would spend hours simply taking in the view and enjoying every minute of it.

For Derek's first Christmas, Aunt Lynne flew in from Houston to be with us. This made the meetings between Derek and my family complete. We spent Christmas day in Romney and opened gifts. Granddad had made Derek a wooden train and a big toy box. It was a struggle to remove the heavy parts from the packaging. "Why did Granddad have to use so much tape on this box?" I signed to Derek. I had the honor of assembling that toy box, and Derek thought watching me sweat over that job was the most spectacular entertainment.

The next day we packed up the car and took off for Ohio to spend time with my brother's family. By this time my nephew, Geoff, was starting to get about on his own. Derek continued to be extremely observant of all that was going on around him. He constantly eyed Geoff in his infant walker until I finally decided to put him in it. It was way too big for him, and he didn't have the ability to sit, but he was delighted to be upright where he could view the world from a different perspective. We propped him up with cushions and rolled-up towels along his sides, and he spent long periods of time batting at the toys on the tray. Once again, his smile said it all: THANK YOU!

Once we returned home, I decided to use a walker like Geoff's in our place. I rolled extra receiving blankets around firmer supports for Derek's trunk, and he spent hours pushing himself around the kitchen and into the hallway to the bedrooms. He never really learned to push it forward but was content to go around backward getting into places that were too small and grinning from ear to ear when being "scolded" for it. I know the therapist didn't agree wholeheartedly with the use of this walker because it was supposedly stimulating the wrong reflex or something. Seeing how much he enjoyed having it and being a bit mobile did my heart good. Most of the time, I carefully followed the therapists' directions and respected their recommendations, but this is one time that I allowed the parent part of me to rule.

On January 3, 1980, Derek had succeeded in reaching the most important goal, celebrating his first birthday. What an exciting day this was for me and for my friends who were able to be a part of the celebration. Derek and I began the day with doctor appointments. The orthopedic doctor felt that Derek's hips were in their sockets and would not need braces or orthopedic surgery at the time. Derek would continue with his physical therapy. Later, we saw the pediatrician. He was pleased that Derek had finally gained weight and was now fourteen pounds. The best news of all was that he thought Derek could be taken off the medications that he had been on for most of the year. Not needing to stop having fun to administer medications would make life so much more enjoyable. I wanted to jump and shout for joy.

After we got home, we went outside to play in the snow. I bundled Derek in his snowsuit, hat, and mittens Grandma knit for him and propped him up in a laundry basket with pillows and towels. Then I put the dog's leash through the handle and pulled Derek down the road and around the neighborhood. All the other children who were outside playing on their sleds would stop and wave to Derek. He would acknowledge them with his "I'm glad to see you" smile. We completed the day by hosting friends for dinner, opening gifts, and eating a birthday cake designed to look like a train. Derek didn't like having a candle near his face. He'd close his eyes, grit his teeth, and stiffen his limbs as if to say, "Move that flickering thing back, please." He was much more relaxed after it had been blown out and taken away. He slept content that night. Derek was a true winner for overcoming many obstacles, one small step at a time.

Sled riding

Just a few days after Derek's first birthday, he started attending the Special Services Center at the public elementary school. He would begin with one full day and one half day each

Derek's first birthday

week. I was a nervous mom sending my infant son to school. *Will he be angry with me for leaving him there? Will he understand I will return later to take him home?* His first day was filled with all kinds of new things: new adults to care and feed him, new children to observe, new toys to look at and play with. When my day of teaching was over, I hurried to my car and drove the few miles across town to find out how Derek handled his first day at school.

When I arrived to pick him up, Derek's body vibrated with excitement when he saw me coming through the classroom door. I felt so appreciated. He was totally exhausted. On the way home he was yawning and almost dozed off. It was only a matter of minutes after I took off his jacket and placed him on the couch that he was sound asleep. Derek had some difficulty adjusting to the busy school schedule, staying awake, and allowing others to feed him. Everyone was concerned about his breathing, which was always raspy. At first, the teachers focused on improving his gross and fine motor skills (lifting his head or rolling over, and reaching for a small toy or holding something small in his hand), visual tracking, eating skills, and socialization. Socialization was his strongest area. It was a real blessing that he loved being around people and observing what others were doing. His smile made everyone happy. Still, few people seemed to understand what Derek wanted to communicate. I don't know how to explain how he and I developed a "silent" communication between us. It was like a gift I had been born with but never had the opportunity to use or develop. All I can say is I was most grateful for our depth of communication.

We had survived and thrived those first six months together. During this time, I felt that much improvement had been made. Derek was now able to move both his arms and kick with his legs. His hands were in a more relaxed position, and he was able to reach out and grasp small objects without using his thumbs. His head control continued to be extremely poor, and he could only turn it slightly, but his eyes were better focused and his peripheral vision greatly compensated for his inability to turn his head. At home, Derek had been exposed to sign language and was much more attentive than when he was first placed in my care. We went most everywhere. We went out for dinner, to church, and shopping. He survived being suddenly dragged out in the cold when I needed something from the store although I tried to become more organized and eliminate those last-minute trips to town. Derek enjoyed having me sign stories to him in the evenings. Best of all was the close, loving bond that had formed between us during our six months together. It was a bond that would lead me to pursue finalizing Derek's adoption.

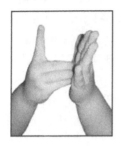

Chapter Four

1 year -
1 year 4 months old

Derek continued to show improvement in his ability to respond and interact with those in his environment. It still took forever to feed him. More times than not, Derek would want to open his mouth for a spoonful of food but just could not get his muscles to respond the way he wanted them to. So, when we were alone and I had hours to kill, we'd just sit at the table and take our time eating. Between bites, I'd sign stories to him, show him pictures, or just tell him about my day at school. I had no idea how much he could comprehend, but I knew he would never comprehend *anything* if he weren't constantly exposed to language. And he paid attention. Why would he pay attention if what I was showing him had no meaning to him?

Other times, when we needed to hurry a bit, I would act like a total fool while feeding him. I would take paper bags, hand towels, or anything that was handy and put them over my head. I'd pull them off quickly and pop the food right into Derek's now wide-open mouth, and he would laugh at my antics.

Sue recalls: **Marian and I continued to do things together and Derek was right there with us. Almost every Friday evening we would go out for dinner at a small restaurant in town. We would always sneak things from the salad bar for Derek. We'd try not to make it obvious that we were sneaking the food, but Derek loved it when I'd hide a small bowl of something under my coat and bring it back to the table. You could just see the delight in his eyes and it was clear to me that he knew we were misbehaving in public.**

Not only did Derek have trouble opening his mouth, but he also had an extremely strong bite reflex. Sometimes I would get the spoon in his mouth and he'd clamp his jaws shut so tightly I couldn't get the spoon out! I learned never to use regular plastic spoons because they could break in his mouth and cause choking or even cuts from the broken plastic. I had a hard time finding a spoon that was the right shape, meaning not too tiny like a little baby spoon, and that was metal coated with plastic. Then, one day when I was not even looking for one, I came upon the perfect spoon in the small drugstore uptown. And it was cheap. (Companies that make things for people with disabilities charge ridiculous prices for some really simple things. Many times you can get them for much less from a regular supplier.) I had the store order fifty of those spoons. When the order came in, the owner said, "These are for Derek. Just take them, please." Derek managed to break the handles on those spoons too, but at least he wasn't in danger of choking on the pieces.

Derek loved his bright orange pacifier, though it was a challenge to those of us who had to keep track of it. He got really frustrated when it fell out of his mouth. I was convinced that it was helping him develop a stronger sucking skill. Still, he wasn't developing the strong, complete lip closure he needed to successfully suck from a bottle. I decided to try using a cup. The cup needed to be hard plastic because of his bite reflex. I found one made by Tupperware. I cut a big crescent on one side that allowed me to see how Derek was managing when I was giving him something to drink and I didn't want to pour liquids up his nose. The cup was a big success. Those of us who fed him held the cup, tipped it gently, and let him suck slowly. This method was much faster than a bottle, and he took in more fluids, which offset his constant sweating.

Much of Derek's time in the preschool program concentrated on his physical development and feeding skills, which seemed to be helping with his drinking and eating. Although I knew this was important, I also believed strongly that language stimulation should be a priority. If Derek had been born with normal hearing, he would have been picking up language every minute from hearing conversations taking place in his presence via TV programs, audiotapes, and so forth. However, his deafness would not allow this natural acquisition of language to occur. So began my battle with educators about the need to sign everything possible with Derek. It was an ongoing issue because he was not able to sign back, so most people felt he was not capable of receiving language in this manner.

I had mixed feelings about the reports that came to me from the school:

He is not really responding to other children nor does he seem to be aware of their presence. Getting Derek to visually attend to a stimulus is our major emphasis right now. Just getting him to maintain eye contact for a few seconds is difficult. The only response I see is that Derek sometimes smiles at different adults.

His first teacher knew little about deafness, and I found it annoying that she continued to believe he was not responsive to the children around him and could not focus on activities in his presence. I had continued to bring my students home from school to play and have time together on the weekends. They would naturally sign everything to Derek, and it was clear that he was aware of their presence and wanted to be included. He would follow their every move in his field of vision.

One friend comments: **Marian was a strong advocate for Derek right from the start. I know Marian was happy to have a child who was deaf, because obviously she knew what to do. Right away she started signing to Derek. I have to say I was a bit skeptical about whether he really knew what she was saying. But she was sure he understood and he did respond in some manner to her signs.**

It's interesting that people commented on my signing all the time with Derek. Don't hearing parents with hearing children talk all the time to their one-year-olds? How much do their young children really understand? My child was deaf. How else would Derek learn language if he was not exposed to it in a visual way? Maybe others were skeptical of my persistence, but I was confident of my choice of communication with Derek. I was determined to model language whenever we were together.

Derek had an excessively strong eye reflex causing his eyes to close suddenly and firmly. Obviously, this affected how he could respond visually to what was going on around him. I reminded the teacher about this and requested again and again that she please move slowly and stand back a bit when interacting with Derek. He just could not handle fast movements that were close to his face. For example, if you held a picture about four inches from his face, his eyes would automatically shut. This gave people the impression that he was not visually alert or didn't want to look at what was being shown to him. However, if you moved a bit slower and held the object or picture more than a foot away, he could focus on what was in front of him. I don't think his first teacher ever understood. I was already becoming frustrated with the educational system, my own profession.

Each day after work I returned home to spend my evenings with Derek. We continued to grow closer and closer on a minute-by-minute basis. It was not long after his first birthday that one more thrilling "first'" happened. I was sitting on the floor with Derek between my legs facing me as we worked on his head control. Using bright plastic blocks I was showing him color signs and stacking the blocks between us. Suddenly, one of the dogs came by and knocked over the stack of blocks. Well, that moment was Derek's *first laugh*. It was not just a smile but a laugh that could be seen clearly for what it was while he used every neck and throat muscle. In fact, he continued to laugh so long and hard that he almost choked. Milestones like that one made me feel so peaceful and satisfied.

Although Derek showed improvement, health problems continued to arise. One issue was the frequent ear infections, *otitis media*, which was difficult to clear up with antibiotics. *Otitis media* is infection of the middle ear that often begins when a person has a cold or other respiratory problems. The small Eustachian tube, which is the passageway between the back of the throat and the middle ear, can become inflamed or infected. In an infant, the Eustachian tube is short and straight. With Derek, formula, food, or mucus from upper respiratory infections could easily pass into the middle ear because of his inability to hold his head up naturally when eating. These infections needed to be treated, regardless of his deafness.

After several painful infections, that caused him to run high fevers, the doctor decided that we would need to surgically insert tubes into Derek's eardrums. The tubes would make it possible to drain any infection in the middle ear and would also help ventilate the air pocket and pressure. This is a relatively minor surgery for most children, but with Derek and his respiratory and neurological problems, it could become a major crisis in a matter of seconds. The ear, nose and throat (ENT) doctor who saw Derek did not practice in Romney, so we needed to drive to Winchester, Virginia. I was more nervous than usual because Derek had not had surgery while in my care. Also, I didn't know my way around the different hospital, nor did I know the nurses. I was worried and stressed about trying to speechread people I had never met.

Derek was irritable on the ride over Route 50 from Romney to Winchester. I was certain he was quite hungry since he was not allowed to eat before the surgery. I didn't know how to explain to him why he couldn't eat. I was anxious and worried. My patience was declining rapidly, especially when we'd get behind a big, slow truck that I couldn't pass on the winding mountain road.

When we finally arrived at the hospital, I did my balancing act of carrying Derek's diaper bag and my purse slung over one shoulder as I attempted to keep him relaxed while carrying him and signing forms with the other hand. There were long halls and elevators to maneuver before I located the same-day surgery area. I collapsed into a chair, dropped the diaper bag onto the floor, and took a few minutes to collect myself. I needed to register and complete a mountain of paperwork before surgery could take place. Just making a legible signature on the forms would be a challenge while holding a rigid Derek. I also needed to use the restroom, but that would have to wait until Derek had been taken into surgery. When would I learn to stop drinking coffee on such mornings? Fortunately Derek's wait was not long after all the paperwork was completed. The surgery itself didn't take long either, as there were no complications. Everything went well, and we were soon back on the road headed toward home.

For the first couple of days after the surgery I could not believe how much infection drained from the tubes. As time went by, it was obvious how much better he felt once the tubes were in and the infections cleared up.

As Derek felt better, he seemed to become more and more aware of his surroundings. One day I needed to take him to a different babysitter because of a scheduling conflict with our regular one. It was the first time that Derek cried when I left him. I guess most mothers would be upset about this event, but I was ecstatic. This was one more indication that he was bonding and that he could express his desire to be in a different place and with a different person. The substitute sitter told me later that he settled down shortly after I left and was fine the rest of the day.

We started going to an indoor swimming pool for physical therapy. Derek's therapist worked with his limbs in the water while I held him. He loved this from the start and soon began kicking himself around as I gave support under his shoulders and head. He also would put his face in the water when I held him upright in a somewhat standing position. He began to lift his head out of the water and displayed an expression of pride with his accomplishment. I tried hard to keep his ears out of the water because of his drainage tubes. Eventually, I bought some small earplugs to decrease the amount of water reaching the tubes. Since I had been a lifeguard years before, the water had been my "second home." Now it was a place Derek and I could mutually enjoy as recreation in the future.

Since Derek's left eye did not appear to move or focus in coordination with the right eye, it was difficult to tell what he saw. Was he seeing double? How far could he see? A new eye exam, for which he managed to stay awake for once, brought terrific news. The ophthalmologist felt that his vision was normal, and he would not need glasses. The doctor also noticed that his left eye was straightening out and strongly recommended that I continue having Derek track toys in every direction possible. I think the mobile connected to the kitchen counter was probably the best visual therapy for him.

Derek loved our dogs, and they also assisted with his physical therapy. For instance, I would put Derek on top of a mattress that I had propped up on a slight slant in my extra bedroom. The goal was to have him learn to roll. I would help him position his arms and legs and prod him on. At the bottom of the mattress sat old, faithful Rocca, a pure mutt. She would sit, wag her tail, and bark as Derek made progress on rolling down the mattress. Once he reached the bottom, she'd lick him and smother him with kisses as if to say, "Well done, my boy!"

As weather permitted, we went for walks in the neighborhood with the dogs trotting along beside us. Derek had a difficult time staying upright in the stroller. How could I help him? Well, being a short person, I needed cushions so that I could see over the steering wheel of my car, so I came up with the idea of cutting a cushion in half to fit in the back of the stroller and give Derek more support. Then I rolled up some towels or small blankets and positioned them along his trunk. This adjustment made our walks more enjoyable and eliminated the need to stop frequently and reposition Derek. We walked everywhere. Sometimes I would even walk him into town, a trip of a couple of miles. Derek would smile to everyone who passed.

That cushion I'd cut in half ended up serving two purposes. It was made of spring-like wire coils covered with a mesh material. I finished the edges of the cut cushion with wide bias tape. It allowed for a bit of circulation between his back and the car seat, where it fit perfectly.

One reason we did so much walking was because my car was acting up. I finally needed to trade it in.

Sue recalls: **We were going to buy a new car for Marian. The dealers had given Marian a good deal on a trade-in. We were just pulling out of the driveway, and the salesman was still standing in the doorway of the place, when that old car backfired so loud that even Marian and Derek heard it! We all just burst out laughing and that included tiny Derek in his car seat! I really felt that he understood what was going on even though he was so small and young.**

Radios were options in cars at that time. When the salesperson asked what kind of radio I wanted, I simply told him no radio. He was startled and I'm sure he couldn't imagine a car without a radio. I told him that most of the people who rode in my car were deaf. I was totally blown off my chair when he asked, "Oh, do you know some deaf people?" Rather than to go into a lengthy, detailed conversation about being deaf, I just replied, "Yes, I know some people who are deaf." Maybe he figured it out after the car backfired!

Winter came and went. Derek continued to struggle with health issues. There were several more hospitalizations we endured together. My friends faithfully supported me. Neighbors helped me with making phone calls. Dr. Giron continued to provide competent medical care close to home. After each hospitalization, there was always a setback in his development. We would need to work to rebuild his body strength. There were times for Derek that just staying awake during the day was a challenge. Some days eating and focusing on who and what was happening around him seemed to be more than he could handle.

There were times that Dr. Giron needed to transfer him out of the small hospital in Romney to larger facilities in other cities. I never could accept this right away without first objecting. Once, while Derek was in a different hospital and under another physician's care, I was crushed by what his doctor said to me. He believed that I was totally wasting my time and gifts with Derek. He remarked that Derek would never amount to anything other than a body that would need to be cared for until the day he died. He strongly suggested that I place him in an institution and further my search to find a "normal" deaf child to parent. I was deeply hurt. To me, it did not matter that I was not his birth mother. We had a strong mother-child bond and I loved him as much as any birth parent could love their child. I was devastated by this conversation. I left the hospital in tears and drove back to Romney to seek out my pastor. Reverend Ellifritz listened patiently when I needed to talk. He always encouraged me to stay strong during times like this, but rarely gave me other advice. I was certain he supported my adopting Derek because he had been a reference for my home study.

Rev. Ellifritz writes: **We wanted to be supportive of Marian and her care of Derek, but our main concern was for her with the tremendous load she had assumed in doing so. What Marian did was almost incomprehensible to me and to many others who knew her. I know he captivated her heart from the first, and that captivation grew to probably become the strongest bond in her life. They shared a special knowing. I find it difficult to believe that the kind of relationship the two had can be conveyed to others academically.**

After Derek was well enough to be discharged from that hospital, I wrote a letter to the doctor who had been the primary physician during the hospitalization. I still have a copy of the letter.

Dr. P:

I do not really want to write this letter, but I feel it is necessary on behalf of Derek Michael Aiken who has been placed in my home for adoption. I have gotten the impression you feel this child should be institutionalized from the two visits I have made to your office and this has bothered me greatly. I have no intention of institutionalizing Derek. However, there may be a time in the future when this might be necessary. At the moment, Derek is being cared for and much love has surrounded him since he has entered my home.

I was pleased with the services provided at your hospital and thank Dr. Zinnia Giron for seeing the need to have him transferred there. The nurses were extremely understanding of Derek's condition and tried their best to fulfill his needs. Without their help this past Monday night, I don't know what the outcome of a very long and strained coughing attack would have been. The nurses were quick to act to his needs and cared for him.

Before I brought Derek into my home, I asked around about a pediatrician. I was given your name by various people because you were capable of handling handicapped children. However, I feel that there needs to be a better understanding between us. Or should I seek another pediatrician for Derek? I would like your opinion on this and would ask for records to be transferred if you feel it is necessary. Maybe you should discuss this with Dr. M. in your office since he has had contact with Derek also. If you feel we can work out a better understanding, then, I will continue to bring Derek to your office.

You might be interested to know that he has been placed in a sitting position since discharged on Wednesday. Needless to say, this is quite a problem for him, but his coughing has lessened in spite of his extremely raspy breathing and slight temperature.

I will be waiting to hear from you. Thank you for considering this letter.

Sincerely,
Marian Aiken

I never received a reply from this doctor. Surely, if he wasn't considerate enough to make an effort to respond, he was not the doctor for us.

There was only one other time that Dr. Giron transferred Derek to another hospital (not the same one) because she felt he needed specialized pediatric care and treatment that was more than the small hospital in town could handle. Once again the hospitalization was tough to handle. The drive into the neighboring cities through the snow and over the mountains was stressful after working all day. Knowing that I could not reach him in a matter of minutes constantly gnawed at me. I finally asked Dr. Giron not to send him away again. I emphasized that even though our small hospital might not have the most up-to-date equipment for Derek's care, it did have a nursing staff that respected him as an individual and also had learned to communicate with me. For me, it was important that the

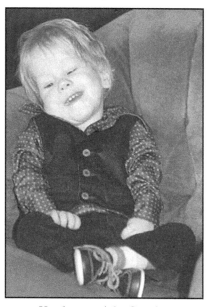

medical staff not only meet and care for Derek's physical needs, but understand the necessity of fulfilling both our emotional needs. That really was a priority. Dr. Giron listened, understood, and agreed to keep him in Romney for future hospitalizations.

For Derek's first Easter, Grandma had made him a vest, slacks, and dress shirt of leftover material that matched my dress. I found a pair of small brown shoes to match his outfit. He looked so sharp! Off we went to church. Normally, Derek sat

Handsewn suit by Grandma

on my lap quietly (other than his raspy breathing) and behaved during services. It was a different story that day. He was excited and wanted to try to jump up and down on my lap, his arms rigid and his floppy head going every which way. After playing with him this way, I finally put him up over my shoulder, and he smiled at everyone behind us. Several people came up to us after the service and just could not believe he was the same child I had brought home several months earlier. These were people who thought I was totally out of my mind to care for him and deal with all the medical unknowns. At last, some people understood there was a person in that body who could share his love and joy for life with others.

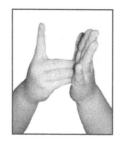

Chapter Five

1 year 5 months - 1 year 6 months old

Once I had made it clear that I was committed to finalizing Derek's adoption, I thought it would be a breeze and things would happen immediately. But more than four months after I had made my desire known, there was no indication that things were moving forward.

Sandy recalls: **Usually, a child has to be in a home for a six-month trial period before adoption can be finalized. In Marian's case, Derek was in her care longer before the agency moved for his adoption to be finalized. I feel that the reason for this was to make sure that Marian did want to adopt Derek and was sure that she was willing to make the commitment to deal with his medical conditions. I knew that Marian was very much ready and would not give up on Derek. It was clear that they had bonded and he was a very happy little boy. What was so difficult was for the agency to be convinced that she was definitely ready and that she was not willing to give up. I had my work cut out for me.**

Soon it was Mother's Day. I so much wanted to call Derek my own. I'm not sure why the paperwork made so much difference to me since it was evident he was going to remain in my care, but it did. Nevertheless, our first Mother's Day was meaningful and happy. I asked my pastor to have a 'Service of Dedication' for Derek. The service is similar to having a baby baptized, but focuses on asking the people in the church to help support and nurture the child throughout his life. Rev. Ellifritz did a nice service for us, and my friend Sue interpreted for me. I couldn't help but wonder about his birth mother and how any woman who had had a Caesarean to deliver a child could forget about her baby. In coming years, I thought often of her on Mother's Day and his birthday.

Sue remembers: **We had gone out to our friends' farm to have dinner and get our hair cut. I recall that I was outside with the others and Marian was in the kitchen with Derek. I heard her talking to Derek and saying that it was Mother's Day and they said a little prayer for his birth mother. I know she prayed for the birth mother but I could not quite understand why at that time.**

However, I am now a stepparent to two children who lost their mother and I now understand those feelings very, very well and how you can feel for the mother of these children. It is not as hard to do as most people would think. You don't want to erase their birth mothers out of their life. You want them to remember their mothers if possible and share any information that you would have about their mothers. I know that Marian shared what she knew, even though Derek would have no memory of his birth mother since he was only an infant when Marian took him into her care.

June arrived, and the academic year was about to end for me and for Derek's program. Derek had successfully completed his first year of infant stimulation with the local school district. Although he missed a quarter of his scheduled days because of his health and his teacher said he'd made little progress, Derek showed he enjoyed his experience by being happy to be there. He adjusted well to his routine at school.

June also brought some profound sadness. My beloved dog, Snooge, died of a brain tumor. This left a large gap in our lives. Derek, Rocca, and I had some adjusting to do. However, Rocca soon took up guard and became most protective of Derek, especially when others were visiting.

Here is a poem I wrote about Derek and Rocca.

My Pet, My Friend

I love my pet, my pet loves me.
We're best of friends, as you can see.

I cannot sit, I cannot walk.
I cannot hear, I cannot talk;
But my pet doesn't seem to care.
She even cleans up my wheelchair!

Sometimes I cry when I am sad.
My pet's right there to make me glad.
Like me, she has no words to say,
But her soft tongue licks my tears away.

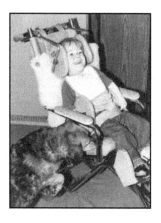

I like to smile, I like to eat,
I like to sleep with her by my feet.
When Mom puts me in my bed,
She likes my pillow to rest her head.

My dog is gentle as can be.
I love my pet, and she loves me.

We took only a couple of short trips that summer. We drove to Ohio to spend some time with my brother's family. It was clear that the developmental gap between my nephew and Derek was becoming wider as time went by.

Jeanann writes: **I remember Mildred, grandma, telling us that doctors diagnosed Derek as profoundly mentally retarded. We wondered about this and what Marian would be able to do for him in the future. In my eyes, Derek proved the doctors wrong when he obviously teased me the next time they visited.**

I was holding him while sitting in a rocker near a stand of dried flowers. Derek seemed to be spastically reaching toward the flowers. I teased him about going after Aunt Jeanann's flowers thinking he really didn't have a clue what I was talking about. Every time after that when we rocked in that chair, Derek would have the most devilish grin on his face as he strained for the flowers. Each time was a profound statement by Derek that the doctors were profoundly wrong!

After visiting with Ronn's family, we went on to the National Association of the Deaf (NAD) Convention. I had entered Derek's quilt in the conference's quilting competition. He was so happy to see his quilt. He smiled broadly as he looked at the animals. His body was full of excitement. However, I was becoming more and more aware that the Deaf community at large was not accepting of him. People congratulated me for taking care of such a child, but they made no effort to communicate with him as they were communicating with the able-bodied deaf infants.

I was hurt. You might even say I was infuriated. The Deaf community in Romney showed greater acceptance of my son. I did not enjoy myself at the NAD Convention and was emotionally drained by feelings of dejection and sadness. I took down Derek's quilt from the display, packed our belongings, loaded up the car, and left early.

That summer I had been granted permission from the landlord to rototill my back yard and plant my

Quilt I made for Derek

garden there. Finally, I would not need to go up the street to care for my garden on another person's land. I could either bring Derek outside where he could watch me from his stroller or, if he was taking a nap, leave him in the living room where I could check on him frequently by peering through the windows. We planted three or four kinds of squash, tomatoes, cucumbers, green beans, and green peppers. I would pick large zucchinis that weighed almost more than Derek. We shared our extra produce with friends. However, we were selfish with the large quantity of winter butternut squash. It was Derek's favorite and I stored them for a long winter's supply.

I spent a lot of time signing stories to Derek over the summer. One of his favorites was a picture book about zoo animals. He loved the lion. He knew exactly when I was about to turn to that page. I could feel a change in his body's tension as he anticipated his favorite animal sign. His reaction when we neared the end of a book made clear to me Derek was involved in the story. I watched his eyes look ahead toward the last page. Then his face would register disappointment, followed by tears or sometimes even a temper tantrum. He held his breath if I didn't find another book to read quickly. *Why would a child who is profoundly mentally retarded react in this way?*

July 27, 1980, marked one complete year of togetherness. Derek and I went to a lovely restaurant, The Upper Room, with some friends. This small, peaceful atmosphere was a perfect setting for our day. After everyone had eaten more than their share, we took a walk in the cool shade of the trees along the dirt road. We had been here often, but today had a more profound meaning, and we stayed longer than usual while we inhaled the fresh mountain air and enjoyed the beauty of the woods before heading home. Below is part of what I had recorded that evening after Derek was sound asleep in his bed:

Derek, I want you to know that you've brought more enjoyment to me than anything else I've ever experienced. It has been a fantastic year and I am sure there are many more splendid years ahead for both of us. I have written about your physical improvements with which I am most thrilled. However, I find the most rewarding feeling in your *smile*. It is precious, and please never stop smiling!

Love,
Mom

63

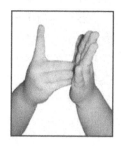

Chapter Six

1 year 6 months -
1 year 8 months old

I hated missing more school than was necessary, so I tried very hard to have all of Derek's medical exams done during the summer while I was not teaching. It seemed like getting the appointments scheduled took forever. I had planned to take him to Baltimore to Johns Hopkins Hospital for a complete evaluation. I started looking for a wheelchair he could comfortably sit in, hoping I could get the Johns Hopkins people to prescribe one for him (the state of West Virginia would pay for it if I had a prescription). I was told Baltimore was not possible because West Virginia had the same services in Morgantown. "Okay then, let's get these things scheduled," I urged.

The day finally came when I drove Derek to his evaluations. It was the beginning of August and many of the people at West Virginia University Medical Center had not seen him for more than a year. I was certain they would be happy to see his improvements.

We met first with the head of pediatrics who did a complete physical exam. She was a warm, caring person who had a zillion questions for me. She appeared to be greatly concerned about Derek's growth. I knew that he was small for his age (more than a year and a half) and only weighed fifteen pounds, but he had grown and was maintaining his weight. She didn't have too many things to say about his progress, which was discouraging.

Derek was also evaluated in the physical therapy, occupational therapy, and speech and language departments. A social worker from the medical center also spoke with me. It seemed like I was asked the same questions by each department over and over again, and I had already completed a long form before the assessments. I felt stressed by the numerous exams as I did not have an interpreter for the entire day and speechreading all these different people was difficult. I simply couldn't understand why they couldn't read the answers I had already provided.

The speech and language specialist continued to emphasize the need to develop speech. I became more and more angry every time I heard them say, "You need to work on vocalizing with Derek. Also work on blowing bubbles with Derek. You should encourage Derek to imitate your mouth movements." How insensitive. They were speaking about a profoundly deaf child who was severely involved with cerebral palsy and had partially paralyzed vocal cords! It was obvious to me that they didn't like my using signs with him, and probably thought I was undermining his progress. I'm surprised they didn't recommend that I teach Derek to sing "Jingle Bells"!

Something else that disturbed me greatly was the neurologist's attitude. I was concerned about Derek's soft spot, the area on the top of his head where the bone had not completely fused. I wanted to know if at his age it should have been much smaller or completely closed. I asked the neurologist about it. He said, "I wouldn't worry about it until he begins to play football." I did not take that very kindly. This was a child who could not hold his head up, sit unsupported, or bear much weight on his feet. He was an infant who had been tickled with feathers in his face and on the bottoms of his feet and had been hammered here and there to test his reflexes. He did not deserve to have such an extremely insensitive remark made about him. "Sir, I do not feel your comments are relevant to my question," I said as I carried Derek from the examination room.

While we waited for other appointments that day, I spoke to a woman who had her twenty-four-year-old son with her. He was sitting in a wheelchair with his head flopped forward and his limbs stiff and rigid. I asked if he was in a rehabilitation program of some sort. She said that she just kept him at home all the time, that she didn't have any way to transport him and he just stayed in his room all day. I thought, *I'll always try to find the best program for Derek, a place where he can feel comfortable and safe and have friends.* Finally, the evaluations were over, and we were called into the office of the director of the Special Children's Clinic to hear her words of wisdom. Derek was exhausted and had just fallen asleep peacefully in my arms when the doctor began her summary of the day. My eyes were tired after the long day of speechreading. I was straining to catch the words she was speaking and to process the meaning and intent behind them.

First, she praised me for the responsibility I was undertaking in caring for Derek. She stressed that everyone was impressed with my ability to speechread and follow conversations. She said my communication skills were remarkable. She felt that although Derek was quite small, he was well nourished and cared for. This was the extent of the positives.

Then the bombs began dropping. The most frequently used phrase in all of the reports was that I had "unrealistic expectations for this child." Each department's evaluation and assessment said the same thing. "Ms. Aiken is totally unaware of Derek's extremely limited condition," was the statement of the social worker. They felt that his movements were seizure activity and accused me of taking him off medications without a doctor's orders. To think that I would want to harm Derek in this manner was incomprehensible. I stressed that it was a doctor who discontinued the medications, not me. I was told that Derek was not able to visually track or recognize common objects. It was so disheartening to grasp what was being said. The director discouraged me from finalizing Derek's adoption, suggesting I keep him in foster care instead. She went on to say that Derek would still be mine, as he was now. "He is a human being and because of this, he has a right to be given the chance to develop and learn regardless of how small the possibilities may be for improvement," she continued. I sat there with tears streaming down my cheeks trying to process all of this as Derek continued to sleep contentedly in my arms.

The doctor wanted one more test, a 'transillumination.' "We think Derek does not have a brain or may only have a brain stem." This was the most drastic statement I had heard. She continued calmly, "We need to go into a dark room to do this procedure to make sure that he has a brain. I will take him and you can remain here in my office."

I felt as if I were going to pass out. No one who has not experienced such a statement concerning an infant who was loved as much as Derek was can comprehend what I was feeling. I felt I'd been stabbed through my heart. I told them clearly I was 150% sure their assumptions were wrong! I sobbed, *"How can a child who responds to his environment like Derek does not have a brain?"* It was evident they could not recognize Derek's personality within the setting that we had been in all day. If the doctor insisted that the test be done, there was absolutely no way that I was going to allow them to take him out of my arms to do it. I insisted that I be allowed to hold him as I was doing at that moment.

It was pitch-black in that exam room, but I was aware that the doctors were talking to one another as they shone a bright light on Derek's head. Thankfully, Derek continued to sleep even as they touched his head with that powerful light. At last, we were ushered back into the doctor's office. For once on this difficult day I was informed I was correct. Derek had a brain.

Just before I left the doctor's office, the director said Derek was clearly one of the tragedies of the sophisticated newborn intensive care program. Tragedy? *Yes, the tragedy is that some professionals cannot comprehend how infants such as Derek bring joy and love to those who care for them.*

I left with my beloved Derek in my arms and together we made the long drive back home. I knew I loved this child with all my heart and that I would do anything for him. But were the specialists correct in their evaluations? Was it worth my time and effort to struggle along day-by-day not knowing what to expect in the future? How would I handle Derek if he became like that twenty-four-year-old who was kept at home in his bedroom all day? I felt sad and depressed for a few days, but each morning Derek awoke with a smile and an expression of welcome as if to say, "Good morning. Mom, let's get on with life!"

Sue recalls: **I remember I was out with Marian one night soon after the long evaluation Derek had in Morgantown and she was driving and talking to me in the dark. Sometimes she would turn on the dome lights while we talked but that night** she left them off and told me about how they had shone a light through Derek's skull to see if he had a brain. I remember she was very, very angry they would even think that about Derek. At the same time they had told her that Derek was mentally retarded and I was sitting there in the car with tears streaming down my cheeks and was glad the lights were off. I had thought that Derek was smart and aware, but now I was being told he was not! I just cried. But, thank the Lord, the next morning I woke up and looked at Derek and he was the same child that I knew and loved! It didn't matter what the diagnosis was. He was still the person I had cared about since I met him and who brought joy to so many people.

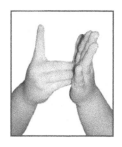

Chapter Seven

1 year 8 months -
1 year 10 months old

When Derek was about eighteen months old, our friend Sue and I decided that it might be nice for her to move into my extra bedroom and pay lower rent so she could save a few pennies for graduate school. Rossie had decided to move out in June, and though he often came for a visit, his bedroom was empty. I knew how much Sue cared about Derek, and it would be a comfort to me to know that she could help care for him at home while I taught a sign language class one evening a week. I had been using high school students to help out with babysitting, and they were wonderful with Derek. I didn't feel completely comfortable with them bearing the responsibility for my son, knowing that he could stop breathing at any time. Also, I worried about how their parents would feel if something really bad did happen while Derek was in their child's care. I could relax with Sue in charge.

I was to begin a new job in August, moving out of the classroom and into the homes of preschool deaf and hard-of-hearing children. It was the first time the West Virginia School for the Deaf would have an itinerant teacher to work in day care programs and with parents in their own homes. I waited until after Thanksgiving, when my classroom position finally was filled, to start my new job. I found the work interesting and enjoyed having to plan somewhat less than I had for classroom teaching. I also found that I could use more materials that were on the market to work on language development with the younger children.

I traveled between 500 and 700 miles a week, and my state

car became my classroom. I'd fill boxes with toys, puzzles, books, and whatever I needed for that day and begin my drive over the mountains in sun, rain, or snow. When I was not on the road, I would prepare information to share with the parents about deafness, sign language, speech development, and options for future educational programs that might be appropriate for their child. I found the work extremely rewarding, but it was stressful being so far away from my son.

Still, my new position required me to become the resource teacher in Derek's preschool. That fall, Derek had a new classroom teacher who was much more aware of his facial expressions than his previous teacher. With my job, I visited the class once a week to work with her on signs and explain various strategies to use with deaf children.

Comments from Derek's teacher: **We attempt to involve Derek in group activities where the children can interact with him. He follows many of their activities with obvious enjoyment. Derek has been exposed to some signs and appears to be attending to what is presented. I personally use facial expressions, basic sign language, and touching when communicating with Derek. It is difficult to tell how well Derek is able to communicate with others, but he is a joy to know.**

Not only did his teachers watch Derek's facial expressions, they also tried to sign as much as possible and could see that he was focusing on what was happening during his time with them. They exposed him to common objects that he used every day along with their signs. For example, a cup was shown with the sign 'DRINK,' a spoon was shown with the sign 'EAT,' a shoe was shown with the sign 'SHOE.' Of course, the teacher was not able to sign complete thoughts or abstract concepts because of her limited signing skills, but giving a sign related to a specific object was a great improvement. I was pleased that at least they were attempting to communicate like this with Derek.

I began to meet new people locally and across the country because of Derek. I attended some of the meetings for his school program and became friends with other parents. We helped each other in times of need. It seemed like every time I went into a store in town, someone would say my name even if I had no idea who that person was.

Sue recalls: **I remember one day Marian came home from the grocery store with yet another story. She had put Derek on the conveyor belt while she was writing her check for her groceries. He still was very small at this time. A woman came up and told Marian that she had had a sister who had been like Derek and went on to tell Marian how old her sister lived to be. I know Marian was happy this lady took so much interest in Derek because of her memories of her sister.**

But this made me start thinking about Marian and I really feared about her future. I knew that when the time came for Derek it would, but I didn't know how in the world she would handle it because he was so much a part of her life. When I brought this up, Marian said every parent worries about their children. She helped me realize that you just can't let worry stop you from loving your children and taking care of them and giving them a home. Fear should not stop anyone from adopting or caring for a child with handicaps. Those children deserve the right to a home and a family too.

That fall, Sue's sister, whom I had never met, had seen a program on *Good Morning America* about a man who was a single adoptive parent of special-needs children. She had heard about Derek and me through Sue and thought the man and I might like to correspond since we were both adoptive parents of special-needs children. Sue wrote to *Good Morning America* and succeeded in getting the name and address of Jim Forderer. She was so excited that she wrote to him about Derek and me and sent pictures along with the letters.

It happened that he would be attending the North American Council on Adoptable Children conference in Houston in 1980 as I had planned to do as well. Sue set it up for us to meet in Houston. I flew there with Derek, and we stayed with my sister for the long weekend. Jim and I met and talked some about our challenges. He had had disabled kids for several years and shared information on medical issues that I might confront concerning Derek's orthopedic condition. This was my first experience of meeting a single person who had adopted a physically challenged child. My sister invited Jim to her home after the conference, and he stayed there until his plane left later in the week.

The night Derek and I arrived in Houston, my sister, Lynne,

and I decided to go to the conference center, register early, and take in an informal session that was about two hours long. We thought it would be best to leave Derek with my brother-in-law, Andy. I figured that since Derek had been awake for the plane trip he would soon go to sleep. Needless to say, I figured *wrong*. When I saw the look on Andy's face when we returned, I wondered if he would ever speak to me again. Derek, who was still about the size of an eight-month-old, was lying on the huge waterbed, breathing heavily, sweating, and his limbs were stiff. I went to sit on the bed so I could comfort him. Oh my, here was Mom Marian who had no idea how to sit on a waterbed! I fell over backward and Derek floated around and thought this was hilarious. He calmed quickly but I felt badly about my decision to leave him with Andy, who had no idea what to do with a child like Derek. He was not yet a parent and his attempts to console Derek hadn't been too successful. (Recently, I reminded Andy of this experience. Thank heavens he doesn't remember it, and yes, he has spoken with me since.)

I continued to struggle with my feelings about the adoption process. I just could not make people understand my feelings, and they couldn't make me understand why I should not go ahead with my plan. Their concerns were about medical care and support funding. The agency reminded me that there was a strong possibility of enormous medical expenses. Also, there was the possibility that if the adoption was final it might interfere with Derek's medical insurance.

(Most states have programs set up to help adoptive parents of special needs children financially. The amount a parent can receive varies from state to state and depends on the child's age, the severity of the child's disability, and the amount of care the child requires. This is called Adoption Assistance Program (AAP). Some children are eligible for Supplemental Security Income (SSI). Usually the child will have medical coverage through these programs as well. I was able to have Derek added onto my insurance plan with my work at WVSD. These support systems help with the extraordinary needs of the children but do not cover basic housing, food, clothing, etc. that any child would need. When I stopped teaching, I began helping with the family income over the years by tutoring, providing child care for non-family members, and sewing.)

I honestly might have had the same worries about finances had Derek not been in my care and bonded with me. I might have questioned why someone would want to give up her freedom and be tied down with an ill infant by choice. My heart said to go ahead and finalize Derek's adoption. I didn't care about the state's monthly $280 for Derek's care. I was comfortable with my own income. For eight years adoption had been my goal, and I wanted to reach that goal legally. Derek and I seemed to be fulfilling a need by being together. His radiant smile ignited my heart. I wanted to make sure he stayed mine.

Another issue that kept nagging at me was being told what to do and how to do it. I had been teaching for several years and spoke as a professional with parents about ways to communicate with their deaf child. I also made suggestions regarding their child's educational needs and program. I shared with Derek's teacher how best to communicate with him and spoke on other issues related to deafness. When people told me how I should hold Derek, how I should feed Derek, how I should position Derek, how I should do therapy with Derek, how I should be doing this and this and that and that, it began to make me feel like I knew absolutely nothing. I was aware that I had no experience, but common sense and creativity can be as important as book knowledge.

Still, I didn't ignore all the advice. I definitely wanted to provide Derek with some of the positioning equipment that would make him more comfortable and allow him to maintain different positions. At this point, he would either lie on his back on the floor with a somewhat curved spine or recline propped in the corner of the sofa for short periods of time. I purchased a special corner seat with a tray for him to try and sit in. The goal was to facilitate upright sitting and some head control. The seat back was designed to help keep the shoulders forward and the arms in front of the child. I could place toys on the tray for him to look at, try to pick up, or to use for receptive language while I signed to him various concepts about the toys or pictures. He could only tolerate the seat for short periods. It was clear from his facial expressions that it was not a favorite position. He was beginning to let me know exactly what he liked and did not like

73

without any use of words or signs.

As I've mentioned, the kind of equipment that might help Derek was, and is, very expensive. Also, many things were just too big for his small body. I approached my neighbor who had a work area in his garage where I might be able to make things for Derek. He even agreed to help me make a new sidelyer positioner. We made it from a sheet of plywood, some foam that I covered with a nice green vinyl, a couple of hinges, a very large "L" bracket and a couple of nuts and bolts. We used the positioner from school for a pattern and adjusted the measurements to fit Derek's body. It cost us only about thirty dollars (three hundred dollars less than the one from a medical supply company). It also weighed less and with the extra bit of padding was much more comfortable than the one at school!

The positioner allowed Derek to remain on his side with his spine straight, his shoulders rounded forward, and his arms midline (centered in front of him), not twisted behind him. It

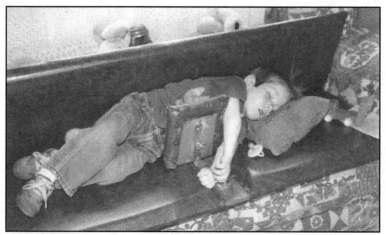

Derek in his sidelyer

also allowed him to have proper saliva drainage and to keep his head from turning strongly to the right. I put the positioner on the sofa so he could see people coming and going, see the TV, and see out the windows. He loved the positioner from the very first time he tried it and spent hours playing and sleeping in it.

Derek, Rocca (the dog), and I continued to travel as time and energy permitted. One Christmas vacation we drove to

Massachusetts to visit my friend Sheila and then down to Long Island to visit our friends Cecilia and Denise. It had been some time since they had seen Derek. They were pleased with the improvements they saw, but they were still concerned about his breathing and other medical issues.

Derek had a cute, white stuffed bunny that his foster mother gave him when she brought him home from the hospital at four months old. Bunny just had to be in his sight before he would go to sleep. It had even gone through all Derek's hospital visits, and of course it traveled with us. One night during our visit, Cecilia, Denise, Derek, and I went out for dinner. When we got back to the house Derek's mood changed suddenly from happy to sad. His chin quivered and his eyes filled with tears as he looked at Bunny.

"Oh my, what happened?" I signed in exasperation. "What did Cecilia and Denise's dog do? Decide to go hunting?"

I picked Bunny up off the floor and gently placed him on Derek's lap.

"Paddington, what did you do to Derek's bunny?" I scolded with one of Bunny's ears in my hand. I closely examined how we might attach the missing ear to Bunny, but it was beyond repair.

"Well, Derek, I guess Bunny is now deaf in one ear just like you!"

He understood and laughed with delight that Bunny was now more like him. I so appreciated how he would accept explanations like that and go on with his life. It seemed he was always looking forward.

He was happy when Snuja, a Boston Terrier, came to live with us when we got home. Snuja was AKC registered as Marian's Little Listener II, and was the second dog I trained to act as a hearing dog for me. Hearing Dogs help increase awareness for people who are deaf so that they can be more in tune with their surroundings. I had missed having a Boston Terrier around, and Rocca was lonely during the day when she was home alone. Derek was delighted to have two dogs to watch and enjoy.

I continued my job on the road and Derek continued his time between the preschool program and the babysitter's. Things were going along exceptionally well when one day Derek began to run an extremely high temperature and developed trouble breathing. Twice, I needed to change his position quickly to get his breathing started again. I was scared to death. Sue called Dr. Giron and she met us at the hospital in ten minutes. A series of X-rays were done immediately and showed another infection of pneumonia. IV's and respiratory treatments were begun, frequent blood draws scheduled to check his blood gases, and monitors put in place as we tried desperately to cool his body below 104+ ° while he struggled to breathe. He kept up his fight but had to be reminded at times to breathe; someone needed either to shake him or change his position.

Again, I questioned my ability to provide the proper care for Derek. I never questioned my love and affection for him, but I wondered if my deafness was interfering with the type of care he required. If I could have heard his breathing or the changes in his breathing better, could I have sought medical treatment earlier before his condition became so serious? The doctor reassured me that she was not concerned about my inability to hear him.

The doctor recalls: **Marian would question me about her hearing and how she was upset that she might not know when Derek needed medical intervention. I tried to explain that even I, with normal hearing, had a difficult time telling if there was a spot of pneumonia in his lungs or not. He was always wheezing and had extremely raspy breathing. Even with a stethoscope it was frequently guesswork and an X-ray would be the only way to make an accurate decision.**

Comforting Derek at times like this was extremely difficult. If only we could have put the oxygen tent over both of us while I held him and rocked him. That would have been comforting. It wasn't possible. It was a constant challenge to position Derek in the oxygen tent. The best upright position that he could maintain was in his cumbersome car seat with all the extra supports that had been added by the therapists. Parts of it began to rust from the moisture in the oxygen tent and it was just too hot for him to sit in it for long periods of time. I finally ordered a therapeutic Tumble Forms seat to take to the hospital. It was not as comfortable, nor did it give as much body support as his car seat, but it could be used under the oxygen tent. Tumble Forms

Derek in the oxygen tent

have seamless coverings that are washable, nontoxic, odor and stain resistant and lightweight. The seat did not rust and allowed him to remain somewhat upright for short periods. Once again, Derek threw off the infection with all his might but returned home a couple weeks later looking very much like the limp, pale child I had first met. My amazing son had done it again, but how much more could his body and spirit handle?

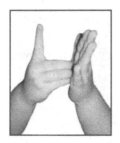

Chapter Eight

1 year 10 months - 2 years 3 months

As Derek had done many times before, he struggled to get better and return to his life of everyday activities. He had to live through the normal baby things, like cutting teeth. He didn't find the comfort in teething toys that most babies do, but he did find some comfort biting on my fingers. He also had to endure some pain from my carelessness, for example, my clumsiness at clipping the nails of his cortical thumbs. Many infants with severe CP have thumbs that are turned inward toward the palms of the hands. Derek's thumbs were so rigid it was almost impossible to straighten them, and one day I discovered there was blood in those thumbs. I think it hurt me emotionally more than it hurt him physically to find that out. From that day on, I took more care when clipping his fingernails and tried to choose a time when he was most relaxed and the least spastic.

I had been talking to the social worker at the Society for Crippled Children about obtaining a wheelchair for Derek. During those discussions it was suggested that Derek might also benefit from a hearing aid to allow him to receive language in some auditory manner. Since he couldn't turn his head to locate people in his environment, would it be possible for him to locate sounds through the use of hearing aids? I certainly had my doubts. Since he had been diagnosed with a profound hearing loss I doubted that a hearing aid could really help. The audiologist at the School for the Deaf attempted to evaluate his hearing in an open field booth. Derek sat in his stroller in the middle of the soundproof booth facing the audiologist who could observe his facial expressions to determine what he might be able to hear. I sat off to the side as an observer and shared my thoughts with the audiologist. (Since I couldn't hear many of the sounds coming through the large speakers myself, I couldn't cheat and help Derek out.) I felt the results were correct when I saw what had been recorded on the audiogram (hearing chart). He had a profound hearing loss. However, the audiologist didn't trust the test results and sent us to Pittsburgh to have an auditory brain stem test done. Derek had to be sedated and hooked up to a respiratory monitor. Electrodes were fixed to his head to provide a better picture of what his hearing loss actually was. That test also showed a profound loss. Still, some school staff and medical staff with Crippled Children's felt it was important that he be fitted with a powerful hearing aid. I finally agreed to give it a try.

We attempted to keep the earmolds in place, but Derek's spastic little fingers would get caught in the cords and pull them out. The receivers were very big and heavy for his tiny ears. His lack of head control and inability to keep his head straight also caused the ear molds to fall out of position. Every time the ear molds fell out they would squeal, but since neither Derek nor I could hear, I wouldn't know it was happening unless I was looking at him. The whistling feedback brought us plenty of stares when we were in public. Those raised eyebrows alerted me to adjust the earmolds. Maybe Derek couldn't talk—but he sure could whistle!

It was practically impossible to tell what he could hear with the hearing aid. Clearly, they didn't help Derek hear speech sounds and when there were extremely loud sounds in the environment, Derek's spasticity would increase along with his anxiety. Trying to keep the earmolds in place resulted in hours of wasted time and much frustration. I agreed to continue to try to use the hearing aid, but I don't know why.

Derek's teacher reported: **Derek seems to show a change in facial expression when there is a sudden loud sound if he has his hearing aids on. However, it is very difficult to keep the earmolds in and not giving feedback. Derek is able to follow objects visually in all directions. He is interested in watching signs done by others and he is giving more eye contact to others while they are signing to him. Derek responds well to**

the attention of others. He seems to recognize others he sees daily.

Once again, Thanksgiving came and we headed for Ohio. Derek was surrounded by the love of his Grandma and Granddad and my brother and his family. The contrast between Derek's development and that of my nephew Geoff, who was only six months older, was profound. Derek was severely delayed in all areas of motor ability, expressive language development, and growth. He still could not sit, roll over, or hold his head up. Geoff was running, climbing, and jumping. Derek had no real functional use of his hands. Geoff could play with any toy that was age appropriate. Derek had no spoken or signed words. His only way to express his needs, likes, and dislikes were through his facial expressions and body language. Geoff was speaking and using verbal language according to developmental charts. Derek's personality shone just as bright as his cousin's as he responded to those who loved him dearly. Witnessing such a vast difference in their

Sitting by the fire

development did not change my feelings toward parenting Derek, nor did it lessen the amount of love I felt for him. Happily, it made me realize these two boys could be loved and accepted just as they were by all members of our family. I feel strongly that love, acceptance, spiritual nourishment, and stability within the home and society are the foundations that all our children thrive upon, regardless of being able-bodied or physically and/or mentally challenged.

I also began to notice how Derek would stay focused longer on things that other children would only observe for a few moments and then be on their way to some other activity. One example was the fireplace. When my brother made a fire, Geoff would look at it for a few seconds and then run off to do something else. Derek would continue to watch the beauty of the flames, and he seemed to relish the warmth. If I would take him away from something he was concentrating on, he would show his disapproval by stiffening his body and making different facial expressions that would indicate he was not ready to be moved, so we'd stay a bit longer. His attention span was beyond what I expected for a child his age.

After our visit, my mother wrote the following poem to help Geoff understand Derek's disability.

My Cousin Derek

Derek's eyes can see;
Derek's ears don't hear;
Derek laughs at me.
He likes me playing near.

Derek's feet don't walk;
Mine run all the day.
Derek sees me talk
But can't hear what I say.

Derek's mouth can eat.
He knows when food is good.
He likes banana treat
As any boy should.

I wish that he could run
And play some games with me.
Oh, it would be fun
To help him climb a tree.

But Derek can't do that,
And he's happy anyway.
Wonder if he knows what
My hands try to say?

Derek's eyes can see;
Derek's ears don't hear;
But I know he loves me,
For he smiles when I am here.

Christmas was coming and it was time for us to pick out our tree. I wanted Derek to help decide which one we would bring home. I parked the car so that he could see all the trees from his seat, then I started holding up trees for him to select from.

"You like this tree?" I signed as I pointed to the tree I was holding.

"No," Derek answered with a pout.

I'd pick another tree. "You want this tree?"

"No," he answered with another pout.

"Come on Derek, I'm sweating," I signed as I removed my jacket even though it was a frigid West Virginia day. I must have held up at least fifteen five-to-six-foot trees for Derek to look at, but he didn't express a desire for any of them. I was getting desperate.

"Okay, just look at the tree you want."

He instantly moved his eyes to the corner. I looked in the direction where he was focusing and saw a lonely, odd-looking tree with branches sticking out in many strange directions. I was dumbfounded!

"You want that tree?" I signed as I pointed at the tree. I got a response! It was unmistakably the tree he wanted. I thought he'd laugh himself out of his seat. After my exhausting work of holding up a bunch of beautifully shaped Christmas trees, he chose that one? It was clear that Derek was proud that he had finally gotten his point across and had gotten his wish.

Once the man selling the trees realized which tree Derek wanted, he simply put it in the back of my car and said, "Please, just take this tree for that boy and enjoy your Christmas!" It was the only free tree I ever remember getting, and Derek was so happy.

We took the tree home, set it up and decorated it. Derek wanted all the ornaments put on, and I followed his visual cues to make sure each was put on the right branch. He was proud and pleased with the way his tree looked. Needless to say, some friends thought I was totally nuts to pick that tree, but after I explained our shopping experience in Derek's presence and others saw how proud he was, everyone supported our choice.

Derek loved to receive presents. Buying gifts for him was a real challenge. He couldn't enjoy the musical toys that a hearing child would appreciate. He couldn't benefit from toys that needed to be manipulated. I bought helium balloons of all shapes, colors, and designs. I deflated some and tacked them on the ceiling over his bed to stimulate his visual development and encourage him to turn his head to observe his balloons. Grandma always found a way to make something for him. She would knit him sweaters, snowsuits, and mittens without thumbs. She had a knack for selecting colors; light blue picked up the color of his eyes, while rust tones made his freckles stand out and accented the red in his hair. Granddad made him a wooden Christmas village complete with trees, animals, homes, a school, and churches.

I also discovered that Derek loved all kinds of stuffed animals. I used them to prop him in various positions on the couch or in the corner of a chair. I bought educational toys that I could manipulate in his presence and use to work with him on his receptive language. That Christmas we began his collection of colorful lights. He found them relaxing to watch before going to sleep each night. And there were books. Books and books and books began to collect in every room of our home. I became quite adept at holding books so Derek could see while signing to him about the pictures. That was a delightful way to spend our evenings and weekends during the cold months of winter.

We continued to thrive on each other's love that winter, although there were hospitalizations every five or six weeks. It was important that the medical staff be aware of how to make Derek as comfortable as possible when in the hospital. Following are notes I had posted on his hospital room wall or on his crib.

Important Information

Derek is profoundly deaf and hears no voices. He responds to lights and vibrations. He has over-reactive reflexes, which cause him to jerk and turn his head away. Please try to move slowly in front of him and when putting the side up on the crib. Derek will not startle as much if he sees you and you touch him lightly before doing medical procedures.

Ways to Position Derek

When awake—try to place him on his side. Roll a blanket to place behind his back. Roll another blanket and put it in front between his legs and up toward center of his stomach. Top leg should be flexed forward. Please put some toys in front of him to see and for him to try and reach. Head should be turned to the left as frequently as possible.

Do not place Derek on his stomach unless you plan to stay with him. Sleeps on his back at night.

Derek's Car Seat
1. Fold two towels to fit lengthwise along Derek's sides.
2. Don't put a towel under his butt.
3. Push his butt down as far as it goes. You need to keep his left knee flexed while doing this and then push him in. You will feel like you may be hurting him but you are not.
4. Place the roller provided under his knees and strap him in quickly.
5. Fold a small towel and place behind his head if he starts to throw his head back.
6. Does not need the red head pillow except for feeding.

Feeding Derek
1. Derek must be positioned correctly in his car seat with the red head pillow in position.
2. Try to keep food below Derek's eye level. This will help to keep him from throwing his head back and reduces his chances of choking.
3. Tongue thrust is worse when he is sick. He gives the impression that he does not want to eat when he really does. Be patient and work slowly.
4. Use only the plastic coated spoon on his bedside stand. Do not use a metal spoon.
5. Place small bites of mashed foods on back left teeth for best results.
6. When giving medications with a syringe, again, place slowly toward back of lower gums.
7. Derek can sip from the edge of a cup but be careful he

does not aspirate the fluids.

Even with the notes prominently placed, sometimes I found Derek in the strangest positions. I would move him, then wait until his nurse came in, call her attention to the notes around Derek, and ask her to please take the time to read the information. Those notes were there for the purpose of helping staff care for Derek and maintain his comfort. If Derek remained in the hospital for an extended period, I would periodically make new signs with different colored markers and add a picture or two. I'd do anything to get the attention of the medical staff, and more times than not, in that small community hospital in Romney, the signs improved the quality of Derek's care.

Chapter Nine

2 years -
2 years 7 months old

*T*hroughout the winter Jim and I corresponded by mail. One of his sons was ill, and we shared stories of our times in hospitals. We decided it would be nice if I could visit him in California and meet his boys. During spring break, Derek and I flew to California for a week's visit. This would be our first of several trips made 3,000 miles across the country.

Jim had four boys living with him in San Jose (about forty-five miles south of San Francisco). We toured around a bit to see some of the local sights, but I had to lug Derek's heavy car seat everywhere. We couldn't leave it in the van because he needed it to sit in when he ate. Derek really needed a wheelchair. Even the smallest wheelchair Jim owned was too big for Derek; however, with some pillows to help him sit comfortably, my son could actually see what was going on around him when we went places. He was alert, happy, and taking everything in. He loved being with Jim's guys and watching what they did.

After we returned home, I was more determined than ever that Derek get a wheelchair. The Crippled Children's Society provided them and I had applied,

First time in a wheelchair

stressing that I needed some way to transport Derek that would allow my hands to be free to sign to him while we were on outings. This was important for maximum language development. Even though he was still small, he was growing, and his body continued to be totally floppy like a rag doll one minute and completely rigid and spastic the next. It was becoming more difficult to carry him. Getting him to stay in a safe and comfortable position in a regular stroller was impossible. Signing with one hand while carrying him was equally difficult, as my signs were incomplete and incorrect. The Crippled Children's Society told me that because of Derek's recurring hospitalizations they believed he wouldn't live long enough to use a wheelchair.

I was furious. "He has a right to have a chair and be more comfortable as long as he is alive. If he should die, I'll return your chair in perfect condition and it can be used by another child!"

That set some minds straight, and it was finally decided that Derek could receive a chair. Once again I was in unknown territory about procedure. I knew I'd have to decide exactly what kind of chair Derek could use and get a prescription for it. Since he would not be able to sit upright all the time, Derek would need a chair that could be reclined and moved to different positions to accommodate how his body might function at a specific moment. Needless to say, his small size also presented a big problem. I didn't have a van, so I needed a chair that would fit into my car. I had to choose something that Crippled Children's Society would agree to purchase. The selection of wheelchairs for young children at that time was much more limited than it is today.

At long last, it was decided he would do best in a TranSporter Travel Chair, which could also be used as a car seat. The front wheels would fit in under the dashboard and the back wheels would fold up under the chair to fit onto the seat of the car. Everything, including Derek, could be swiveled around to fit in the car and be secured with a seat belt. Perfect! My patience was tested as we waited for all the paperwork to be done, and the chair to be approved, ordered, and shipped. In the meantime, I was still lugging that heavy, bulky, miserable car seat.

About this time I was starting to think about adopting another child, even though Derek's adoption still was not finalized. I saw how much Derek enjoyed being in the presence of other children. I continued to bring students home from school on weekends, and Derek delighted in their attention and signed communication. It had become clear to me that he would most likely never be able to physically participate in most activities and would play the role of "The Cheerful Observer." Yet, this made him no less a person. He was someone who truly appreciated being in the presence of others where he could sow his own small seeds of love.

Derek's love radiated to everyone who entered our home. His desire to live could not be explained in words. His willingness to share was evident by his acceptance of other children. Loving another child could never break my bond with Derek. There was absolutely no possibility that another child would replace him or lessen the amount of love I had for him. We both had much to share with any child who joined us.

So over the next several months I began searching for an able-bodied deaf child, the kind of child I had been looking for when Derek entered my life. I found Doris, who lived in New York and had become deaf from meningitis. She was placed with a married couple in her home state. Then there was Kerri in Texas, who was deaf and had a seizure disorder. I was told that we didn't have the proper medical facilities for her in my home. There was Johnny, who lived in Tennessee. We went to visit him, but for many reasons he wasn't the child for our family. Passion and David were siblings who lived in Pennsylvania. Passion was deaf and David was hearing, but they were placed with another family. There were a lot of disappointments. Maybe I needed to change my focus?

I had learned so much from having Derek and unquestionably I enjoyed our relationship. *Why not adopt another physically challenged child so they can appreciate the presence of each other?* I gathered information about several children. My social worker and I updated my home study to present to other states where several possible adoptees lived. This kept us busy for the next several months.

In the meantime, school had let out and Derek and I were

basically free for the summer. All kinds of fun things were planned. We took a short trip to Pennsylvania to visit some relatives and were coming back across the mountains in West Virginia on a beautiful, clear afternoon. Suddenly, I noticed Derek was greatly excited in his seat. I could not imagine what was going on, as there were no tunnels, bridges, or flashing road signs ahead, all of which he loved. I followed his gaze. Sure enough, there were my parents driving up the mountain in their motor home! How could he have recognized it? We had passed every kind of vehicle imaginable for more than 300 miles, yet he knew this one was theirs. Yes, it was different because my Dad had built a box on the back, but for him even to have a clue who was in that motor home was beyond anything I could have imagined! He genuinely loved his grandparents and knew he was in for another special time with them.

Other exciting news involved Derek's wheelchair. Finally, it was approved and was to be delivered soon. Fortunately, someone brought to my attention that I would need a ramp. Most homes in West Virginia are not built on flat ground. Once again, Granddad (who was still visiting), neighbors, and friends measured, sawed, hammered, and painted a ramp that would tolerate the snow and ice of winter, rain of spring, and hot sun of summer, all for the cost of the materials. Everyone was happy to see the sparkle in Derek's eyes as they worked. The ramp was ready, but we had to wait just a little bit longer for his wheelchair to arrive.

When it finally came, there was an enormous problem: it was just too big for Derek. He still weighed only about fifteen pounds and was no more that two feet tall. If his hips were back in the seat, his feet were where his knees should have been. I made pillows and foam supports that would fit the chair and allow his body to be moved forward but the footrest could not be raised high enough once his knees were at the front edge of the seat. My dad and neighbor cut, sanded, and finished some boards to raise the platform high enough for his feet. Then his feet could not stay in position and would slip off the sides. Once again, they sawed, sanded, and finished more supports for the sides of the footrest.

The side supports that were part of the chair's construction were almost the full length of Derek's trunk and were necessary to help keep his spine straight and provide him with trunk support. The head supports were also quite big. They certainly were not attractive but they did keep his head turned forward so that it would not flop back and up to the right. Still the problems continued. The armrests were so high that the wheelchair tray came to the middle of his chest and not at his waist.

The strap that was supposed to keep his hips in position was much too long. Off we drove to the man who taught shoe repair at the School for the Deaf and asked if he could make large, sturdy, snap fasteners for the strap so we could shorten it. He smiled at our request, dropped everything he was doing, and went straight to his shop to make the modifications.

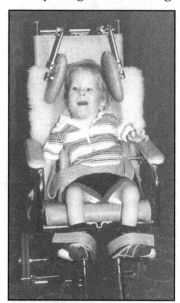

Finally, after almost a year's wait, Derek had his first wheelchair. He was thoroughly proud and delighted at being able to be in an upright position with the adequate support his body needed. I was eager to go for an outing and have my hands free to sign to Derek about everything we experienced. We were both thrilled with our new freedom. Also, Grandma and Granddad were able to take Derek on several walks around the neighborhood before they left to return to Arizona.

Derek's new chair arrives

Soon after Derek's chair arrived, so did more company. Jim had been traveling cross-country in his van with his three boys. (It had been necessary to return one of his boys to his home state.) Both of us had made an effort to keep in contact with the foster families where our children had lived before moving into our homes, and Jim was making his summer visit to his boys' families. He stopped in Romney for a couple of days, and we had a great time together, despite being a bit crowded. None of his boys could communicate with signs, but it did not seem to bother Derek. He just soaked in all the action, and I felt that he knew how much Jim's family accepted him. We went on some trips, and Derek fit right in with the group now that he had his own chair. It was heartwarming to see him interact with everyone who entered our home.

Derek taught me many things that summer. He actually encouraged me to slow down. For those who do not know me, this is almost an impossible undertaking. One day as we were eating (remember, eating was like a hobby for Derek and he took hours to finish a meal), Derek shifted his gaze from me to his plate. As always, my eyes followed his and sure enough there was a tiny ladybug inching its way around the rim of his plate. He watched that small, delicate insect with the greatest interest. I gave up with dinner and signed to him what I knew about ladybugs: they could fly, they were red, and so forth. Eventually it flew away.

When we traveled, we would stop along the roadside to enjoy a gorgeous sunset. I would take Derek out of the car and hold him in my arms. His entire body would relax as he took in the spectacular hues of the distant sky. Often something would catch his eye as we went for walks, such as a flower, a butterfly, or a squirrel. Once again, I would be encouraged by Derek to take time to appreciate the beauty of our environment. After all our struggles together with medical issues and dealing with many kinds of stress, I found it incredible that this petite child, without words, had the power and unique ability to instill and nurture peace within my being.

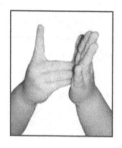

Chapter Ten

2 years 7 months - 3 years 3 months old

We spent the remainder of our summer relaxing, going for long walks with Derek's new chair, working in the garden, sharing and eating the large quantities of produce we grew, searching for a sibling for Derek, doing daily therapy, and just enjoying being together. Once again, I was not looking forward to the start of school even though I loved my job.

As school began for both of us, we adjusted to our schedules once again. I was still working the itinerant preschool position and driving daily, so I decided to stop teaching ASL class at the college. I didn't want to be away from Derek more than necessary. Sue and I wanted to take an aerobics class two nights a week. It would have been costly to have a babysitter for both nights, so we decided to bring Derek with us. He sat on the sidelines and seemed to take pleasure in our activity. I don't recall that he ever complained during our hour-long sessions. He was thrilled by our entertainment and had a way of encouraging me to continue when I was winded and the aerobics were getting the best of me.

Sandy had worked throughout the summer with her department to have Derek's adoption approved. I had hired a local lawyer to prepare all the required documents. At long last we received a court date. On September 21, 1981, I carried Derek up the many steps of our county courthouse to present our case before the judge. It was an exciting moment for me to know that Derek would now legally be mine and known as Derek Michael Aiken.

Sandy recalls: **Adoptions are things that most judges enjoy** doing because they are happy times. I remember that Judge John Hamilton was very impressed with Marian's desire to accept all of Derek's medical conditions and adopt him. He was also very impressed by the fact that she was a single parent and very devoted to this child. During the adoption proceeding, Judge Hamilton took time after the normal question and answer session that is involved in the adoption proceedings to talk about Marian's devotion and commitment to her small child. The speech that Judge Hamilton gave was very touching. Normally judges do not take the extra time to recognize such a special occasion.

Following our time in court, Derek and I went home and waited for our friends to finish their workday so they could help us celebrate over dinner and dessert.

I had kept in touch with the head of the Pediatrics Department at the hospital where Derek was born. I could only imagine the stress of a job in a neonatal Intensive Care Unit.

Sandy, social worker, with Derek

Many infants do not survive even after the best care possible. Some survive and live active lives as full-term babies might, showing no effects of being born prematurely. Still others survive with varying degrees of disabilities, such as Derek. However, most leave the hospital to live with their birth families. I had never been in the neonatal ICU. Nor had I had the opportunity to meet those who had cared for my son. Here is a letter I sent to be shared with the people who had taken care of Derek during his first few months of life.

September 23, 1981

Dear Dr. Phillips,

I am writing to thank all those who helped care for Derek during his first several months of earthly life. It must be an extremely strenuous job for those of you who work in the neonatal unit to care for such sick and helpless babies. Would you please share this with the staff in the neonatal unit?

I can't imagine life today without Derek. He has brought so much enjoyment to me. It is true that he will always remain severely handicapped, but his radiant smile, as seen in this picture, reminds us that these children deserve to live a life of happiness and love.

There is something about caring for a child such as Derek that enables us to grow along with that child. I find that my patience, love, sensitivity toward and acceptance of others have grown tremendously. I realize that this will not be true of all those who care for children as severely involved as Derek, but it is true for Derek and me.

Derek's adoption was finalized on September 21st, and he is now known as Derek Michael Aiken. He has a busy schedule for such a young child. He can be outgoing when he knows the people he is with. And, if he could, I know that he would very much want to express his thankfulness to those who helped him struggle and survive during the first several months of his life. Please accept our words of gratitude for your dedication to your work.

Sincerely,

Derek and Marian Aiken

I continued to look for a sibling for Derek. I had already begun inquiring about other children who were physically challenged. It was not difficult to find such children since there were many. But it wasn't easy to decide which one might have the best personality for our family and be able to receive our love. I found Patrick, Sean, Robbie, Phillip, Josh, and Rusty. Sandy, who continued to be my social worker, sent out information to their social workers. Phone calls went back and forth from state to state. I even drove to Minnesota to visit one child, only to learn that his social worker would never even consider placing a child with a single parent. Wow, that blew me away. Why hadn't we been told of the social worker's position before I made such a long trip? Many of the other children I considered were placed with families in their home states or permanently with their foster family.

But Rusty was still a possibility. He lived north of New York City in a foster home with an older couple. Like Derek, he had cerebral palsy and also a mixed seizure disorder. I felt it was worthwhile to obtain more information about him and I wanted to meet him in person.

Despite the many conversations Sandy and I had with Rusty's social worker she just couldn't seem to understand that although I was deaf and single, this adoption was something I felt I was capable of handling. One day at Sandy's office while she was talking to the social worker, I took the phone out of her hand and spoke through the receiver myself. I explained clearly why I wanted to make the trip to New York to visit Rusty in person and why I felt adopting another child was something that everyone involved could benefit from. Then I handed the phone back so Sandy could hear the response. I really don't remember what it was, but I do know that we had more positive contact after that conversation. Many times, it was not the child's worker who was so much concerned about my deafness and being single, it was the supervisor. This was the situation in Rusty's case.

While we waited for decisions to be made about Rusty, we continued with our regular schedule. We faithfully did Derek's daily therapy but he showed only slight improvements in his physical development. In fact, it was hard to tell if there was any progress at all. Still, it was a challenge that we enjoyed together, and it was a rewarding way to give and receive love. Each small sign of improvement was like overcoming a gigantic hurdle for Derek.

There were so many "cannots." Derek cannot sit, cannot stand, cannot hold his head up. Derek cannot feed himself, cannot help dress himself, cannot toilet himself, cannot bathe himself. Derek cannot communicate his needs with words or signs. The list seemed never to end.

Nevertheless, there were also the "cans." Derek can keep his head a bit straighter than three months ago. Derek can sit in the corner seat and in the corner of the sofa when propped up correctly. Derek can eat three meals a day of ground foods and soft, chewy cookies. Derek can drink from a cup. Derek can follow moving objects with his eyes and hold small toys in his hand. Derek can kick his feet in the swimming pool and bat at his mobile. Derek can enjoy the dogs. Derek can watch and attend to stories signed to him. Derek can radiate love and appreciation through his cheerful personality, and Derek can interact with those in his environment.

One day in November I arrived for work at the home of one of my preschool children and was given a message that Derek was terribly ill and I should return to Romney as soon as possible. I had never before been called in from my job on the road. I was completely panicked. I jumped back in the car and took off for home. I made record time over the West Virginia mountains, got to the school, left the school's car keys in the office, and ran to my own car.

I sped across town to where Derek was. My heart was racing, my palms clammy as I gripped the steering wheel. I relaxed a little when I got to Derek's classroom and saw him smile at me. Sue had already called the doctor, and she was expecting Derek. She checked him over, listened to his lungs, sent us to the hospital for a chest x-ray, and said she'd call us later with the results. After this episode, I made the decision that I would not travel the following school year but return to the classroom to teach. I did not want to be hours away from him.

Sue recalls: **While Marian was on the road, things weren't looking as bad as they had been with Derek, although he was still seriously ill. Of course, there was no way to get that news to Marian. I was in the office when Marian came flying back from miles and miles away with tears in her eyes. I had never seen Marian so distraught over Derek as this. She had always taken everything with a tremendous amount of strength, every little step of the way with Derek. He had been through many things and so often I thought, *Will he make it?* I had watched Marian shoulder it all. Now, I felt the burden of her having to travel and be away from him was just too difficult for her to handle.**

We were delighted to have Derek's wheelchair, but it wasn't without problems, especially during the winter months. One day when we came home from school, I was taking it out of the car as I normally did. It was a long, complicated process, and just as I went to lift the front wheels off the floorboard and out of the car, my feet slipped right out from under me. Boom! Derek and I were down on the ice. Thankfully, he was still in his chair, safe and sound, but my shoulder was really painful. As I lay there trying to figure out if I'd broken it, dear Derek, with his wonderful sense of humor, looked me in the eyes and laughed! Fortunately, my shoulder was not injured and the pain went away almost immediately.

Occasionally, I'd wrap the dogs' chain-link collars around the chair's back tires to give it some traction up the ramp. This wasn't very smooth riding, but it did provide some safety.

Snow and ice could also be the cause of school closure for Derek. Since I taught at the state School for the Deaf and the children lived there, there were no "snow days." If I could not drive to work, I could walk in. But how would I know if Derek's school was closed for the day? Closures were announced on the radio, and I could not hear them. My neighbor and I created a solution: if Derek's school was to delay starting for two hours, my neighbor would close one side of her curtains and I would take Derek to her house until school began. If his school was canceled for the entire day, she would close the entire curtain and I would take him to the babysitter. This "code of the curtains" worked pretty effectively. If I couldn't drive to the babysitter's, then my neighbor would keep Derek for the day.

I was finally granted permission to make the trip to meet Rusty during Christmas vacation. We stayed with our dear friends, Cecilia and Denise, on Long Island. Cecilia drove Derek and me into New York City to meet the social worker. It was so nice to have Cecilia along to help out with communication, as she was fluent in ASL. Rusty, who was two and a half months younger than Derek, was in the hospital with bronchial pneumonia. He had lived in the same foster home since he was an infant and his foster parents loved him dearly, but it was not feasible for them to continue caring for him because of their age and health. After meeting with his social worker and her supervisor, it was agreed that I could visit Rusty on Christmas Eve at the hospital.

Sadly, Derek couldn't meet him that day (hospital rules

about visiting children). Derek and Denise waited in the lobby while Cecilia, Rusty's case worker, his doctor, and I went into Rusty's room. I had only seen a couple of pictures of him and they didn't do him justice. I couldn't have selected a child who was more the opposite of Derek. Rusty lay fast asleep in his hospital bed with beautiful, shiny, dark hair and an olive complexion. When we woke him, he looked up at me with huge brown eyes that took my breath away. He was so big and hearty-looking that I asked the nurse if she was sure this was Rusty. Derek was older but Rusty weighed ten pounds more and was almost a foot longer than Derek. I sat Rusty over the edge of his bed while I held onto him and studied his face.

He could not sit alone, but he had some use of his right hand and good head control, compared to Derek. In fact, he put his right arm up around my neck to hold on. Clearly, he had a lot going for him physically and I thought he would be able to improve greatly with more therapy. I took him out of the crib and rocked him in the rocker that was at his bedside. I really don't recall much more about our visit that evening. I wanted to go back to Derek and tell him about Rusty. I didn't really know how much Derek understood about the new adoption plans, but he continued to pay attention to my conversations and responded in a positive manner. After Christmas Eve services, Cecilia helped me phone my parents and tell them my news. I was in tears trying to describe Rusty over the phone to them. Soon after Christmas Day, we returned to West Virginia with our report to Sandy. Of course, she had already spoken with Rusty's worker on the phone about him joining our family.

Rusty's worker shares her memories: **I never had any misgivings about placing Rusty with Marian. He was a child with special needs who required an exceptional home. We had some inquiries about him, but when the prospective parents were told more details in terms of what caring for him would be like, they backed out. We felt it was important to be as up-front as possible about his difficulties rather than place him with someone who would not be up to the task. The first thing I remember about contact with Marian was a telephone conversation with her social worker in West Virginia. The social worker explained to me about Marian's adoption of Derek and her knowledge of and ability to cope with handicaps very** similar to Rusty's. Nothing I said about Rusty had deterred Marian. So, since she would not be dissuaded, we scheduled a meeting in New York.

I remember her wheeling Derek into the agency and back to my office. What struck me then is what always strikes me when I look at the faces of her children, and that is how happy they are. Derek looked like a very happy and loved little boy.

I remember a comment made by one doctor during our meeting that she felt Derek was having seizures and was concerned about his breathing. My sense at that time was that she may have underestimated Marian's knowledge and her sophistication when it came to Derek's medical problems. I, however, was very impressed and conveyed this to my agency. After our meeting, I think everyone involved with Rusty's case was delighted in our good fortune of finding a home like Marian's for him. I know that her handling of Derek and his obvious flourishing in her care put us at ease when we considered what she would be facing with Rusty. I strongly suspect the placement would have been more complicated had it not been for our meeting Derek and seeing how well he was obviously doing.

While we waited for the final paperwork for interstate adoption placement to be completed, there was much to keep me busy. I corresponded with Rusty's foster family on a regular basis. I wanted to learn more about his everyday schedule, what he liked to eat and do. Unfortunately, they had never accepted that Rusty had limitations and much of the information I was given was not accurate. For example, I was told his seizures were under control and he didn't have or need a wheelchair. I sent them pictures of my home, Derek, and the dogs to help ease the anxiety of separation from the child they had cared for.

Assuming Rusty would become my second son, my greatest problem would be how to transport two children in wheelchairs in my small station wagon. I learned Rusty actually had a chair very similar to Derek's, but it was larger. Neither of them would fit comfortably in the back seat. One of my neighbors and I went to the Ford dealer with the idea of buying a van. My neighbor explained to the dealer, without my knowledge, why I needed one. The salesman was touched and sold me a new van at cost. I didn't need anything fancy. I ordered an empty cargo model with the idea of fixing it to accommodate two wheelchairs. We found a remnant of carpeting that fit. A neighbor and I went to a junkyard and when we explained what I needed, the manager told us to take whatever we could find that would work. When we got back home, we cleaned up the seat belts we'd found, drilled holes through the van floor, and bolted them down securely. Now I could secure the wheelchairs in place. Naturally, there was one seat belt between the two front seats for Derek right smack in front of the air conditioner.

I also had to rearrange our bedrooms. Derek's room was too small for two beds, so we swapped rooms. The bigger bedroom would be perfect for the two boys.

"Mom put Derek's bed here," I signed to Derek. "I will put bed here for Rusty." Derek watched with interest as I moved the chest of drawers, his wall decorations, and the deflated helium balloons from the ceiling. Rusty was too big for a crib so I bought a nice youth bed from another neighbor. We were all set with our sleeping arrangements. Derek practiced sleeping alone in his new room for several nights before Rusty arrived. He seemed to take all the changes in stride.

Word came that all the paperwork had been completed, a date was set for us to travel to New York to bring Rusty home, and I was excited about adding another child to our family. Suddenly, a completely different feeling struck my heart: this was the last weekend Derek and I would spend together as a family. *Am I doing the correct thing? Do I honestly want to follow through with this? How will I manage with two wheelchairs, two young children who are totally dependent on me to meet all their needs? Will I have enough energy to care for both of these beautiful children?* My heart kind of sank to my stomach.

I decided I had to do something special with Derek that weekend. The weather was cold and windy and the roads were covered with snow, but Sue had read in the paper about a small petting zoo scheduled for that weekend. So Derek, Sue, and I drove extra carefully to the mall in a neighboring town. The man in charge of the petting zoo refused to let Derek and his wheelchair inside the enclosed area. Sue stood up for us and before I knew it, we were ushered into the animal area. Then I understood why the man was so concerned about the wheelchair. Goats began munching on the sheepskin in the back of his chair, the tires, and the tissues and loose dollar bills in my pocket! Derek thought it was hilarious and laughed so hard he could barely breathe. A llama that had been lying next to Derek's chair stood up and touched Derek's hand, which was hanging over the armrest. Derek's fingers got stuck in the llama's fur. He loved it, and his eyes followed every move of the creature with delight. I picked up a young lamb and held it on his lap. Derek cherished every moment he was with the animals. He was so radiant and expressive. I am so thankful that I followed my heart and did something special with Derek that weekend despite the awful weather and bad road conditions. It's extremely meaningful

At the petting zoo

for children to have special times with their parents before a new family member is added, for no other reason than just to let them know they are cherished.

The following weekend, we loaded up our new van and drove to New York to bring Rusty home. We spent part of the time with Cecilia and Denise, then stayed with other friends, Mary and Maureen, who lived closer to Rusty. Mary had been one of Derek's preschool teachers and Maureen had taught the older class at Special Services Center in Romney. We had a wonderful time together. I was able to leave Derek with Mary or Maureen when I needed to go somewhere alone. I had made arrangements to visit Rusty's preschool program, meet his therapist, and sit down with his neurologist to discuss his seizures and all of the medications he was taking to control them. All the while, Rusty's elderly foster parents followed along watching my every move with hawk eyes. They totally disagreed with the placement, but Rusty's social worker realized they wouldn't be able even to lift him for very much longer.

Early the next morning we loaded Rusty's things into the van. The separation was particularly difficult for his foster mother. It was obvious that he'd had a lot of love from her and her husband.

In retrospect, it was crazy to even think of traveling from New York to West Virginia that day. The weather was terrible. I wanted to take my boys home. I didn't know if Rusty understood what was going on. I wanted to begin familiarizing him with his new family life. So, on April 6, 1982 we left New York on a long and tedious drive of several hundred miles back to West Virginia.

Maureen M. remembers: **I couldn't believe that Marian wanted to adopt another special-needs child because I thought she had her hands full with Derek. But she felt she had enough love and energy to share with another child, so the adoption went through.**

I remember on the day she was to pick Rusty up there was a major snowstorm in the New York area. My friend Mary and I told her to wait another day to get Rusty. Did she listen? No!! Marian was determined to get him and go back home. She strapped Derek in her van and took off for Rusty. I went with her: cars were sliding all over the roads. Marian said she felt New Yorkers could not drive well in the snow. I pointed out to her that this was a major snowstorm, there was a lot more traffic in New York than West Virginia, the parkways were a bit narrow, and she was driving like there was a double lane where there was only a single lane! Did she care? No!! She picked up Rusty and set off. Fortunately, she arrived home safely. Determination and stubbornness are two of her most noticeable characteristics. And I'm sure they have become a necessity in all her dealings for her boys.

Derek was about to have his first experience taking the back seat. I put his wheelchair in the middle of the van and secured Rusty up front in Derek's spot. I explained to Derek that I needed Rusty there so I could keep an eye on him. Amazingly, Derek smiled as if to say, "Yes Mom, I understand." I watched him in the rear-view mirror, and every time I caught his eye, I signed to him how much I loved him. He smiled right back.

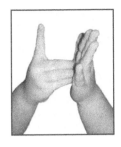

Chapter Eleven

3 years 3 months - 3 years 8 months old

Wearrived home late at night. It had been such a tedious trip and I was beyond exhaustion. I unloaded the boys only and left their wheelchairs in the van. Derek was glad to be home and seemed to be proud of his new brother. Sue was sleeping but came out to the living room when she heard us come in.

Sue recalls: **I had already gone to bed when I heard Marian come in. I got up and went to the living room. Marian had put Rusty down on the floor and amazingly he rolled over!** *'That boy will really be able to do a lot,'* **I thought, but of course things would prove differently as time went on. I was surprised that Derek never showed any jealousy toward anyone else, particularly his brothers. He seemed genuinely happy to have a new brother and never appeared to mind moving over and making room for another.**

I made sure that both boys had their medications and enough food to last the night and I put them in their beds. I was pleased that Derek smiled through the entire event and shared me without any protest. It was not easy for me to go to sleep that night because of all the excitement of having my new son home.

There were numerous adjustments to make now that I had two sons to care for, but I'd always been a person who does best with a structured schedule, and that quality would serve me well. The biggest adjustment was the morning routine. Derek had always been patient enough to remain in bed while I took a shower and got dressed for work. However, I quickly discovered Rusty had an entirely different personality and once he awoke, he would fuss, whine, scream, and bang on whatever was within his reach. He wanted to be out of bed and to eat breakfast immediately. It took a lot longer to dress and feed both boys but Rusty was able to finger-feed himself dry cereal and pieces of toast. He could also chew, and choking was a minimal concern. These factors helped tremendously in speeding up the morning breakfast procedure. Still, I also needed to master the routine for his anti-convulsant medications.

Rusty was able to do more physically than Derek. Derek could scoot himself about on his back while lying on the floor in a slow and somewhat random manner, but Rusty was able to drag himself on his right hip while pushing with his right foot and pulling with his right arm, and he could roll around on the floor. He also liked to grab things that were within his reach. So began the relocation of breakable knickknacks. Out went the coffee table with pointed corners as Rusty could hurt himself if he had a seizure while he was on the floor. I also found I had to be attentive when Rusty wanted to play with Derek.

He liked to pat Derek's face and pull his hair. Derek was unable to defend himself but took it all in stride, as long as I was able to move Rusty before he got too rough. Occasionally, if I didn't reach Rusty in time, Derek would manage to get in a good kick or two to push Rusty away. I can't imagine what

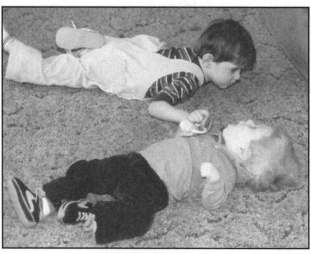

Rusty taking Derek's toy

was going on in his mind when he was so tolerant of Rusty's behavior. I do know that my tolerance level was not nearly up to Derek's.

What I found most interesting was how capable Derek was of sharing me. Previously, when Derek was in the presence of other children in our home, it was only for short periods. I expected him to show some jealousy at having another child in the house all the time, but I saw no display of concern or irritation. Derek was simply full of smiles and happiness that he now had a brother to watch, one who definitely entertained him. Derek also showed the ability to take pleasure in other's accomplishments such as things that he would never to be able to do physically, like sit on the floor without support. When Rusty finally learned to balance in a sitting position, Derek glowed with pride that Rusty was able to do this though Rusty would still topple over sometimes, Derek perceived this as entertainment.

With Rusty, it was the opposite. Every time I paid attention to Derek or picked him up to hold him, Rusty became jealous, demanded my attention, and wanted to be up. I cannot overstate how relieved I was that Derek could share as he did. Derek knew I loved him no less than before. In fact, his ability to share and know that he could always receive what he needed from me strengthened my love for him. It was an incredible gift Derek gave me.

Derek and I managed to finish out the school year while Rusty went to a sitter during the day. I began feeling comfortable with our new routine. I would wake up, shower extra quickly, dress and feed the boys, load them into the van, go to work, pick up the boys, come home, and fix dinner. One of the most challenging tasks was shopping. Thankfully, Sue or a neighbor or other friend would often come to my place and stay with the boys while I went to the grocery store. We continued to go out for dinner with friends, although not quite as often.

Sue recalls: **Marian did not seem to slow down much after Rusty arrived but her activities did change some. I remember going out to dinner with other friends and not having Marian and Derek along. The people in the restaurant asked if something was wrong. No, nothing was wrong, but Rusty's**

behavior prevented Marian from going to some places. She still went on her trips with her boys and dogs and wasn't the least bit afraid.

Summer vacation of 1982 was finally here. My parents had only seen pictures of Rusty, but they had never met. As soon as school was out, I loaded up the van and off we went. The van was crowded with Derek, Rusty, two dogs, John, a former student with whom I had become very close, and me. He was eleven years old the summer he traveled with us. Derek idolized John and vice versa. John would come home with me on weekends and help me with the boys. His joining us on the trip was a wonderful experience for him as well as a great help to me. On our way to Arizona, we spent a night or two visiting friends. At first when I traveled with both boys, I found it easier and felt more secure to stay with friends rather than spend the night in motels. Sometimes we would pull over at a campground and sleep in the van. It was crowded but cozy knowing that my little family was together and happy.

It could take hours to stop and feed both of the boys. With my sons, it was not a matter of removing a seatbelt, having them climb out of the van, run into Wendy's, order a hamburger, sit in a booth, and enjoy a meal. You can only imagine how long it would take to unbelt and unload their wheelchairs from the van, push them through doors that did not have automatic openers, find enough space at a table in a restaurant for two wheelchairs and two able-bodied people, then go and order food, feed the guys, clear our table, reload back into the van, and belt their chairs to the floor again. It was just too much work. Derek did not do well in these types of places, and he would become more spastic than usual. People who did not know our little family stared at us. Therefore, I carried a cooler filled with ice and plenty of yogurt for Derek. We'd also carry other soft foods like pudding and applesauce. Eating the same foods got a little boring and it certainly was not a nutritionally balanced diet, but Derek rarely complained. Sometimes we'd stop and I would run into a store or fast food place and buy meals while John stayed with the boys in the van. Derek was always happy when I brought him a milkshake or a cup of ice cream, but Rusty's tastes were different. Ice cream and milkshakes were not on his list of favorites. Rusty liked crackers, dry cereal, French fries, and other finger foods, but he made quite a mess. Thank goodness the dogs had good appetites and would clean up around his wheelchair. Because I did most of the feeding in the van, I was constantly banging my head on the ceiling. This gave Derek some good laughs.

Other times we'd pull over at a rest stop or picnic area to take a break to refuel our bodies and stretch. I'd get the boys out of their wheelchairs to take care of their toileting needs. Sometimes we'd just stretch out on sleeping bags on the van floor during our stops. Other times we would unload and eat in a shady place. After a short time, I would lift and belt the boys back into their wheelchairs and then hit the road again. All this in our dear little cargo van with two seats in the front, two wheelchairs, two dogs, and all our necessary belongings in the back...and I loved it.

We stopped in Houston to visit my sister's family. She now had children of her own and the physical abilities of her children far exceeded those of mine, even though they were younger. Nevertheless, we always enjoyed being together and just hanging out on the living room floor. Acceptance of my children in the homes of my family was the most rewarding part of my visits.

Onward to Arizona! I thought we'd never get across Texas. My boys weren't accustomed to the heat and dry air. Rusty took the trip fairly well. He didn't enjoy sitting for long periods of time in any chair, much less his wheelchair, but I hung things from the ceiling of the van for him to bat at to help keep him amused and it seemed like John was constantly picking up the toys that he had dropped on the floor. Derek's wheelchair was positioned between the two front seats in front of the air conditioner and where I could keep lifting his head up when it dropped forward. He would visually take in John's and my conversations. If we were not involved in a conversation, he was content to observe everything outside our van: the desert, the cacti, farms, cities, the sunsets, and the differences in all the scenery. He just seemed to soak it all in with delight.

At last, we reached our destination at Grandma and Granddad's house. Oh, what joy filled Derek's heart to be with them. My heart overflowed to see my two sons receive so much affection from my parents. Although Rusty had very limited eye contact with others compared to Derek's, he quickly captured my father's love in a different way. Rusty could hear, and he had a delightful laugh when he was being teased. And Granddad knew how to tease! Derek was still Grandma's boy and took in her every move and attempt she made to communicate with him through signs. Once again, I was glad Derek was willing to share those he loved dearly.

Grandma recalls: **What I think was special about Derek was that he was the first child there and it was his home, but he never appeared to resent others coming into the family. He enjoyed the fellowship so much. He never seemed to have a shred of jealousy and he enjoyed life.**

Two very special things stick in my mind about that visit. One was going to the fireworks display in Phoenix with my father, John, and Derek. Derek had never seen fireworks. (Rusty had to stay behind with my mother because the noise would cause him to have seizures.) It was a treat to see Derek watch the beautifully lit up skies. His body would stiffen and quiver with excitement. As the fireworks fizzled down and disappeared, Derek's body would relax until the next spectacular sight. I remember how much enjoyment my father received from watching Derek. Derek truly knew how to bring pleasure to others' hearts.

The second vivid memory is of the circus. Grandma and Granddad treated us to the circus in Phoenix. We were ushered to the wheelchair section through an area that included space where the animals were kept until they went on. I thought we were never going to get through all the

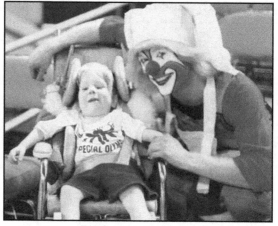

Derek at the circus

animals, clowns, and acrobats. Derek took it all in with excitement. It turned out that the wheelchair section was up high and far from the center of action. Derek's eye control was still quite limited, and he couldn't look down for long periods. He needed to be lower to really be able to focus on the action.

Dad went to the manager. I was totally embarrassed, but my father was determined that Derek was going to see this circus from a better seat. We were in our new places just in time for the beginning of the circus parade. Derek was trembling with excitement. (Excitement, however, frequently affected Derek's comfort. He would sweat excessively and his breathing would become quite raspy. I would cool him off with wet washcloths and offer him fluids.)

The acrobats, horses, the clowns, the other animals—everything and everybody marched right past us. Then, the lead elephant stopped in front of Derek. The lady on top was waving to the crowds. Then she shifted her focus to Derek who was sitting there in his little blue wheelchair with his arms spread wide and a broad smile on his face. He made perfect eye contact with this lady. She sat for a long time and waved to Derek, and he smiled back. Eventually, the people behind her began to yell for her to get moving. I think she had completely forgotten what she was supposed to be doing.

This was a big moment for me. I was still having a difficult time figuring out what my child really understood and how much he could actually interact with others. At times, I felt he was highly intelligent, but then school reports told me I was wrong. *Could a child who could focus for such a long time— more than two hours—do so if he were profoundly retarded?* There were children around us who were playing with this and that, running around, and not even paying attention to the circus. Derek, however, was totally absorbed in the activity in front of him, concentrating on what was happening, laughing at the clowns' silly antics, holding his breath when the man on the motorcycle rode overhead on a tightrope. His eyes were ready to pop out when he saw the lions and tigers. His hands were in fists and he was gritting his teeth while the tightrope walker did a fabulous balancing act. *Could such a child be classified as retarded?* In my opinion? Definitely not.

All too soon we left Arizona to continue on our way. We drove on into California to visit Jim's family for a week of low-key activities and servicing the van. At last, we set out for the long journey back across the states to our cozy home in West Virginia.

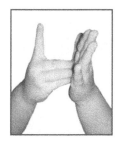

Chapter Twelve

3 years 8 months - 4 years 6 months old

*W*e returned home safely from our summer travels. The school year was almost ready to begin, and I had decided to return to the classroom and not travel for work. I just didn't want to be far away from the boys. Rusty had shown improvement in his physical strength and could now sit independently. He tolerated his leg braces for longer periods of time and continued to finger-feed himself. He also was doing most of his own spoon-feedings. I was pleased that he could be more independent. He was sleeping better and not waking up as frequently during the night. His eye contact had improved as well. It was encouraging to see Rusty improve in so many areas.

Where Rusty showed great strides, Derek continued to lag behind, but there were improvements.

Derek's physical therapist noted: **Derek was out of town with his mother all summer, so I did not get to see the "little rascal" until school started. He seems more alert and active than ever now. The biggest change is the notable increase in tone and active movement of his neck flexors, which allows him a little more stability of the head while seated. Derek seems to have more body awareness and tries to use his extremities as much as he can. The tonic neck reflex is still evident but not as prominent as it was last year.**

Rusty was ready to begin school in the same class as Derek. It became more and more clear that his seizures were not being controlled well despite the fact that he was on several anti-convulsant medications daily. As each day went by, the frequency and duration of his seizures increased. I had trouble finding a pediatric neurologist who was prepared to treat him under the medical insurance that had been arranged with Rusty's home state. Sandy, Dr. Giron, and I worked diligently to find the proper physician. In the meantime, Rusty had gone into *status epilepticus*, which is continuous seizure activity (or a series of seizures without returning to consciousness between seizures). So began a long, stressful year of hospitalizations.

It started in a local hospital in Cumberland, Maryland, about a forty-five minute drive from home. After several days there, he awoke and seemed to be himself and was discharged. However, just a couple of days later, he slipped back into *status epilepticus* and was transferred to West Virginia University Medical Center in Morgantown. I was extremely concerned about his care and not being able to remain near him. He was in ICU and parents could visit only for very brief periods. Sometimes I found someone to interpret phone calls to the hospital for me. Many times, I simply found someone to care for Derek and took off for Morgantown, a two-and-a-half-hour drive each way.

Rusty contracted a very serious case of pneumonia, his left lung collapsed, and he needed to have chest tubes inserted. He had to be tied to the bed because he would pull on the tubes and IV's. He had to be fed with a nasal tube. His coloring was ashen. I drove back and forth and sometimes was permitted to visit with him for only fifteen or twenty minutes. He could not be held or sit in his wheelchair. The neurologists began experimenting with different medications. When he was awake, he was constantly screaming, fussing, or thrashing around in the bed. However, most of the time, he was not aware of what was happening around him. He stayed in Morgantown for weeks. Fortunately, I had some friends in Morgantown I could stay with on weekends. They also helped to check up on Rusty during the week.

On the other hand, Derek was doing exceptionally well health-wise. He continued to attend his school program for five full days a week. He was gaining strength in his legs and becoming more active. A couple of weeks after Rusty was admitted to the hospital, Derek began to withdraw and his eating became sporadic. He indicated through his facial expressions and gaze that he missed Rusty. He would look at Rusty's place at the table and then back to me with an expression as if to ask, "How is Rusty? When is he coming home?" I tried my best to explain that I did not know when Rusty was coming home.

The next time Rusty was out of ICU I took Derek with me to visit. Derek couldn't see Rusty from his wheelchair so I picked him up and put him beside Rusty in the crib. Tears welled up in my eyes as I watched what happened next. Rusty lay completely still and Derek, who was normally the less mobile of the two, lay next to his brother, trying to reach up to touch Rusty's face. When he succeeded, his smile was full of happiness and contentment. Then Rusty opened his eyes and looked at Derek and smiled. My friend Marsha had come with us, and both of us were really stunned. Even the nurses were in shock. It had been weeks since I had seen much response from Rusty. It was obvious that a bond had developed between the boys in less than six months. Yes, Derek could receive but he also could give. How grateful I was for that fine trait.

That winter was a very emotional time. There was so much going on and I was full of conflicting feelings. I was elated Derek was doing well but desolate about the condition Rusty was in. I was exhausted with worry. Rusty was always on my mind and I struggled with the fact that he might need to be returned to New York. We could not leave him in the hospital forever. *Who can care for him while I am working?* He certainly would not be able to return to the preschool program if he were discharged from the hospital now. I needed to work full time and care for Derek. Rusty was now dependent on a nasal tube for nutrition that he would pull out frequently and, when he was home, I would have to reinsert it while he screamed, bit at me, and tried to push my hand away. This was not the child I had brought home a few months earlier.

Because the adoption was not finalized at that time, the State of New York had the final say about his medical treatment. However, some of their decisions did not match my opinions. The biggest problem for me, personally, was how Rusty responded to me. Even when Derek had been extremely ill, he was always aware of who I was and when I was present. Rusty, on the other hand, showed very little recognition of me or my role in his life. I felt it would comfort him if he knew who I was and we had a stronger bond. I worked on building that bond when he was able to come home for short periods. He inevitably needed to go back to the hospital for medication changes, pneumonia, bladder infections, and finally to have surgery for a feeding tube placement.

I learned how to replace feeding tubes and mix formulas that would give him a balanced diet and that were of the right consistency to get through the tube. I also learned how to handle his seizures, which continued to be frequent. I became aware of what caused some of his seizures: sudden loud noises, clicking sounds of a toy, the dog barking, and the doorbell. Most of these sounds I did not hear myself, but I became visually aware of them and would try to prevent a sound from happening if I could. The doorbell was the easiest because I simply told my friends to walk in and not ring it first.

Should Rusty be returned to New York? What a difficult question to contemplate. It was something that needed to be addressed and dealt with. If it was decided that he needed to go back I would not only need to try and explain the decision to Derek, but I also would need to live with it myself. There were a huge number of considerations. *Is it fair to Derek that I need to spend so much time away from him to visit Rusty in the hospital, or when Rusty is at home, the time required for his medical care? Can I actually return this child to his home state and into an institution, a child I have chosen to join my family? Can I admit to myself that I am not capable of handling this situation much longer?* The social workers were willing to go either way with my decision, but I needed to be the person to make the decision. I struggled for several weeks. I searched for a spark of awareness in Rusty. He was too ill to be transported back to New York anyway. I continued to bring him home and care for him when he was well enough to be out of the hospital.

Through all of this, Derek was holding his own. After so many hospitalizations and illnesses the first years of his life, he plugged right along this year, still struggling to breathe at times, but missing only a couple days of school and spending no time in the hospital. He also continued to sustain me with his engaging personality and eagerness to face each day with the desire to make every moment count.

We continued our daily routines as much as possible with school, story time, playing outside in the snow, language exercises, and physical therapy. The physical therapist still was not pleased about Derek being in that infant walker, but I wanted to keep him in an upright position at least part of the day. I began to use some creative skills I didn't know I had. I decided to make him a standing board. It was very simple but served the purpose just fine. I bought a large

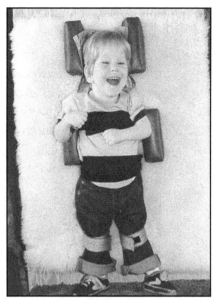

Handmade standing easel

sheet of plywood and sawed it in half. Then I added a long hinge at the top. I made a platform for his feet that fit near the bottom of the board. I padded the board with foam and a layer of sheepskin, put on some side supports and some straps to hold him at the waist, chest, and knees. I'd position him on it while he was lying down and then raise him to standing position, it looked like he was the painting on an easel. He loved this standing board and was up high enough that he could see out of the windows. I had the freedom to stand him at different angles depending on the amount of head control he had at the time. When he wasn't using it, I simply closed it flat and tucked it out of the way behind a chair or the sofa.

One weekend when we were in Morgantown, we stayed with our friend Marsha. I was showing her how to make pompoms. Her attempt with bright orange yarn was a total flop! The yarn wasn't wound tight and was uneven. Nonetheless, Derek thought it was the most splendid thing to play with. It was lightweight, colorful, and soft. He'd pick it up with his tiny fingers and swing it around with his right arm. He'd get his hand near his face and rub it on his cheek, or if he were sitting in his chair near me while I was reading or not paying attention to him, he'd try to brush my arm or face with it. That simple thing

115

brought him hours of entertainment and pleasure. Marsha was grateful to Derek for turning her failure into something positive.

Communication is always an issue with children like Derek. Finding a way to let him express himself, what he wanted, how he felt, or even what he understood seemed impossible at times. I continued to search for products he might be able to use. His deafness complicated the situation because he needed to be able to see the signs of the person he was communicating

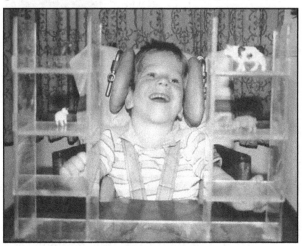
Derek's eye gaze box

with. I finally came up with a Plexiglas object box that I made to fit on his wheelchair tray. It consisted of six compartments where objects could be placed to Derek's left and right, but it was open in the center so he and another person could see each other. It was heavy, bulky, and breakable, but it would work. I wanted to help him learn how to make his desires known. We began by placing two objects in the top compartments, a cup for drink on one side and some pudding on the other, for example. The goal was for him to look at whichever he wanted and hold his eye gaze there for a short period. Then I would reward him by giving him his choice. I would also place two toys on the upper shelves and ask him to look at a specific toy. This would help me know what sign vocabulary he was retaining and comprehending. It took great patience for both of us and progress was slow, but evident. Later we were able to add more objects, as he understood what was expected of him.

The Christmas season was upon us again and our friends from New York came to visit us. Cecilia and Denise were among the first of my friends who had met Rusty before he moved in with Derek and me. They were surprised by Rusty's condition and just as frustrated as I was about his changes and care. We celebrated Derek's fourth birthday, which was quite a milestone for him. I decided he should be dressed in something other than baby clothes since he was now four years old. He was still considerably small for his age. Finding clothing that was age appropriate, that fit, and that was made of a fabric that was not too rough or stiff could be a challenge. He definitely did not need pants with reinforced knees. (These types of pants were popular during the early 80's.) Dressing continued to be difficult at times, especially when his left arm rotated back and stiffened. Fortunately, getting pants on him was not a problem, but I learned that all the pockets needed to be smoothed out and not balled up under the seat belt of his wheelchair.

It also continued to be difficult to find toys from which Derek could benefit. I had come across a book with how-to directions for making special toys for children who were physically challenged. (Today, several companies develop and sell such toys for special-needs individuals.) I set out for the toy store to find some battery-powered toys that would visually reinforce a physical activity that Derek might learn to perform. They would need to hold his interest but move slowly enough not to set off his defensive eye reflex. The toys then needed to be modified by bypassing the on/off switch so Derek would be able to play independently with it. A new switch that Derek could manipulate would have to be created.

I went to Radio Shack and got the materials: copper wafers, wiring, mercury switch, pedal switch, and soldering supplies. I would need to adapt the toys as described in the book. I had no idea what I was doing, but I soon learned that many of the things suggested were not sturdy enough to stand up to Derek's spasticity. I needed to modify them to meet his needs. For example, a suggested lightweight cardboard box would need to be made of plywood covered with fake fur.

Once modified these types of toys would help him learn

cause and effect. For example, if he touched a kitchen spatula that was wired to switch a toy off and on, it could activate the toy and reinforce the activity of reaching out and holding down on the spatula. Or, I'd place Derek prone on a therapy wedge with his bright red knit hat, specially made by Grandma, with a lightweight mercury switch secured. As he raised his head, the level of mercury in the switch would change and the toy would activate. I could position that switch in different places that would

Playing with a spatula switch

encourage him to raise his head as much as possible. For Derek this was therapeutic *and* fun at the same time. It was quite a challenge to decide where to place the switches and what position he should be in. *Do I put this switch near his left or right hand, by his left or right cheek, near his left or right elbow, by his left or right foot, or on his head?* Derek's ability to focus on things was to his advantage in succeeding at these tasks, but even though his visual tracking skills showed steady improvement, his ability to have much physical control over his body was so limited. One day, he would seem to have fairly good control over his right hand, but the next day it seemed like he could not make that hand do what he wanted it to do. At times he became frustrated and upset.

Using a mercury switch

I would have to put the toy away because it was completely defeating the goal of having fun while learning. However, on his good days, he would entertain himself for long periods and become upset if I needed to stop an activity.

Derek's progress report from school states: **In visual motor skills, Derek has improved on following moving objects eighteen inches or farther in front of him, using only his eyes. He has been exposed to four to five new signs each week throughout the year and his attendance has been great! He is much more responsive and has expressed his likes and dislikes more consistently.**

Spring came and things for Rusty began to improve. Once again, he smiled frequently. He became more attentive to his surroundings. His skin coloring changed back from green or ashen to his normal olive complexion. His seizures were under better control and he was able to remain awake for longer periods. He continued to be irritable, but I could deal with that most of the time if I just didn't wear my hearing aids, which was not a problem for me since I didn't especially like them to begin with. Rusty's crying and complaining didn't bother Derek since he couldn't hear him, but it did bother the dogs and the neighbors. Sue discovered that if we played an audiotape of his favorite TV program, *Family Feud*, he would quiet down immediately. And at last, Rusty began to eat again. His intake of fluids was still extremely limited, and I continued to give him liquids through his feeding tube. It must have been about three months later that he began to drink from a cup and to feed himself again.

Sue and I worked hour after hour with Rusty and Derek doing all kinds of therapy and stimulation on the living room floor. We gave them spontaneous language experiences, speaking and signing everything we said about every activity that took place. Sue and I did the physical acts of completing puzzles, stacking blocks, and sorting pictures while the boys were supposedly attending to our every move and receiving our comments as we went along. Rusty began to roll around, to sit unsupported, and to torment Derek. His eye contact improved day by day and his awareness of his environment began to return. We were able to resume our walks around the neighborhood. When spring arrived, Rusty celebrated his fourth birthday. The accomplishment that was of utmost importance to me if Rusty were to remain in our family finally happened. Rusty showed recognition of who I was. He smiled when I entered his line of sight and reached out with his long right arm to hug me around the neck. He turned his head in the direction of my voice. What a pleasure it was that Rusty was able to bond again with Derek and me. The decision was made that Rusty would stay. Derek was glad to have Rusty home and to have more time with Mom too. Once again, we could continue to be an active, contented family of three.

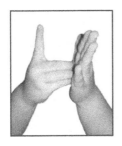

Chapter Thirteen

4 years 7 months - 6 years 5 months old

*A*fter that challenging winter of medical problems, Rusty regained his weight and tolerance for being around people. I felt a need to travel further than between home and hospitals and to leave some of my worries behind. Jim and I had continued to correspond throughout the year and decided we would hit the road together with our families. We'd meet at my house and caravan from there. I had my van serviced and made preparations for our trip. I learned the previous summer that the air conditioner did not serve the back of the van well. So my neighbor hooked up fans along the ceiling to help circulate cool air from the front. We had to be extra careful where we placed the fans because Rusty could reach far with his right arm. He was good at randomly reaching, pulling, and throwing loose or lightly-secured objects. Instead of hanging toys for him as I had the year before, I secured things tightly to his wheelchair frame or the tray on his chair.

Jim and his boys had driven to Connecticut to visit Alan, a child he was thinking about adopting. Then he had some trouble with his van and was delayed in arriving at my house. Once Jim, Jay, Tom, and David eventually arrived in Romney, my home overflowed with three power wheelchairs and their battery chargers, stacks of clothes, and boys. Instead of stepping over only two bodies as I walked around the living room, I was stepping over four or five. At night, we put sleeping bags on the floor for Jay, Tom, and David. Rusty and Derek slept in their own beds. Jim decided to bed down in his van, where he had more room to stretch out. Once Jim had done his family's laundry, we packed up our vans for our cross-country trip of 1983. Sue and the neighbors waved good-bye as we drove off. Jim usually took the lead, pushing his old van a bit beyond the speed limit. I followed in my more reserved driving style, staying within the speed limit even in Texas. As much as possible, we stayed with friends along the way, but it was never easy. Places where I had stayed with friends before were more or less wheelchair accessible since Derek and Rusty's chairs could be lifted and carried up steps by two people. However, Jay, Tom, and David were using heavy power wheelchairs that could not be carried up the steps. We parked their chairs near the steps and Jay, a nineteen-year-old non-ambulatory dwarf, was able to crawl into homes. Tom and David needed to be carried in. Tom was thirteen years old and had cerebral palsy which affected his lower body. He could drag himself across the floor once he was carried into someone's house. David was twelve years old and also severely involved with cerebral palsy with extremely limited use of his left hand and no use of his other limbs. This was definitely an eye-opening experience. I had carried Derek and Rusty up steps to Sue's apartment, but they were still small. I had also carried them up two flights of stairs to the doctor's office because there was no elevator (this was before the Americans with Disabilities Act). I hadn't thought anything of it at the time because my boys were small, but what would I do when they got older? Would I need to change doctors? As we traveled, I began seeing more and more physical barriers.

Jim liked to unload his boys for meals. I preferred to feed my boys in the van. Jim's old van had a side door that opened downward, creating a ramp for the wheelchairs. My van didn't have a ramp or a lift. I physically lifted Derek and Rusty, in their wheelchairs, in and out of the van. Jim and I compromised, agreeing to eat only our evening meals in restaurants, unless we were spending the night with family or friends. We startled people with our group of five boys, all in wheelchairs, as we held doors open, filed into restaurants, moved chairs, rearranged tables, and got situated. This was complicated. Tom and David were both left-handed, Jim needed to help David with his meals, and Tom's footrest needed to be clear of table posts. Jay could sit most any place at a table, but we liked to put him by Rusty to lessen the chances of Rusty throwing a spoon or tipping over a glass. I needed to position Derek and Rusty at an angle and close enough so I could feed them. Derek's positioning was more complex because of his strong tonic neck reflex, which caused his head to turn toward the right. He liked to sit beside Tom, who rubbed his head or gently touched his arm like a loving older brother. It always took several minutes to get settled, but everyone seemed to have a great time and accepted each other's presence.

Tom and Jay could read the menus and order for themselves. Jim read the menu to David. I decided what Rusty would eat. I signed to Derek the items on the menu I thought he would like to choose from (then hoped I ordered the right thing). As we waited for our meals the boys munched on crackers or chips, except for Derek (who couldn't chew). To hold him over and help keep him relaxed, I fed him a cup of pudding that I brought along. I also carried a handheld electric mixer to grind his food into the correct texture and consistency so he could swallow it. Eating in restaurants drained me. It was extremely different from eating at home where I prepared and put the food on the table before I brought Derek and Rusty to the table. Going to restaurants with friends in Romney were more for social outings than a chance for new cuisine. I fed them something at home first and ordered small portions of side dishes or desserts when we were out.

Jay, Tom and David could all speak. I could understand Jay's and Tom's speech fairly well, but not David's. I needed to ask someone to repeat what David said. I tried to keep Derek included as well by signing as much as I could to him.

Onward we traveled, loading and unloading wheelchairs. As we traveled south to Louisiana, Jim arranged to visit another child, Ben, who was available for adoption.

Ben lived with a foster family on the bayou in the city of Franklin. Although he was eleven months younger than Derek, they were about the same size. Ben had much the same coloring as Rusty. He was another beautiful child. His eyes were as big as saucers and they actually moved together and focused normally. He was highly alert and attentive to activity around him. His facial expressions were strong and, like Derek, he expressed himself with his eyes. Ben also had cerebral palsy. He had little control over his body, but had much better head control than Derek. He also had normal hearing and appeared to have considerably good receptive-language skills. He left me with the impression that he was extremely bright but trapped in a body that would not function physically as he desired.

He was reluctant to leave his foster mother's arms so that Jim or I could hold him, and he didn't have a wheelchair.

"Ben doesn't have wheelchair. Can Ben sit in your chair?" I signed to Derek.

Derek's delight in sharing was clear as he gazed at Ben and acknowledged my request with slightly raised eyebrows and a smile. I lifted Derek out of his chair and put him on the sofa. I showed Ben's foster mother how to put him in Derek's wheelchair and then took some pictures of Ben. At first, Ben was

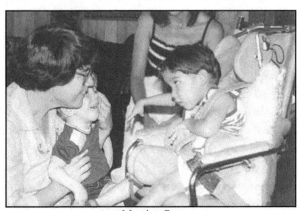

Meeting Ben

unsure about sitting in Derek's wheelchair, but he gradually decided he liked it. Rusty became restless and Derek was uncomfortable, so after about an hour, I took my boys to the van while Jim talked with the social worker. Members of Ben's foster family smoked, and the smoke was very hard on Derek. It was also a really hot, humid day. I couldn't do anything about the weather, but I could get my son away from the smoke. I directed the fans on Derek and tried desperately to make him drink extra fluids to keep him hydrated.

Eventually, we made it to my sister Lynne's home in Houston. Again, we were challenged with steps at the front door, as well as bathrooms that were not easily usable for Jay, Tom, and David. (Bathrooms were not as much of an issue for Derek and Rusty.) The boys liked to stretch out on the floor where my nephew Marc, who was a little over a year old, crawled over them. Lynne and Andy enjoyed meeting Jim's boys. They'd heard me talk about them for several months. This was a "get to know you" stop before we continued to my parents' in Arizona.

It was incredibly hot. We stopped at a motel so that Jim could bathe his guys in a wheelchair-accessible bathroom and give Derek some time in air conditioning. Jim took his boys to see a movie, and I stayed behind with Derek and Rusty. I needed some time with my own guys to focus on them and give them my full attention. When we arrived in Arizona, my parents received everyone with open arms, as was their nature. Derek delighted in being in their presence. Grandma took him swimming, fed him ice cream, held him, and read him stories. Granddad enjoyed talking with Jim, Jay, Tom, and David and learning about each one. One evening they had a surprise birthday picnic for me. They put trick candles on the cake. Naive as I was, I didn't know anything about trick candles. I blew and blew and blew but the candles wouldn't go out! Derek laughed and laughed until he could hardly catch his breath. He got a big charge out of this joke. Our visit was short but long enough for Derek to stay connected to Grandma and Granddad.

At a stop on the way to California, Jim talked about Ben.

"Marian, would you be interested in adopting Ben?" he asked.

"Adopt Ben!" I exclaimed. "I haven't finalized Rusty's adoption. What state would allow me to adopt another child until I finalized Rusty?"

"Well, I plan to go through with adopting Alan (the boy he'd visited in Connecticut). I know Ben would fit your family. You could help him reach his potential," Jim continued.

Actually, I was interested in Ben from the minute I saw him in his foster home, but I had no intention of adopting another child. *How can I handle a third child who will be totally dependent upon me to meet all of his physical needs like toileting, dressing, nourishment, mobility, etc.? How will I manage alone with three children in manual wheelchairs? What will Derek make of having another brother?* Still, the issue of space at home was not a concern. There was plenty of room for another bed, small wheelchair, and clothes. And the van could easily hold another wheelchair.

"I'll think about it, Jim, and let you know."

I had to discuss the idea with Derek and get his approval before moving forward with another adoption. Before leaving California to return to West Virginia, I developed the pictures I had taken of Ben in Derek's wheelchair. I used them when I talked to Derek so I could be certain he knew exactly whom I was talking about. I didn't want Derek to confuse Ben with one of Jim's boys.

"Derek, did you like Ben?" I signed to him one day when we stopped at a rest area to have lunch. I needed to do this "consultation work" slowly. I didn't want to give him the impression he would have less attention from me again so soon after Rusty had joined us (just a little more than a year earlier).

Derek raised his eyebrows as he smiled. This facial response meant "yes."

"I think Ben is a nice boy too," I signed to Derek.

I took a more northern route home. It was a long drive, but the scenery was beautiful and the temperature a bit cooler. Some evenings, I would pull into a campground, and we'd sleep on the floor of the van. Other nights, I would stop at a hotel where we could actually sleep on beds. While traveling, I always slept near Derek with one hand close to his chest to monitor his breathing. I still feared he might forget to breathe while sleeping. Each day, I refueled the van, fed my sons, made certain Rusty had things to entertain himself with and tapes in the cassette player so he could listen to music. Derek and I appreciated the scenery, and I frequently thought of Ben.

"Derek," I would sign, "I think Ben liked your wheelchair. You like Ben?" I'd ask again and again, hoping to get a consistent response.

With his eyebrows up, a smile, stiffened arms, and his eyes on Ben's picture, he clearly meant, "Yes."

"Ben join our family, you want?" I'd sign. "Derek, Rusty, Ben, Mom, family, you like that idea?" I signed with lots of facial expression, including raised shoulders and eyebrows, to make it clear I was asking him a question.

Each time I mentioned Ben, Derek focused on my signs with great intensity. His body would quiver with excitement and I interpreted his responses as meaning "yes." When we arrived home, I contacted my new social worker, Nancy, about the possibility of Ben joining our family. She had lived in Romney for years, knew some ASL, and was open to the possibility of bringing Ben into the Aiken family.

Even though Rusty's adoption had not yet been finalized, Nancy, the Department of Welfare, and Rusty's social worker understood that it had been delayed because of his medical issues the year before and not because I didn't want him or wasn't able to care for him. Also, Ben's social worker had already met Derek, Rusty, and me. We weren't just a file he was handed. He was impressed with how I handled the boys and communicated with them. He was also pleased with the services offered in our small community and school. The decision was made officially, Ben would join our family in Romney as soon as possible.

As the social workers completed the interstate paperwork, I went about my daily life with Derek, Rusty, and work. I purchased another bed and chest of drawers. I bought bunk beds and made a railing for the bottom bed to make sure Rusty couldn't fall out. Since he was the longest of the three, he would use the standard size bed mattress. Ben would have the youth bed that Rusty slept in. Once again, I included Derek in the changes to the room arrangement.

"Derek, come here," I motioned, encouraging him to roll his infant walker down the hallway so he could see my effort to fit all the furniture in the same room. The boys had to share a room because it had the baby cry signal. Each boy's bed had to be placed against one wall with a railing on the other side of the bed. I used extra-long sheets to fold over the railings and under the mattress to prevent their spastic limbs from becoming stuck or bruised on the railings. As I worked and Derek watched, I stopped and signed to him what I was thinking and doing.

"I put your bed here. I put Rusty new bed there. Ben sleep that bed," I signed. "You like your bed here?" I'd ask. I wanted Derek to feel included in the process and to make Ben's placement as easy for him as possible.

I did something to make the move easier for Ben, too. Ben gave me the impression that he was bright and understood what was happening. So, I sent him short letters every week.

I enclosed pictures of our home, family, and dogs. He was accustomed to hearing his foster mother being called "Mama Ruby." I didn't want to be called "Mama" and signed my cards and letters "Mom Marian." (With Rusty, my correspondence before his placement was to ease the apprehension of the foster family, not Rusty's, as he didn't have the cognitive ability to comprehend. Today, there are many more options families can use such as social media, webcams, videotapes, computers, and all types of technology to make the transition easier for the children.) One weekend I arranged home care for Derek and Rusty so I could fly to Louisiana to spend the weekend with Ben. We received permission for Ben to spend two nights with me at my friend's house in Slidell. It was a wonderful way to learn more about each other before his move to West Virginia.

At home, we went about our usual routine. Derek's progress in school seemed to have plateaued and his physical strength remained about the same. His breathing continued to be labored and raspy, but I was greatly relieved there had been no pneumonias or hospitalizations for several months.

The first week of December 1983, I received word that Ben's paperwork was completed so he could join us in Romney. Sue cared for Derek and Rusty while I flew to Louisiana to bring Ben home. On December 19, 1983, Derek shared his home for the first time with his second brother.

It was Christmas vacation. I had two weeks to adjust to life with three sons before I had to return to work. Sue was not around to help; she was spending Christmas vacation with her family. Feeding Ben without a wheelchair was close

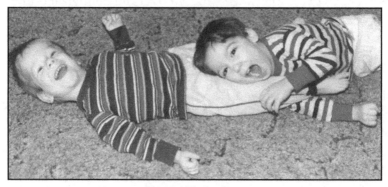

Happy to be brothers

to impossible. I decided to rotate feeding the boys. This way each had some individual attention, and Ben could use Derek's wheelchair while I fed him. However, it was definitely time consuming. I never imagined it would take so long to feed three boys. Each needed three meals and snacks every day.

Rusty was the easiest to feed and dress, but he had no patience, and would not wait. I started the mornings with Rusty, and his food was always, always there when I brought him to the table. It was a toss-up who would be next, Derek or Ben, so I had them take turns. Derek's body would alternate between being rigid or floppy. Ben was always rigid with his hands fisted, legs and arms stiff. He also had little control over his oral skills. Once he got his mouth open for a spoon, his tongue would thrust forward, making it difficult to get the spoon into his mouth. Keeping the food in his mouth so he could swallow it was also challenging. Like Derek, he could not chew so his food had to be ground or mashed. Ben was better able to take liquids than Derek, but he was accustomed to drinking sodas, which I didn't give Derek or Rusty.

It seemed like I would just finish breakfast when it would be time to begin preparing lunch. *What time will I need to start my day when vacation is over? Will I be able to feed these guys and get to work on time after driving them to their school program?* I hoped Sue would help me for a week or so when she returned from vacation, even if she wasn't a morning person.

When I told Jim how I had to rotate Derek and Ben for meals, he shipped an old wheelchair from California for Ben to use until he got one of his own. Mealtime was still time consuming, but we could all be around the table at the same time. I just had to remember which spoon went into which mouth!

Derek loved being a brother, but Ben wasn't so sure. Whenever I turned from Ben to do something with Derek or Rusty, Ben would pout and cry. It never occurred to me that Ben would be jealous. This could be a major problem in a family with a single mom. I let him know that I did not appreciate his trying to manipulate others with his "basset hound face." It took some time for him to learn that if he wanted my attention, he would have better luck if he found a positive way to let me know.

Sue returned and we celebrated another milestone in Derek's life, his fifth birthday. He had won the love of many people during his first five years. He continued to find joy in the smallest things. Then, shortly after that birthday, his health took a major turn. Since he had been generally well and hadn't needed to be hospitalized for over a year, I had almost forgotten how ill he could become. Once again, I was running back and forth between work, home, and hospital. I had to make arrangements for both Rusty and Ben when I was at the hospital. Sue covered for me much of the time at home, but it was not right to depend on her day after day so I had some high school girls come to care for Rusty and Ben.

One day Dr. Giron spoke with me frankly. "Marian," she said as she showed me Derek's chest x-rays. "I need either you or someone else who is close to Derek to remain with him if he is to stay in the hospital here in Romney. The nurses can't be with him the entire time. And, Marian, I'm not certain he can survive this case of pneumonia."

Stunned, I choked back tears. I could only nod to acknowledge that I understood. I also didn't know if he would survive, and I was frightened beyond words. His struggle was greater than anything I had ever witnessed. The weight he had slowly gained over the past two years was gone in a matter of weeks because he could no longer eat. He was on IV's for fluids and medications. Respiratory treatments left him exhausted. He tried to cough but was too weak to do so. He could barely move. My mind raced as I tried to figure out how I could stay by his side, work, and continue to care for Rusty and Ben at home. I wanted to do it all. I was tired and felt I had let all three boys down when I could not be with each of them. I realized I had to do something I had not done before: call my mother for help.

But first I had to ask for help to make the phone call. I wanted to call as soon as I arrived home that night, but Ben was still awake. I had to be careful what I said around him because he could understand conversations. Rusty's ability to understand language was profoundly delayed, and it would not have made any difference if he were in the room. I spent time with Ben and Rusty and put them to bed before I had Sue make the call.

I dialed the number as Sue held the phone and waited for an answer. She cradled the phone on her shoulder as she interpreted the call for me, and I spoke a little louder than usual so we did not need to pass the phone back and forth.

"It's your mom," Sue signed.

"Mom, I need to ask a big favor of you," I spoke, my voice quivering.

"Yes, Marian, what is it you need? You sound upset about something," Sue signed as my mother spoke.

"It's Derek, Mom. He is in the hospital and very ill with pneumonia. The doctor wants someone to be with him all the time, and I just can't do it," I said as I tried to hold back tears. "Can you come and help me?"

Without hesitation, my mother made arrangements to come. There's no airport near Romney, so I needed to drive about two and a half hours to Dulles Airport near Washington, D.C. to pick her up. Her plane came in the late evening and it was close to midnight when we returned to Romney. She wanted to stop by the hospital to see Derek before we went home. I peeked in the doorway of his room to see if he was awake before going in. To my surprise, Dr. Giron was by his crib, swinging her stethoscope back and forth like a pendulum to entertain him. I commented on the late hour and told her I was surprised she was still at the hospital.

"I wanted to check on Derek and decided to stick around to play a little while," she said with a peaceful smile. Then she left for the night.

I scolded Derek in a teasing manner, telling him it was too late for him to be awake. He was able to grin, then his eyes focused on Grandma. (He had been sleeping when I left for the airport, so I had not been able to tell him where I was going.) After a few minutes of handholding and some kisses, I explained that Grandma would be back in the morning to stay while I went to work. I drove Mom home, then returned immediately to the hospital to spend the night with Derek.

For the next several days, Mom and I alternated between home and hospital. I spent the night at the hospital while she stayed with Rusty and Ben. Early morning, I'd return home to get Rusty and Ben up, dressed, fed, and ready for school. I took my mother to the hospital, and she would stay there with Derek for the day while I was at work and Rusty and Ben were in school. After school I'd reverse my route, pick up the boys, pick up Mom, and take them home. Mom had never met Ben. He was delighted that his new Grandma came to visit. We discovered Ben liked coffee when Grandma shared some sips with him, even though he'd just turned four. I'd grab a bite to eat, feed the dogs, and go back to the hospital for the night. Mom and Sue would cover at home.

Derek labored for more than two weeks in the oxygen tent. It was difficult to make him comfortable. He struggled to eat because of excessive mucus, other secretions, and coughing. The hospital staff focused primarily on keeping his temperature down, suctioning his airway, keeping him hydrated, and doing respiratory treatments around the clock. At last, he was weaned from the oxygen tent and able to breathe room air. Slowly he began to eat and regain his strength. After a month, he was discharged and came home to recuperate.

Home seemed to be the best medication. Derek could sleep in his own bed or on the living room sofa. He could be held

Grandma visits Ben, Derek, and Rusty

and fed whenever he needed to be. My mother stayed on and Derek soaked up all of her attention. Eventually, she made arrangements to return to Arizona and once again I was a single parent. Sue had moved next door. We were still close, and she made herself available if I needed help.

During the spring of 1984, I felt tension with the administration where I taught. I decided to take a sabbatical the following year to develop teaching materials at home. I looked forward to spending more time with the boys, both at home and at their school program. We didn't travel cross-country during the summer, but we did attend the North American Council on Adoptable Children's Annual Conference. Workshops, children's programs, social time, and day trips were all part of these conferences. Tables filled with books listing children waiting for a family stood in the display room. Most of the children listed were considered "hard to place" because they were sibling groups, mixed-race, older children, and teens or they had severe disabilities and medical needs. I was flipping through one of those books one day, and came across a child who caught my eye. His name was Sean, he was from Illinois, had cerebral palsy, and was born in 1979. A couple of years earlier, when I was looking for my second child, I had inquired about a child in Illinois whose name was Sean. I was informed that he was to be placed with a family the following week, so I didn't leave any contact information. Was this the same child I had called about more than a year earlier? I made a copy of his page to compare with my notes when I returned home after the conference.

It was the same Sean. The family who planned to adopt him backed out just a couple of days after I called. Sean was still in foster care with the family he had lived with since he was born. They felt they couldn't offer him a permanent home to meet his needs while meeting the needs of their own children. *Should I still consider adopting Sean? How can I leave a child in foster care if I had earlier considered adopting him?* One weekend my friend Marsha traveled to Illinois with Derek, Rusty, Ben, and me and even drove through a tornado to meet Sean. By now, I was used to the pattern: meet with social workers, meet with foster family, answer lots of questions, speechread people I had never met before, and try to hurry to get Derek away from all the people who smoked. Even after only a few minutes, his breathing became more labored with the heavy air. I had to get him out of there. I loaded all four boys into the van and Sean joined us in our hotel room to spend the night.

Rusty and Sean seemed to enjoy each other. Rusty loved to pull off Sean's socks, which made Sean laugh and laugh. It was fun to see them interacting. Derek enjoyed sharing a bed with Ben and me. He thought Sean and Rusty were great entertainment. The next morning, rather than exposing Derek to more smoke, I returned Sean to his foster family while Marsha stayed at the hotel with the boys.

I had the same questions as when I met Derek the first time. *Why do these wonderful people who offer their love, care, and homes smoke when they're around children who are medically fragile?* I will never understand. Even though it was cold, I rolled down the van windows to make sure it was completely smoke-free before we loaded up to return to Romney.

Derek and Rusty liked Sean. Derek approved of him joining the family. But Ben was not so certain he wanted to share his space and Mom.

"Ben, do you think it would be nice for Sean to move in with us?" I asked one day.

He responded with his basset hound face and an eye gaze to the word NO written on his wheelchair tray.

"Well, Derek thinks it is an okay idea. Rusty and Sean like each other. I think it will be okay because I am not teaching this year and will have more time to be with you guys." I brought up the topic at dinner every so often, signing for Derek and speaking for Ben and Rusty. After some more discussion, Ben decided it would be okay to just let the social workers decide.

Derek, Rusty, and Ben continued to attend the Special Services Center where each progressed at his own pace, though in Rusty's case, it wasn't much. He disliked physical therapy. His ability to understand language was profoundly limited. He did make progress in learning to better spoon-feed himself, and at home he learned to pull himself up on the couch or rocking chair. Ben was able to use an icon (picture) board on an easel with a head pointer I made for him out of leather and Velcro straps. It had drawbacks, but he did great communicating in this way. It gave everyone a better sense of what Ben understood and what he wanted to express. How I wished Derek could control his head like Ben. I wanted others to believe me when I said Derek understood language in sentences and not just one sign here and another sign there. For now, I had to settle with the plexiglas object box I had made. It was better than nothing.

For Christmas of 1984 I flew with my three sons to California for a week's vacation. I have no idea what I was thinking when I made the plan to fly with Derek, Rusty, Ben, and three wheelchairs. Just packing for the week was a challenge. I had to bring clothes, medications, diapers, toys to occupy Rusty, soft foods for Derek and Ben to eat in-flight, metal or plastic-coated metal spoons, special cups, and a car seat for Ben on the plane. Once I parked the van at the airport, I had to make several trips to unload luggage and wheelchairs, get our tickets, and tag all the wheelchairs. (They would need to go in the plane's cargo hold once we boarded.) I had some assistance from the airline employees, but they were not accustomed to carrying children like mine and Ben and Derek were reluctant to have strangers carry them to begin with. But first, I managed to have someone watch them while I used the bathroom.

When it was time to board, I had to figure out how I was going to get all of us on the plane. Once I got my mind organized, I was ready to go.

"I'll put Rusty on the plane first and come back to get you in a minute," I signed and spoke to Derek and Ben to let them know the plan. I carried Rusty to our assigned seats, making certain his right arm would be next to me. Rusty could sit on a regular seat without any problem, but his right hand could cause problems. As I took care of Rusty, the flight attendant secured Ben's car seat.

Then I went back for Ben who was to ride in his car seat, allowing me to hold Derek, who could not sit in the smaller car seat or on the regular airplane seat. As I was unfastening Ben's wheelchair straps, Derek was showing signs of anxiety at being left alone at the door of the plane. His body stiffened and his facial expressions showed great worry.

"Mom will come back to get you. I will hurry," I signed with one hand while I held Ben with my other arm. I had to reassure him a couple of times before I could carry Ben onto the plane. When I reached our seats I was shocked to see that Rusty had already taken the magazines, air sickness bags, and airplane literature out of the seat pocket in front of him and scattered them around. *Oh Lord, help me keep my sanity*, I prayed. I quickly grabbed the scattered materials and stuffed them in the pocket in front of Ben. Then I went to get Derek.

When he saw me, his entire body relaxed. Before taking him out of his chair, I made certain all the belts and straps on Rusty and Ben's chairs were secured as well as possible before they were stowed under the plane. Then I did the same with Derek's, but one-armed, as I had him in my other one. Off we went to our seats. I climbed over Rusty with Derek in my arms, kicked the diaper bag out of the way and plopped into the seat between Ben and Rusty. Now, to fasten the seatbelt while holding Derek. *What will my next challenge be?*

I had been worried that Rusty would be a problem, banging and kicking during the flight, but he was an angel. It was Ben who decided to give me problems. He didn't want to sit in the car seat. He whined and fussed which stressed me out and rattled my nerves.

"Ben, I know you don't want to sit in the car seat. Derek would gladly take his turn in that car seat if he could sit there. You should be happy you can even sit in the car seat and see what's going on around you." But my words did nothing to comfort him. Instead, people began turning heads as he fussed more and more. I finally gave up trying to reason with him and asked the flight attendant for a blanket. She gave me two, which I folded along with our jackets and put on the floor in front of me. That's where Derek ended up for the remainder of the flight. Ben was on my lap.

We didn't have a direct flight to California and had to change planes in Chicago. Once we landed, we waited for all the other passengers to leave the plane. Before boarding, I had requested that the boys' chairs be brought to the door of the plane because I would need them during the stop in Chicago. When the flight attendant told me that the wheelchairs were ready, I put Ben back in the car seat to wait while I carried Derek to his wheelchair. I almost dropped him when I saw what wheelchairs were waiting for us. They were the adult airport chairs—not the boys'. I tried not to make a scene as I explained there was no way my sons could use these chairs. They had to have their own. After several calls by airline personnel, Rusty's chair was finally delivered to where I was still waiting with Derek. I was nervous and anxious as we waited. Derek's breathing became labored. The flight attendants encouraged me to sit Derek in this chair. I explained Derek's chair was the blue one and this brown chair was for my other son who was still on the plane. After more than twenty minutes, Derek's chair was finally brought to the door. Although the headrest had been jarred out of position, he was delighted to be in his chair. He smiled from ear to ear and his body shook with excitement. I made a mental note to carry tools to adjust chairs with me on the return flight home.

"I will bring Ben," I signed to Derek as I left.

I unstrapped Ben from the car seat and carried him to his wheelchair. I hurried—I almost ran. Rusty was beginning to wake up, and I didn't want to leave him sitting alone on the airplane. Besides, I only had an hour to toilet and feed the boys before we boarded our connecting flight to California.

After I gathered all our belongings from the plane, airport volunteers pushed Rusty and Ben while I pushed Derek. I was loaded down with the diaper bag, my purse, and car seat, but zipped along to our gate nonetheless. I looked over my shoulder to check on Ben and Rusty as the airport volunteers pushed them at the speed of a stroll around the park!

"Please hurry," I pleaded. "I have to feed all these boys before our next flight."

We neared our gate, I thanked the volunteers for their assistance, and planned what to do next. Changing diapers was a priority. Derek and Ben were small enough for me to use a changing table in the restroom, but Rusty was not. I put my jacket on the floor for him. Next, I needed to feed Derek and Ben. If I didn't have time to feed Rusty, I could easily do it on the plane. As I fed the boys, I kept my eye on our gate to make certain we wouldn't miss the plane. Nerves overcame pride and I asked one of the airport staff to please let me know when we needed to board.

Just as I finished feeding Rusty, an airline employee came over.

"It's time for you to board. Please give me your tickets and I'll assist you to your seats," she said.

Can I go through this again so soon? Why did I even think of making this trip? Had I gone off the deep end when I planned it? I was tired and my arms ached from carrying our things and holding Ben and Derek, but there was no turning back. We were half way to our destination. I forced myself to focus on positive thoughts of the good time we were going to have with Jim's family and my parents who planned to drive to California to spend the holiday with us. Then I repeated the procedure of carrying one son at a time to our assigned seats. Before others boarded the plane, I stressed to the airline employees the need for each boy's wheelchair to be brought to the door when we landed in California. I did not want a repeat of what I had just gone through. Unfortunately, the flight was a repeat in one respect, Derek ended up on the floor. Ben was on my lap.

Once we landed and all the boys were in their chairs, things went a bit more smoothly at the airport when Jim met us. He knew how to push a wheelchair with gusto.

At his house, everyone was happy to be together. Christmas was filled with excitement and gifts. A person from Jim's church learned Ben's birthday was Christmas Day and brought a cake for a party at dinnertime. We had a wonderful visit, but on Derek's birthday, we boarded the plane for another demanding journey back to West Virginia.

After a day of rest for Derek, Rusty, and Ben, they went back to their school program. I felt I needed about five days of rest to catch up on lost sleep and let go of the tension from flying before I continued to work on my projects at home. Never again would I attempt to fly alone with those three children. Yet soon I was on another plane alone headed for Illinois to bring Sean home to join our family.

Although I was looking forward to having Sean join us, I hated having to plan the care for Derek, Rusty, and Ben, who would be staying behind. I had to write down everything in detail, the order to get them up in the morning, medications, what each boy ate for breakfast, what to pack in lunches, how many minutes it should take to do this and that, plus I had to arrange for someone to drive them to and from school. Our daily schedule was routine for me. For another person, or sometimes more than one person to take over, I had to be specific. I also had to list contact information in Illinois if there was a need to reach me while I was gone. This was long before TTY machines in public, pagers, and e-mails. I didn't like this part of parenting. I finally got all the details on paper, hugged each son good-bye, and took off for the airport.

Sean was attached to his foster family, and I wasn't certain he fully understood that he was moving to my home. His family had a big party for him, and he was excited. I imagine it seemed like a birthday party with cake and going-away gifts. I spent the afternoon and early evening at his foster home and went to a hotel for the night. I needed to rest for the flight home, but rest did not come. Instead I tossed and turned with excitement. Early the next morning, we packed Sean's things into the car and off to the airport I headed with a one-way ticket for Sean. Traveling with one child was a breeze compared to the December trip.

Derek, Rusty, and Ben were in bed but not asleep when Sean and I got home. I was excited as I carried Sean to his new bedroom. Derek and Ben understood the concept of Sean being a new brother. For Rusty, his smile was most likely because I was home and not because Sean was in my arms.

Morning came quickly. I now had four sons to toilet, dress, feed, put in their wheelchairs, load into the van, and drive to their school program. Sean would not begin school right away, but I still had to take him when I left with the others. The teachers and aides came to the van to meet Sean. He was all smiles when he heard people say his name. Ben began the morning being jealous and wanted to be the center of attention. With a quick reminder that his "basset hound face" was not an acceptable way to seek attention, he settled down. Derek, as usual, was willing to share with another brother and seemed glad to have more entertainment to make his life more enjoyable.

WNPB-TV of Morgantown, West Virginia, learned about our little family. They had become interested in our story and over the previous year had done several days of filming for a thirty-minute documentary, *Do You Hear the Rain?* The cameras had followed us to school, doctor appointments, hospital, and around our home. During the filming, Derek was the first person to realize the hot lights were making the ceiling warp! Thanks to his laughter and eye gaze, I looked up and was able to let the camera operator know.

The last day of filming, May 29, 1985, the camera followed us as I carried Rusty in one arm and Ben in the other up the steep steps of the courthouse to finalize their adoptions. Russell Francis Aiken and Benjamin Patrick Aiken legally became my sons.

I still wonder how I became a single parent of these four boys, all of whom had cerebral palsy, were non-verbal, in wheelchairs, were totally dependent on me for all of their physical care, and were all born in the same year. We lived each day at a time. We developed our own system of communication, which was not always understood by people who came into our home. Rusty was the most limited intellectually but the highest functioning physically. Sean learned to point to pictures. Ben used a head pointer with pictures placed on an easel, his super-sharp eye gaze, and his facial expressions. Derek, who was the most limited physically of the four, continued to rely on his eyes, facial expressions, and body language to make his needs known. Where many people may not have felt comfortable communicating this way, I felt at ease, content, and secure. I didn't need to rely on hearing or speechreading to understand them. Looking back, I remember the feeling of peace that we had within our family of five. I'm so proud that Derek's will to live and his impulse to share his love had led me to create my family thus far. Thank you, Derek.

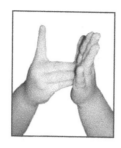

Chapter Fourteen

6 years 5 months - 6 years 7 months old

*T*he boys completed their school year. We packed up the van, left Romney, and headed west. We made our usual stops in Houston and Arizona. It was a long, hot drive across the country with the four boys and two dogs. We had planned to spend a month in California with Jim and his family, but shortly after I arrived, Jim and I decided to get married and set a date for August.

After corresponding for the past three years and traveling together during the summers, Jim's and my relationship had become more than just friends. I was pleased how Jim's sons accepted my sons and me, and I was able to make myself understood to Jim and his sons since I was able to speak. However, for me to understand everyone was difficult since Jim knew little ASL. He attempted to sign some when speaking directly with me but speechreading him was very hard. Communication was going to be challenging.

I insisted that since I was going to move to California and leave my home and friends in Romney, we must be married in Romney. I started planning my wedding from 3,000 miles away. I planned to wear a suit since I was not the typical young bride, but this plan didn't go over well with some of the older boys. They wanted me to wear a full-length wedding gown. Once again, I was challenged to do something I hadn't done before: sew a wedding gown on a sewing machine that was not mine in a house with ten boys (while I was adopting Rusty, Ben, and Sean, Jim adopted more sons too) and Jim was out doing errands or teaching horseback-riding lessons. I managed to finish it with a one-of-a-kind veil that would not fall in front of my face—I needed to see the interpreter. I made the veil over a margarine bowl covered with the same material as the gown, with lace attached so that it could only flow back. It was unique, as was the wedding.

My next challenge was to find clothes for the boys. Jim and I had decided that they should wear matching suit jackets. I spent many hours shopping around the neighboring Bay Area cities of Mountain View, Sunnyvale, Palo Alto, and San Jose, getting lost in the area since I didn't know the cities and streets well. Making matters more difficult was the difference in sizes that we needed to fit nine boys with jackets and a vest for Tim (who had only short stumps for arms). Derek was the smallest and needed a size 3T jacket. As I was walking through a store one day, right before me was a rack of navy blue suit jackets on sale! I had been in this store many times but hadn't seen them.

"Where did all these jackets come from?" I asked the clerk.

"Oh, they've been in the back of the store because they're not complete suits. We decided to put them out for sale," she answered.

I found a size 3T, two size 4's, and a size 5 and continued to find more correct sizes. I hung them on the back of Derek's wheelchair to free my hands, so I could continue to look.

"Why do you need so many jackets?" the sales clerk asked as I continued to search.

"For my sons to wear in my wedding!" Fortunately, she didn't pass out before I could explain. Kind as she was, she gave me another twenty-five percent off of the sale price. I thanked her and left the store happy I had gotten a fantastic bargain.

To go with the jackets, all the boys would wear pale yellow shirts, but I couldn't find them (many of the ones in the shops had long sleeves, which would not do for an August wedding in West Virginia). I cut off sleeves, hemmed, and dyed them. Each boy was to wear a different-colored tie. The older boys who were to be the ushers wore dark blue slacks and the others wore tan. With that task accomplished, I felt a bit more at ease.

While I was preparing clothes, Jim searched to find a used motor home that would hold everyone for the trip across country for the wedding. Eventually he found one and we made do with some modifications, such as an extremely steep wood ramp for the wheelchairs. Packing all our necessary things for this trip was not easy. Where do you store all the suits, a wedding gown, Jim's tails, and all the everyday things for so many children when each one needed to have his own wheelchair? We packed and repacked until we found a place for everything.

The first leg of our trip ended at Albuquerque for the annual conference of the North American Council on Adoptable Children. My parents met us there and helped with my four younger boys. This also gave them a chance to become more acquainted with Jim's boys. After the conference, Jim and I had three days to drive from New Mexico to West Virginia to get blood tests for our marriage license. My parents planned to drive in their motor home with Derek and Ben, who were the slowest eaters and would need more time for traveling. Also, they were small enough that my parents could still lift them and get their wheelchairs in and out of their motor home when necessary. Although my parents dearly loved these boys and were capable of taking care of them, I still worried about Derek becoming dehydrated. As it turned out, everything was fine, and the trip was quite a treat for Derek and Ben. It was a truly special adventure with Grandma and Granddad.

Granddad recalls: **As for a special time with Derek, we would have him at our place and he was so bubbly and loving in his own way, that we felt a unique attachment to the young man. Of course, we went back for the wedding of Jim and Marian and had a great time going across country.**

Grandma writes: **That trip in our motor home with Ben and Derek was really special. Surprisingly I only have one picture of them during the trip. They were in my bed to get warmed up that morning and they were both laughing! They thought it very funny. I guess I was too busy taking care of them, feeding them, and so on, to take pictures. That was a really special trip.**

Jim and I and seven of the boys arrived in Romney in time to get our blood tests, hang out our wedding clothes, make last-minute preparations, and try to catch a wink of rest here and there. Tim, Tom, and David were to stay with friends of mine, whom they had never met, while Jim and I went on our honeymoon. Alan's foster family would come from Connecticut to take care of him, and Donald, Derek, Rusty, Ben, and Sean would stay with my parents. Mom and Dad arrived two days later with Derek and Ben. Dad arranged the flowers for the church as well as for my wedding party and me. Jim's family, including his parents, sister and brother, their spouses, and children, all came. Of course my relatives from the East Coast were there as well. I had so many mixed emotions. I had grown to love the Romney community and the people who lived there. I had great respect for the doctor who cared for my children. I needed to say many good-byes and there was just not enough time. People came and went. They wanted to help, but I wanted to sit and talk.

The weather on our wedding day, August 17, 1985, was in the nineties and humid. Jim and I worked nonstop to get the boys ready for the ceremony. We bathed, fed, dressed, and tried to keep everyone cool. Jim took some of the boys to the hotel where his parents were staying to give baths, as it was too crowded at my place. Grandparents helped out here and there, as did friends. After everyone was dressed, we loaded nine boys into the RV and headed to the church. Jay rode from the airport with my interpreter. My sister, Lynne, was to be the organist during the ceremony, but her plane was very late. I asked the church organist to play pre-wedding music until she arrived and went to put on my wedding gown and veil. Under the direction of my brother, the older boys took seriously their ushering duties. All the younger boys were pushed into the church, followed by the wedding party. Derek was unhappy in his suit jacket (which I had spent an incredible amount of time finding), but Uncle Ronn gave him a stern look, motioned "smile and go," and pushed him down the aisle. Derek was my ring bearer. Pictures show him smiling proudly!

Our wedding was unique, as was our family. I waited for Rusty's "EEEEEEEEEEEEEEEE" to fill the church. Or, "Dad, I need to use the bathroom!" But all the boys sat patiently and attentively throughout the entire service. Jim and I had written our own vows and had not shared them until that moment. Jim had practiced frantically to learn to sign and speak his at the same time, and I really appreciated his effort. I also wrote words for a song that we shared on that special day. Jim sang and played his guitar and I signed. I spotted a frown or two on Derek's face. I think he must finally have realized he was actually going to need to share his Mom with not only nine other siblings, but also a Dad. The words for our song follow.

Our Sons

You are our sons and our love you have won,
Thank you for giving your love.
You've come into our lives and have helped make us one,
Thank you for being our sons.

We want to continue to give you love,
Support you in all ways we can.
We want you to grow in body and soul,
To be happy, well-functioning men.

Each one of you has special talents and gifts
To share with your family and friends.
We love you so much 'cause you give us a lift.
With your jokes and your laughs and your grins.

You show your needs in your own special way.
If you have no words you use smiles, frowns or tears.
We strive all the way to know what you say,
Be it pleasure, pain, gladness or fears.

Let us continue to grow in our love,
As a new family learning to share.
We have searched near and far in this country of ours
Because your Mom and Dad care.

You have shared the joys to be found in life.
Thank you for giving your love.
How blessed we are to have sons so nice.
Thank you for being you. Thank you for being our sons.

The organ music played after we were pronounced "husband and wife." We turned and walked down the aisle. I smiled at family and friends. As I approached the back door of the church, I was startled, shaken, and saddened. Lynne had

145

just arrived. She had missed the entire wedding. I had not been able to see who was at the organ while I was standing, but I had taken for granted that it was she. My heart was heavy and I felt bewildered and disappointed. I gave her a big hug, which was the best I could do under the circumstances. Following the ceremony, we greeted our guests, took pictures of Derek surrounded by his nine brothers and parents, and attended the reception at the West Virginia School for the Deaf. I went home to change and spend time with Lynne before Jim and I left for a thirty-two hour honeymoon.

Then we came back to pack my things. Since the wedding was more or less a last-minute decision, including the permanent move to California, none of our belongings had been packed. Possessions had accumulated over the years and there was a lot of packing to do. Everybody seemed to be getting under my feet and in my way. *Why can't people leave me alone and let me do my own packing? I want to know where my things are. Please just bug off.* I finally asked Jim and Mom to take the boys out on a trip while Dad and I stayed behind to pack in a somewhat organized way. Books, teaching materials, clothing, therapy equipment, dishes, furniture, medications, sewing machine, fabric, bedding, keepsakes, and photos were boxed and loaded into a U-haul that we would tow with the motor home back across the country. As we pulled out of town, tears flowed steadily for a long time as I left the life I had lived for the past several years as an educator, single parent and small town resident. In less than three months from the day we left for our California visit, Derek, Rusty, Ben, Sean, and I began our third 3,000-mile trip across the United States.

Shortly after we arrived in California, a letter arrived from my parents. Enclosed was the following article, which had been written by our wonderful, smiling, grandma-like hometown family friend, Gift Storms.

News About A Family of God
Wedding of Marian Aiken and James Forderer

On August 17th, 1985, at 4:00 pm in the United Methodist Church in Romney, West Virginia, a most unusual, unique and beautiful wedding took place. Rev. Howard Ellifritz, a former pastor of the Romney Church was the minister and Jane Watts from Ellicott City, Maryland was the interpreter, since not only the bride was deaf but also many of the guests. This was not unusual in Romney since this is where the West Virginia School for the Deaf and Blind is located and the bride taught in the School for the Deaf for several years. The most unusual and unique thing about the wedding was that it not only joined together Marian and James, but also formed a family of Mom and Dad and ten handicapped brothers in wheelchairs. With James came Jay, Tom, David, Donald, Alan and Tim Forderer and with Marian came Derek, Rusty, Ben and Sean Aiken. Derek, the first boy adopted by Marian Aiken, was the ring bearer and was brought up the aisle by Ron Aiken, brother of Marian, with the pillow and rings resting on Derek's lap. Three of James' boys, Jay, Tom and David (in their wheelchairs), were ushers, as was the bride's brother. The bride and groom wrote their vows and then the groom spent many hours learning to sign the vows, which he spoke and signed to his bride. Another thing which made the wedding unusual was a song written by the bride and groom to their ten sons. The groom sang the song while accompanying himself on the guitar while the bride signed in lovely flowing sign language.

I'm sure not all the boys understood just what was happening as they have various handicapping conditions, but the smiles on their faces and the love in their eyes as they looked at their parents would have moved a heart of stone and as I looked about I saw many damp eyes and even a tear or two on the faces of the guests.

There are all kinds of mission fields near or in far and distant lands, but here before my eyes was a mission field that was so unusual and unique that I could not help but feel that if crowns are given out in heaven with jewels in them, these two people will have beautiful ones with many, many jewels. These are two very special people and I pray God will bless them in a very special way as they continue to serve Him and care for these boys.

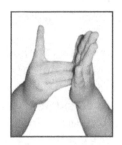

Chapter Fifteen
6 years 8 months -
7 years 6 months

Starting life in California was much more of an adjustment than I had expected. The boys and I had visited several times and our visits were pleasant, but the actual move threw me for a loop. It was culture shock. Ethnic diversity in the stores, restaurants, and just about any place I went was a relatively new experience for me. Fenced yards, countless stoplights, street names in Spanish that I couldn't remember or pronounce, and neighbors not knowing each other contributed to the strain. These were external changes that I needed to adjust to, but internal changes were draining my patience as well.

We were thirteen people and three dogs in a small, rented house. Jim and I now occupied the larger bedroom upstairs, but I didn't like being that far away from my sons at night. Alan needed to adjust to not sharing a room with his Dad. Jay shared a bedroom with his dog, Thai, and a friend from high school who lived with us. Tom and David shared another bedroom. The bathroom between their rooms had a large tub where we bathed all the boys, so it was occupied constantly after school hours. Donald, Alan, and Tim shared another small bedroom that was off the family room toward the back of the house. On the other side of the house, Derek and Ben slept in the laundry room area. There was no wall space to decorate or places to put their things. Rusty and Sean were in an extremely small room, where I also needed to find room for Derek's and Ben's clothes. There was a small bath with a shower off the laundry room that the boys could not use because of their physical challenges, but Jim and I used it since there was no bath upstairs. I found it frustrating that I could not find places to put all of my boys' clothes, toys, and books.

Most of my personal things stayed packed in boxes in the garage, as did the therapy equipment. I missed my pots and pans, which would not fit in the little kitchen. It was a real stretch to squeeze ten wheelchairs, Jim, and myself around our dining room table while placing those we had to feed within arms' reach. My family was accustomed to eating dinner early in the evening. Jim's normally ate later. I also had to adjust to different and spicier foods.

At first, it didn't bother me that I couldn't follow conversations at the table, but as time went on, I became frustrated and hurt that I didn't know what was being discussed. With Derek, Rusty, Ben, and Sean, I had been the only person who could speak so I knew exactly what was being said. But this new situation was entirely different. I was even jealous when people would talk with Ben and ask him questions because I had no idea what the topic of the discussion was. I felt trapped at dinnertime.

There was a fairly large family room where the boys spent most of their time after school and on weekends watching TV and videos. I became aware of the different programs the boys saw and was upset when the younger ones were exposed to programs I felt were not age-appropriate. There were no captions for TV at that time, and I could not follow the dialogue. I felt I had lost control over issues that were important to me.

It seemed that Jim's boys adjusted much better to our marriage than my boys did. I think that was mostly because Jim's boys were accustomed to living in California, had their friends, and didn't need to change schools. (Soon after we returned to California from our wedding, it was the start of the new school year.)

I wasn't prepared for what was involved to find the correct school program for the boys and have them enrolled. Where I grew up in Pennsylvania, there was only one elementary school for us to attend and one class for each grade. In West Virginia, there also was only one option, and fortunately the school in Romney served my children well. In California, I was stunned that there were so many schools in one area. The high school that the older boys attended was almost as large as my college.

Jim felt that certain schools were appropriate for my boys, and I felt differently after visiting various programs. It took weeks before they could even begin school, and Rusty, Sean and Ben started several weeks ahead of Derek. We couldn't find a program close to where we lived that would accept kids with his physical limitations and also had staff members who were knowledgeable about deafness and knew some sign language (at least at a level I felt was acceptable). Jim scheduled visits to several schools to review the programs each offered. Derek came with us to observe the classes. I tried my best to follow conversations by speechreading, but I missed most of the information, so I couldn't explain much to Derek. Everything was completely new to him, and I could tell he was tense and nervous. We found a program with children who had similar physical challenges and a teacher who could sign, but I was impatient with everything that was going on.

I am not certain if Rusty, Sean, and Ben remembered riding a school bus while they lived in their foster homes, but it was an experience Derek hadn't had. He was used to a short ride in our van to and from school. Now, in California, he was expected to ride on a bus with a driver who could not communicate with him. To make matters worse, he was put on the bus before 6:30 AM, in the dark, and didn't arrive at his school program until more than an hour and a half later.

Initially, Derek had a teacher who could sign fairly fluently, but at Christmas time, she left for the remainder of the year and was replaced by a substitute. Derek's desire to attend school began to wane. He became less active at home and appeared to be somewhat withdrawn. I was concerned about his emotional health. His eye contact became sporadic. What little head control he had gained after years of therapy was decreasing and his head was turning strongly to the right again. He also was poorly positioned in his wheelchair when he arrived home in the afternoon. I had written to the school of my concerns and they assured me that he was receiving what he needed.

One day I had forgotten to send his lunch to school. Ben happened to be off from his school that day, so I loaded him into the van and took him with me to drop off Derek's lunch.

We stopped by the office and were told to take his lunch to the classroom. Was I in for a shock! All the children in the class were more or less stationed in areas alone. Ben and I stayed for more than an hour and the entire time we were there, the teacher spent a total of five minutes with Derek. The rest of the time, he was left with a toy that he couldn't interact with and positioned in such a way that he could not see the other children in the class. This didn't go over well with me at all, especially because of his deafness. I immediately understood why he was becoming withdrawn. Social interaction and observing others were his strengths. I told his teacher that I was going to gather his belongings and take him home. Not only was I upset about this, but so was Ben who was very close with Derek. I wrote a letter to the school administration expressing my disapproval of Derek's educational setting. I needed to search for another program, but in the meantime, I kept Derek at home for the remainder of the school year and worked with him myself.

Many people came and went in our household. Various members of Jim's church, which would become mine and the younger boys', United Methodist Church of Los Altos, had been volunteering at his home for some time. They were wonderful people who had assisted Jim's boys with schoolwork or on outings, or helped clean house or make and serve dinner. I became friends with them, but also was very stressed by their presence. I was a "do it all alone" person who was not accustomed to others entering my home to do chores. I guess you might say I felt an invasion of privacy. None of these people knew sign language and to speechread everyone was almost more than I could handle. I also sensed that Derek and Ben were having some trouble adjusting to all these new faces. Some of the volunteers continued and others stopped. I just felt that I needed more time to adjust to my new family without so many people coming and going. I wanted Jim's six boys to get to know me better and learn what expectations I had for them. I didn't want to turn the volunteers away, but I needed some time without them.

Ben adjusted fairly well to his new school, although I needed to encourage the school staff to focus a bit more on his academic strengths. Rusty did okay where he was placed, but it was harder to find the right place for Sean. Once he was in a program that was appropriate for him, he did well. Derek and I continued to work at home, and he became my shadow. His eye contact improved and his head control returned to what it had been. I made him a new communication board. It was once again made out of Plexiglas with a shelf on top and slots that would allow me to present pictures of the objects at the same time I signed them. I exposed him to as many icons as I possibly could. Derek began to use his gaze to select pictures of what he wanted to eat, where he wanted to go, what he wanted to do. I was encouraged by his progress. He so enjoyed going places with me, and our little jaunts allowed for much receptive language development.

I had stayed in touch with John, a student at the West Virginia School for the Deaf, who had helped me tremendously with my boys back home. So in June, we packed up our van and headed back east for his graduation. Derek, Rusty, Ben, Sean, and Tom rode together in the van for the entire trip. Tom was several years older and helped entertain his brothers while I drove. He read books like *The Great Brain* and *Super Fudge* to Ben. He had also learned many signs that he could use with Derek and me. Tim, who was three months older than Derek, rode with us as far as Oklahoma, where he was to stay with some friends whose son was also a congenital quad-amputee. (Tim was born with no legs and only short stumps for arms.) It was pleasant having Tom and Tim along to talk with as we traveled (I speechread, and they signed—even Tim, with his stumps! Sounds impossible, but it worked). The six wheelchairs were packed snugly into our little van, but we had to make frequent stops to eat and keep hydrated. Tom and Tim used power wheelchairs and I carried a set of motorcycle ramps to get them in and out. I also used the ramps for Sean's chair which was wider and heavier than those of the other boys. For them, I lifted them in and out of the van as I usually did. It was faster. Toileting and meals took more than an hour each time we stopped. Tom tried to help as much as he could with what use he had of his left hand. Once we left Tim with his friends, we had a little more space to move around, but it was still crowded.

After four days of driving, unloading, loading, sleeping in

hotel rooms (since I didn't know people to visit on the route we were traveling), filling the gas tank, checking the oil and radiator frequently, we were finally close to Romney. My heart pounded with excitement. I knew I had been homesick, but when we arrived in Hampshire County, the impact was more than I had imagined. Ben knew where we were and so did Derek. I hadn't thought about Derek being homesick. Was I in for a surprise. We were a few miles from town when he began to get choked up. As we drove past the road we used to turn onto to go home Derek was a total mess. Tears, sweat, secretions in his throat, and his limbs so stiff I thought he was going to slide out of his wheelchair.

"Derek, we'll go to school to inform Maureen we are here," I signed. "We will not sleep at our house. We'll sleep at Maureen's house." I tried to calm him by resting my hand on his knee, but it was impossible to get him to settle down. I drove toward the back entrance of the School for the Deaf campus and parked close to the building. By this time, Derek's face was flushed and beads of sweat covered his forehead. His hands were fisted, his limbs were stiff, and arms were clammy. He gritted his teeth and his breathing was so heavy that I had to get him out of his wheelchair. I explained to the others I would be back soon and asked them to please be patient as I lifted Derek out to take him in the air-conditioned building with me.

Once in the high school building, we went to the home economics room to find our friend Maureen. More tears from Derek. I couldn't tell if they were tears of joy or sadness. Maureen gave us each a hug and then wiped Derek's flushed face with a cool washcloth. After a few minutes, he calmed down while Maureen and I made plans for me to drive to her home. She walked us to the van and said hello to the other boys while I loaded Derek back in and belted his chair to the floor. Maureen and her family lived several miles out of town in a log home off a dirt road. I was anxious to get there and unload the boys, but first we had to make one stop at High's to buy Derek's favorite ice cream, mint chocolate chip. He had lived on this ice cream for many years but High's ice cream wasn't available in California. Ben also wanted his favorite, chocolate peanut butter cup. It certainly is amazing how ice cream can calm a child.

Maureen's husband, Jim, had made a ramp for us to use at the house. After almost a week on the road, I felt an incredible feeling of "being at home" as I unloaded the boys from the van and placed them on the floor in the house to stretch out. Derek and Ben knew this home well and were at ease. Maureen and Jim's daughter (who was almost the same age as Derek) and two sons had grown up around Derek, Rusty, and Ben and everyone felt comfortable being together. Even Tom, who tended to be shy, opened up and felt comfortable. We all experienced warm, welcoming, West Virginia hospitality.

The next day we attended John's graduation. Derek was excited to see John and smiled from ear to ear as John walked across the stage to receive his diploma. He posed for pictures with John after the ceremony. The memories stirred me when I recalled times that John, Derek, and I had spent together traveling, spending weekends at my home in Romney, and visiting with my sister and her family, or when John had come to the hospital to visit Derek when he was ill. John had been a part of my life for more than thirteen years and part of Derek's life since he came into my home. Trying to remain composed, I hugged John good-bye, hoping this wasn't the last time we'd be together.

After the graduation ceremony, we visited the boys' old school, talked with Dr. Giron, and went to our old neighborhood. I didn't take Derek inside our West Virginia home, which our former neighbor and friend had bought, because he was already highly stressed. I felt guilty. It had never crossed my mind that he could be so homesick. Every time he saw someone he knew, he cried. He did better when friends came to visit us at Maureen's house, especially Sue, who came and held him for hours as we sat on the floor and visited. Then all too soon it was time to say good-bye once again to Romney.

Derek, Rusty, Ben, Sean, Tom, and I headed to Ohio. My parents were at my brother's on their annual trip to the East Coast. We took a long detour through Squirrel Hill Tunnel in Pennsylvania, one of Derek's favorite places to drive. Tom got a big kick out of how something so simple could bring Derek pleasure. It was exciting to see Derek bonding with his older brother on this trip. In Ohio, we spent time with relatives and relaxed with Grandma and Granddad. My nephew, Geoff, was doing everything that was appropriate for a six-year-old. He weighed three times as much as Derek. There was no way to compare them any more. Each boy was just loved for who he was. As always, they shared Grandma and Granddad's love and attention. We stayed in Ohio for only two days since we had to return home to Los Altos so the boys could begin summer school. Once again, Derek's reaction to our visit reinforced my belief that he could not be profoundly retarded as specialists believed.

That belief was supported after we returned to Los Altos and Derek attended four weeks of summer school. The county had hired someone to work with him during the summer months at the school he had attended the previous fall. The bus ride was still long and hot, but for once, there was an adult waiting at the school who had the experience of raising a deaf child, communicating via ASL, and had more knowledge of nonverbal communication than most regular school staff. She signed everything, including stories, group language lessons, music, and instructions from the physical therapist as she worked with Derek as his classroom aide. Derek formed a special friendship with a classmate because she signed conversations between the two. I am convinced her short experience with Derek forced the school district to begin to acknowledge that Derek understood someone who signed fluently. Meanwhile, Derek's sparkle returned, along with his desire to go to school.

Chapter Sixteen

6 years 7 months -
9 years 6 months

The new school year soon began. We decided that Derek would attend a class that was closer to home, even though the teacher had very little knowledge of deafness and limited signing skills. In her favor was that she was a wonderful teacher and truly concerned about the well-being of her students. Since summer school had proven to be a positive experience for Derek and someone had finally seen that he could respond to people who could sign fluently, the school district reluctantly agreed to pay for a part-time classroom aide who could sign. I managed to find someone from church to fill this position. Derek was in heaven. He became much more expressive and enjoyed each day.

Months earlier, I had decided to take Derek to the California School for the Deaf in Fremont to have a comprehensive assessment performed. There was a Special Needs Unit at the school and I had hoped that Derek might be able to go there with other Deaf students. When I'd visited the unit I saw that even though the students could walk and had the physical ability to sign, some had social and cognitive skills that were lower than Derek's. The assessment was one of the most thorough evaluations Derek had had to date. However, as usual the examiners questioned what he understood beyond basic signs. Although this frustrated me, I could understand why, it was close to impossible to take Derek into a new setting with new people for a short time and have him relax and feel comfortable enough to obtain accurate results. As a result, people saw his physical problems as his primary disability and not the deafness. But even though the assessment team gave several suggestions to encourage communication skills and strongly recommended that he continue to be instructed in his full-day program through ASL rather than speech, they felt the school was not prepared to handle his physical needs with the lack of therapy equipment, lack of wheelchair bus, lack of trained staff to assist with lifting, toileting, and feeding. This was probably true. Yet, it was so disappointing that Derek continued to be isolated from other deaf children.

Meanwhile, Jim had been looking desperately for a house we could buy. After months of searching he found a four-bedroom, three-and-half-bath house located in a beautiful part of Los Altos. Typical of most houses we considered buying, it didn't meet the unique needs of our large family, but it did allow us to spread out a bit more and was on a large corner lot that would make future expansion possible. We went ahead with all the paperwork and help from Jim's parents. I was at a total loss during the process. I couldn't follow the conversations with the bank and Jim's parents, but I finally went along and signed where they told me to.

The previous owners of the home were heavy smokers. One bedroom appeared to have been painted tan, but it was actually stained from the smoke that covered the ceiling and walls, it had in fact been painted yellow. I washed down walls during the day while the boys were in school, but gave up on the living and dining area. Painting would be the quickest remedy for those rooms. Likewise with the room Derek, Rusty, Ben, and Sean would share. I worried about the boys being exposed to the secondhand smoke in the house. I wanted the house to be free of contaminants before we moved in, so I painted whenever I could find time including after I put the boys to bed. When I drove at night I almost always got lost trying to find the house in the dark and sometimes would panic. It was a busy, challenging, and frustrating time.

Before we could move the family, we built a steep ramp so we could get the wheelchairs into the living room. A sliding shower door was removed from the large tub in the master bedroom where the older boys could bathe. We made do with the rest of the house the way it was, which required lots of patience.

I knew we needed a larger house, but I was worried about my sons. How much more change could my younger boys take in such a short time? How much more change could I take? Jim's and my days started at about 6:00 each morning with getting all the guys up, toileted, dressed, fed, and out the door on buses within a two-hour period. Sometimes we crashed wheelchairs as we moved from one space to another or accidentally bumped in the kitchen as we rushed to make sure everyone had breakfast. Rusty and Sean had learned to spoon-feed themselves, but Derek and Ben still took a lot of time to feed.

The boys went to four different schools, but Derek, Rusty, and Sean all had to be ready at the same time because they rode the same bus. Tom and David went to the same high school. Donald and Alan went to a different school in San Jose. Tim and Ben rode a bus to yet another school. Sometimes there were two or three buses in front of the house at once. Jim and I continued to care for the boys as we moved into the home we had just bought. I don't think anyone can even picture what a tremendous task this was.

A typical day might look like this: after all the boys had gone to school, I'd take care of the dog Snuja (my old friend Rocca had left us at eighteen), get a quick breakfast, and wash the dishes. Then I'd load several of the unpacked boxes from West Virginia into the van and drive to the new house and find a place to store them. If time permitted, I might paint a couple more walls or clean the kitchen. It never failed that one of the boys had a wheelchair, therapy, or doctor's appointment. That meant driving to that child's school, signing him out at the office, getting him from class, loading him into the van, driving to the appointment, taking him back to school afterward, unloading him from the van, signing him back into school, taking him to the classroom, and then climbing back into the van. Lots of climbing in and out of vans for Mom and Dad, and I still was lifting boys in wheelchairs because I didn't have a wheelchair lift. I shopped for food for dinner, did laundry and yard work, completed paperwork for all the schools, and packed more things in between all the other activities.

When the boys came home from school, many needed to be toileted, given a drink or snack, and set up with homework. Derek, Rusty, Sean, Ben, and Tim would want out of their wheelchairs, so they could stretch out on the floor and move around. Two afternoons a week Jim took some of the boys to Westwind Barn in Los Altos Hills where he led groups of physically challenged children in horseback riding lessons. Dinner had to be prepared and served, all the boys brought to the table, which meant lifting them back into their wheelchairs, and then feeding those who could not feed themselves. Shortly after the table was cleared, food put away, and dishes washed, it would be time to bathe the younger boys and get ready for bed. I would then pack more things, go to the new house and paint or clean for an hour or two, return to the rented house, check on Derek and Rusty before retiring for the night at about 11:00. Sometimes I would be so exhausted I would fall sound asleep but other nights my mind would continue to race with things I knew had to be done. Nonetheless, it was worth it. I loved my family and wanted the best for them. They needed a larger house with more bathrooms, and I was determined to see them in it.

After several weeks of preparation, some of the rooms in the new house were ready. Jim and I decided to move in shifts. Some friends helped move beds while the boys were in school. Chests of drawers came the next day. I moved with Derek, Rusty, Ben, and Sean to the new house first, which messed up the school bus schedule because Tim was at the rented house and Ben was at the new house, and they both rode the same bus. Friends also helped move some of the boys' personal items, like toothbrushes, which wound up mixed together. Which toothbrush belonged to which boy? I was totally frustrated the next morning.

Derek, Rusty, Ben, and Sean shared one of the larger bedrooms. It was a tight squeeze with four beds, four chests of drawers, and four wheelchairs. Nevertheless, Derek was delighted to have walls decorated with pictures and to have one of his lights nearby at night. He adjusted well to the move.

Each day we set up another bedroom moving in another son or two until we were all sleeping under one roof. By "set up" I mean the basics of beds and chests of drawers, not organization. That part of moving was ongoing for months, even years for some things, and never for others. Jay wasn't with us any more. He had moved into a place of his own in a neighboring community. Donald, Alan, and Tim shared a second bedroom.

Even before we bought the house, we had been housing children from Mexico who came to the area for short-term medical care. Some would stay with us for a few weeks before being admitted to Shriner's Hospital in San Francisco, and then for a few more weeks before they returned home to Mexico after their surgery. One boy, Alberto, became a part of the family and lived with us for several years. He moved with us and shared a bedroom with Tom and David.

Alberto entered our home not knowing English, and I knew a total of maybe five words in Spanish. At first, we used Sean's icon book to communicate by pointing to the pictures. Alberto learned English quickly. In fact, he became trilingual, fluent in Spanish, English and ASL. Derek loved Alberto as he was one more person who could sign at home. Derek didn't care if the signs were perfect. He just appreciated people trying to communicate with him.

The kitchen of our new house was extremely small with only two working burners on the stove. The refrigerator was hopeless. We needed to shop twice a day since we couldn't store enough food for both dinner and school lunches. The living room was large and basically served the family well. Jim and I carried meals from the kitchen to the dining table. We moved the dining table into what had been the family room so that everyone could fit around the table at the same time. Getting meals on the table was complicated. We carried two plates at a time for our boys, some of whom needed special plates with rims or cups with handles. We had to remember who was left or right-handed and place the silverware on the correct side of the plate because most of the boys didn't have enough range of motion to reach a utensil on the wrong side. Some of them used spoons and others used forks. Some used straws and others did not. All food had to be cut or ground. It was challenging.

I missed teaching. I missed being around adult conversation. Since all the boys were in school during the day, I decided to try working outside the home and became a substitute for several of the local schools in the county's Special Education program. Some of the classes were at the school Derek, Rusty, and Sean attended which was about a twenty-minute drive from home, but my favorite classes were at the mainstream program for the deaf in San Jose even though the distance and early morning traffic was a problem. I enjoyed my time in the classrooms, but it was short-lived.

Just as Derek was having his educational needs met fairly well, he started having health problems. How I longed for our doctor and the hospital we had left behind in West Virginia. In California, we had a wonderful family doctor from church whose office was only ten minutes from the house, but Derek's medical needs were beyond what he felt capable of handling. I took Derek to what was the old Children's Hospital at Stanford for his outpatient care with a respiratory specialist. Within a week he had to be admitted for pneumonia. I could tell that Derek missed his former doctor, nurses, and hospital in Romney, as did I. Once again I taped large signs on the walls near his bed so the medical staff would know how to make him most comfortable. They let the staff know to allow him to see them before touching him to lessen the startles, position him in his wheelchair in this way, and so forth.

In Romney all I needed to sign was, "We need to go to x-ray" and Derek knew where we were headed since he knew the floor plan of the hospital. Now going to x-ray meant quite a walk from his hospital room, down several halls, and a ride on an elevator. Even I got confused going there and would have to backtrack which made Derek upset and anxious. His limbs would stiffen, his breathing would become more labored, and he'd break out in a sweat. I didn't like to leave him alone. I was continuously needed at home as well as at the hospital. I was under significant stress and found myself very short tempered when I met new medical personnel. In Romney, the drive from home to hospital was five minutes; in Los Altos it was thirty minutes at best, providing there was no traffic and I didn't get lost on the way. Needless to say, I managed to make a wrong turn several times that first week of Derek's hospitalization.

After he was discharged he needed respiratory treatments every four hours for two weeks.

Derek's new doctors were not encouraging about his prognosis. The pulmonary specialist said his aspirated pneumonias were being caused by reflux into the esophagus. She also said his lungs were weak, and each time he had pneumonia it would take longer for him to recover. Since he had remained remarkably well the previous couple of years, it was nearly impossible to accept what the doctors had to say.

When Derek was cleared to return to school, I called the office to let them know the good news and that Derek's doctor wanted him to have a small blue suctioning bulb with him in case he had excessive secretions in his mouth and throat. The office person said I would have to talk to the school nurse about that. The nurse made a home visit with Derek's aide.

"You can't just send Derek back to school with a suctioning bulb in his backpack," the nurse informed me.

"Why? It's not that difficult to use. Just squeeze it and put it in his mouth if he seems to have some mucus in the back of his throat and get it out," I responded, dumbfounded.

"Marian, we need to have a written procedure of when and how to use the suctioning bulb in the classroom. We must have written permission from the doctor that states Derek is well enough to return to school. We need to train the teacher and Derek's aide on how to use the suctioning bulb. I must have it in writing that it's even safe for him to ride the bus without an adult with him," the nurse continued.

I couldn't just put the suction bulb in his backpack. Obviously, this was going to be another learning experience for me: "Understanding School Nurses and Medical Procedures!" What I felt was trivial definitely was not trivial to the school system. It would take me another week to get a letter from the doctor and to train Derek's teacher and interpreter/aide. Meanwhile, he was bored staying around the house all day while the others were in school. Very few people understood how much Derek enjoyed school. It was hard to explain to him why he couldn't get on the bus with Rusty and Sean in the mornings.

Meanwhile, John was not happy at home in West Virginia, and decided to move to California, live with us, find a job, and further his education. He moved in and shared a bedroom with Tom, David, and Alberto. Having John around was a big help because I was able to leave Derek in his care while I ran errands. John understood Derek's communication, and Derek understood John. He also helped with Rusty, Ben, and Sean if I needed to be at the hospital with Derek.

Derek would return to school for short periods of time and then would need to go back to the hospital with another respiratory infection. When he had those infections, his body would become entirely spastic, and he would grind his teeth. The medical staff believed he was having seizures which meant another EEG to find out for sure. I continued to believe that he was not having seizures but that much of what people witnessed were spasms or startle reflexes. During one EEG when Derek was alert, I threw small stuffed animals around the doorway to test if what others felt were seizures were actually seizures. No seizure activity registered on the EEG. However, we did start him on a muscle relaxant to decrease the spasticity in his limbs. Derek had a hard time adjusting to the medication, and I was frustrated when he spent long periods asleep. True, his spastic limbs would be relaxed, but then he'd not be alert and would have more secretions in his throat. After several months of trying different dosages, the doctors finally found the one that worked best.

Derek attended school as his health permitted. He enjoyed having a part-time interpreter in the classroom. He loved lessons related to science and animals. Every morning he would watch a hands-on science program on TV while waiting for his bus. He also took his *My Backyard*, a science magazine, to class to share. Derek would also go horseback riding with Jim as his health allowed. He continued to be a sports fan and joined the other boys watching the games on TV. Occasionally he'd even get to go to a San Francisco Giants game with the family.

Derek also liked going to church. He went to the church service that had an ASL interpreter instead of going to Sunday school with the other children. He sat in the front and watched the interpreter. I don't know how much he understood, but one

163

Sunday his behavior told me that he had paid attention. The interpreter signed about an upcoming pancake breakfast with piles of pancakes dripping with lots of syrup. Derek still loved to eat, and he enjoyed pancakes (when time permitted on a Saturday morning). Something was wrong. Since sign language has regional variations, the interpreter used a different sign for syrup than we used at home and Derek's excitement about eating pancakes quickly turned to tears. What Derek saw in his language was "Eat large stacks of pancakes with lots of honey," not syrup. To complicate matters further, to Derek the sign "honey" referred to the bunny in the classroom at school. He was totally devastated that anyone would think of eating Honey, the bunny rabbit. I turned him to me and tried to get him to understand that the sign the interpreter used for "honey" also meant "syrup!" I thought I would never get him settled down. I had to take him out of church to calm him and explain again what the interpreter meant. I'm sure we left a good number of people confused in our corner of the church.

Jim and I would take several of the boys to various conferences or technology groups to learn about new equipment to help people like our sons, but nothing seemed to be appropriate for Derek. I continued making different switches for Derek to try to use to control toys. Choices were few because of the profoundly limited control he had over any part of his body. The therapists and I had tried positioning various switches near his hands, fingers, head, and chin, all with little success. One day while Derek was on the living room floor, and I was reading nearby, I glanced up and saw that he was lightly touching a toy with his foot. His foot! We hadn't tried a switch at his feet! I was so eager to give his left foot a try that I immediately picked him up and put him in his wheelchair. He was a bit startled because I didn't take time to explain what I was doing.

"I have an idea," I signed. "You can try to play with your foot," I continued. "Come," I signed as I pushed his wheelchair near the area where there were several battery-powered toys.

I took off his left shoe and propped up his leg with a couple of pillows. Then I took one of the switches Ben and Alan used for computer games and connected it to a battery toy of a bright yellow bear that played a drum. I put a thick magazine on top of the pillow for a bit more support and held the switch near his big toe.

"Push. Try to push," I signed as I took his toe with my free hand to help show him. Derek tried to focus on his foot and wiggle his toes,

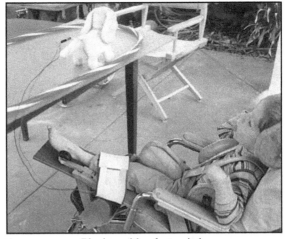

Playing with a foot switch

but he couldn't. Then, I tried the ball of his foot. He could activate the switch and we both got excited, but once he had his foot extended he could not relax enough to release the pressure from the switch. Attempt number two was not successful, either. On the third try, I held the switch on the outside of his foot near his little toe.

"Push. Try again," I signed. "Do you understand?" I signed.

Just as I was about to give up, Derek turned his foot ever so slightly outward and touched the switch! He then turned his foot back away from the switch. My heart was pounding with excitement.

"Derek, do it again," I signed. He did. He smiled from ear to ear and his eyes held an expression of real satisfaction. Thanks to all the skills my Dad had taught me, I was able to mount the switch on a special board I created to fit on his wheelchair footrest. It took me several days to measure, saw, sand, glue, and finish the switch mount, however, soon Derek could activate the battery-powered toys. We had a computer and some special games that required him to use the switch and helped him learn about cause and effect. Initially, Derek's favorite game on the computer was to make a little man walk up the steps until he reached the top. When the man fell off the top of the steps, Derek laughed and laughed, and then would start again. He entertained himself for hours playing this game. We had several other games and special programs that required him to attend to the computer monitor and to touch and release the switch. The goal was to see if he could gain enough control to communicate with others through a computer.

Even though Derek had missed quite a bit of school, his vocabulary continued to grow and the part-time interpreter in the classroom was really helping. Derek continued to use his Plexiglas language board at school and at home, and we still had to follow his eye gaze to determine his answers. By the end of the school year, Derek recognized 100 icons consistently. I could now read him stories and then ask him about the story. I wanted to know what he actually comprehended. It took a while for him to figure out what I was asking of him, but he was eventually able to answer the questions by looking at the correct pictures. This type of improvement convinced me to continue to insist that his communication needs be met in his educational program.

In May, Jim had taken some of the boys to a wheelchair soccer group. One day while they were at practice, he met a parent who had a deaf son. The next week Jim took Derek to see if he enjoyed being pushed around the soccer field in his wheelchair, and to meet the nice woman, whose name was Cindy. They came home excited, so I went along for the next practice. I immediately sensed that Cindy would be perfect as Derek's classroom interpreter/aide. I didn't even know if she worked or wanted to work. I didn't give her much choice, and I encouraged the school to interview her for the job.

Meanwhile, Derek needed to change campuses for summer school. A young girl who had just begun to learn sign language was hired as his aide. I wasn't happy with her because she was just too inexperienced, yet other things required my immediate attention.

In July, an infant was born at Stanford Hospital with various complications. Jim was asked to speak with his parents and discuss how the baby's needs could be met and what type of care he might need. Somehow, things got turned around, and he joined our family in August when he was discharged from the hospital.

Having Ilan join the family was a totally new experience for me. His birth family was still involved in his life and this was the first time I would be dealing with an open adoption. He was critically ill and needed twenty-four hour care. Ilan was in the living room with an oxygen tank, suctioning machine, feeding supplies, and everything else that goes with a critically ill newborn. He was fed through a nasal tube. He vomited almost every time he was moved which meant lots of laundry. His birth parents came to visit almost daily. Medical care personnel came and went. (We had a home nurse at night so that Jim and I could get some rest.) Having all these different people in our home was overwhelming. The older boys felt their family privacy was being invaded. I felt ill at ease when I took Ilan for medical appointments accompanied by a nurse carrying a large binder of information. Frequently the birth parents would also attend the appointments. Eventually, Derek, Rusty, Ben, and Sean would have to move over to make room for Ilan in their bedroom.

While I continued to work to get Ilan settled in, I also continued advocating for Derek's needs, including my desire to have Cindy work with him. Derek's new school was close to her home. Without doubt, Cindy was an angel sent Derek's way.

Cindy recalls: **The first time I saw Derek, his smile just messed me up! I loved the gleam in his eyes and I was surprised he understood my conversations. So after about the third time Marian asked if I would work with him at school, I decided to check it out. It was my first time to be hired to work with a physically challenged child.**

Cindy went from the soccer field to become a classroom interpreter/aide, and Derek was overjoyed. She understood deafness and quickly began to read Derek's nonverbal communication. I was so relieved that someone else could see that Derek did understand conversations when presented in fluent sign language, not just a sign here and there, and that he could make decisions, answer questions, make his basic needs known, and so forth. At last, I felt comfortable sending Derek to school again.

Cindy comments: **At first it was hard for me because I wasn't certain about Derek's physical abilities. Was I signing too fast, too slowly, too much, or too tediously? It was kind of a guessing game for a while, and then we were fine. I was frustrated because I didn't get a whole lot of help from the** staff when I started. Here I was, a person literally off the grass of the park coming to work with Derek, a child who was deaf, to whom I could sign. The teacher didn't include him much in the group and I was expected to work solely with him. I remember asking his mom what I should be doing since I was not receiving much guidance from the staff in the classroom.

Communication. It wasn't that difficult. Why didn't the teachers share more information with the aides working in the classrooms? When we took Derek to the California School for the Deaf for a comprehensive assessment we received a long list of recommendations that was never shared with the classroom aides. Many times the aides who work daily with one specific child are not included in the Individual Education Plan meetings. It just doesn't make sense.

I shared ideas with Cindy about what she might try with Derek, and before long I realized we were on the same page in terms of communication and expectations. As she began to feel more comfortable with Derek, I was able to stay in the background.

Cindy explains: **After an adjustment period, I felt I understood Derek better. I could see that he was expressing things through his eye gaze, facial expressions, and body language. We had our little secrets when we would get frustrated because he would know by the expressions on people's faces how they perceived him. He was very intuitive as to who was respecting his way of doing things. They would make statements such as, "Why are you communicating with him? He doesn't understand what you are saying." And he knew! When things like this happened, I would turn around and sign something like, "They don't know what they're talking about. Just ignore them." He would feel good that I knew the difference. He needed to understand that.**

The bus ride to Derek's new school was about forty-five minutes, but he rode with two of his siblings and was not alone like he had been when we first moved to California. His academic work became more advanced because he had a full-time interpreter/aide. He also began using a computer with single-switch games more consistently at school and home. The goal still was to find a communication device that he could use to share his feelings and express his needs at a higher level than through just eye gaze and body language. At home, I fixed him up to practice with Ben's new speech output computer. Eventually, he was able to spell out his name, but for all practical purposes, his severely limited muscle control prevented him from advancing further with that system.

Derek remained very small, weighing only about twenty-five pounds when he was nine years old, but his therapist felt that he needed a new wheelchair with a different seating system. It took a lot of adjustment for Derek (and me) to accept a new wheelchair. His first chair had become a part of him. The upholstery was in excellent shape, and even the wheels still swiveled like they were new. In my opinion, the chair continued to serve its purpose, but the therapist felt differently. Cindy came to interpret for Derek and me as we spent long hours having an evaluation done for a new seat that would give Derek maximum physical support and allow him to sit comfortably and as upright as possible. We were trying to design a seat for a child who could not sit at all, could not bear much weight on his feet and could not lift his head or hold it upright. His muscle spasms created other challenges as well.

Constant adjustments to his straps, seatbelt, and head supports had to be made depending on the degree of spasticity. His arms could get stuck under the lap tray or armrests where he would rub sores if someone didn't notice and move them.

Derek began having more trouble eating, and he would choke frequently. Even with his food ground fine and with plenty of time in the morning for him to relax, breakfast was a problem. Many days I needed to send his breakfast to school with a note that asked if Cindy could finish feeding him when he arrived. I struggled with positioning his head during meals, the position we used during instructional periods wasn't appropriate for feeding. We tried various types of head supports, neck collars, and other restraints to position his head. The neck collars would slide out of position and the straps would end up around his neck and could choke him. I was extremely frustrated with these issues, and I can only imagine how frustrated Derek must have been. Fortunately, Cindy was able to continue to feed him breakfast after he arrived at school. She was also more flexible about Derek's new chair than I was. (I often used his old chair at home during meals.)

At the same time, we embarked on a year-long major remodel of our house. We tripled the size of the kitchen and converted the double garage to a wheelchair-accessible bathroom and laundry area. We added two large bedrooms, another adapted bathroom, and a bonus room. We expanded the room where we charged all the power wheelchairs at night and replaced the ceiling. We created a large office area and added a new double garage although it was too small for the vans. Finally, we installed a new roof. Derek enjoyed watching the changes and didn't even seem to mind that we were without a kitchen for four months. Eventually, he moved into a different bedroom, which he shared with Ilan. Ilan made a lot of noise, but with Derek being deaf, it was not a problem. Derek continued to adapt fairly well to changes in his life.

Even though he had had low tolerance for heat most of his life, during late spring and early summer Derek began to have greater difficulty during his bus rides and in the classroom where there was no air conditioner. He would sweat profusely and become dehydrated quickly. I investigated the possibility of a cooling vest that he might be able to use during the day. I had talked about it with the people who worked on his seating evaluation, and one day they arranged for us to try one.

At first Derek was agitated and reluctant to let me to put the vest on his body. He had to wear a cap, and that sent him into a temper tantrum. However, once we had it on and the cooling system was running, Derek's spastic muscles relaxed, and he appeared to be most comfortable. This was something Derek could truly benefit from. When it was time to take off the vest and

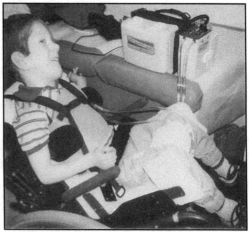

Trying a cooling vest

170

go home, he threw another temper tantrum, but this time it was because he did not want to have the cooling vest removed. I managed to get a prescription to purchase a system, but we never got it.

There would have been complications, but they could have been resolved. The vest would have had to be in a child's size, which was not available at that time. His new seat would have had to be changed to allow for the thickness of the vest, and a battery would have had to be mounted under his chair to power the cooling system. His entire chair would need to be rebalanced to accommodate the battery. Unfor-

tunately, the one obstacle that I never was able to overcome was that Derek's medical insurance would not cover the cooling system costs. The company didn't

Relaxing in the pool

accept the doctors' and therapists' recommendations. I felt I had let him down by not being able to purchase the system for him. I would have to continue to try to cool him with wet cloths, keep him near a fan, and give him as much liquid as possible. Fortunately, we had a large swimming pool where Derek could float around and be as free and content as an eagle soaring in the heavens.

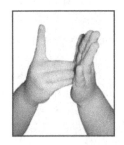

Chapter Seventeen

9 years 7 months-
10 years 7 months old

The fall of 1988 brought Derek his fifth teacher in less than four years. Cindy continued as his interpreter/aide, for which I was most thankful. Marvis, Derek's new teacher, didn't know much about deaf children but seemed to include Derek a bit more in class activities than the teacher from the previous year.

Marvis writes: **I learned some basic signs but mostly communicated through Cindy. As a result, I didn't feel as effective as I should have been. What stands out most in my memory is his good nature and sense of humor. So many times when something humorous happened, he was right there with a big grin and aware of what was going on. Years before I met Derek, I had visited a State Hospital and saw many children just lying in cribs with absolutely nothing and able to do nothing. Then I think of Derek and of all the love and care he received and of all the love that he therefore was able to give to others.**

Cindy explains: **I don't remember Marvis doing much sign language, but what was neat about her is that she would say, "Cindy, please teach this reading group and work on these IEP goals." We did it as a group, which made Derek very happy to do something with two or three kids at a time. He loved doing this and what amazed me, he just knew the answers before the others did!**

Two of those 'others' Cindy mentioned were Derek's siblings, Sean, and our new son, Raymond, who had joined the family during the summer. Like Derek, Raymond couldn't speak, walk, sit unsupported, or have much physical control over his body. He had been born without physical challenges however he became severely disabled at a young age when he nearly drowned. Raymond was extremely spastic, and I had a tough time understanding his communication. I felt helpless caring for him. Fortunately, he bonded with Jim who became Raymond's primary caregiver. When the morning bus came for Derek, Raymond, Sean, and Rusty (who was at the same school in a different classroom), it was a challenge to get their chairs situated so that Rusty wasn't kicking someone, opening the emergency exit, or pulling someone's hair, or that Raymond and Derek were not getting their arms stuck in one another's wheelchairs. No matter how hard we all tried there were times when Raymond's long arms unintentionally smacked someone in the face. Sean didn't bother others physically, but he became seriously upset if someone bothered him. Thank goodness they had a bus driver who was relatively patient and the boys mostly got along well. Although Derek was the oldest of this group, he was much smaller and more medically fragile.

Derek's ability to continue eating orally diminished. He choked repeatedly and could not relax well during mealtime. Doctor visits became more frequent. It seemed every other week we would go to some doctor or specialty clinic. I started with the pulmonary specialist, Dr. Palmer, because I felt Derek's problems were respiratory in nature. Dr. Palmer was highly competent and caring. I began regular respiratory treatments with Derek using nebulizers and chest physiotherapy. These treatments seemed to help him temporarily, but he continued to have frequent pneumonia or low-grade infections in his respiratory tract causing coughing and respiratory distress. Dr. Palmer eventually sent me to gastrointestinal specialists, who sent us to the ear, nose, and throat (ENT) specialist. I was extremely impatient waiting at all these appointments. Often I needed to bring Ilan and a child for whom I provided day care. I'm a person who is rarely late and it irritated me that I arrived on time but had to wait for long periods to be seen. I became so frustrated at times that I asked to have appointments rescheduled because I wasn't willing to sit and be kept waiting for such a long time. Derek also became irritable, his breathing became raspier than usual, and he sweated profusely. I could see that other parents worried about his breathing. They pulled their children closer to them. Often, all eyes appeared to be on us—except the doctors'.

A battery of tests was ordered to determine why Derek was having so much trouble swallowing. First was the nasopharyngoscopy exam with the ENT specialist, who used a flexible scope to examine the airway passages to determine if there were any blockages in the upper airway. The scope is pushed through the nose and down the back of the mouth and throat.

This test was done at Stanford University Medical Center, where Derek had not been before. Most of the patients there were adults. I tried to hide my own anxiety from Derek as I remembered similar tests I had undergone as a child and teen. Derek was awake for the exam. He panicked. All color drained from his face. His body stiffened, his hands clenched, his teeth clenched, his eyes darted from me to the scope to the doctor, and his head turned strongly to the right. I felt like I had a rock in my stomach as I held his sweaty arms and tried to comfort him.

As soon as the nasopharyngoscopy exam was completed, I rushed Derek to the van, undid his seat belt and straps, and lifted him out of his chair. Tears streaked my cheeks as I held him close and repeatedly signed, "I'm sorry, I'm sorry, I'm sorry," until his body went limp with exhaustion.

The next week a barium study was done to determine if Derek's system was able to digest and eliminate his intake. I despised putting him through all of these tests. The X-ray technician handed me a large cup of thick, chalky barium.

"You need to drink," I signed to Derek and pointed to the cup.

The X-ray room was dim. My hands shook as I held the cup to Derek's mouth. He choked after several swallows, and the doctors told me to stop, take him out of his wheelchair and put him on the X-ray table. I wanted to explain to Derek what to expect before I took him out of his chair. People were impatient with me as I asked them to repeat instructions. I couldn't speechread well in the dimly lit room, and Derek needed to be included in the conversation. I finally took him out of his chair and lifted him onto the X-ray table. The doctors turned him every which way under the X-ray machine as they followed the movement of the barium on a monitor. I tried to hold him in the unusual positions the doctors needed. This prevented most communication aside from eye contact, and even that was not possible at times. He would become completely spastic and rigid during these tests and although I tried to be gentle, I felt as if I were torturing my son.

The barium moved slowly, so slowly that the doctors decided to do the test in stages. After taking several pictures of Derek's throat area, we were told to go into the waiting room until called back for more X-rays. We waited for more than an hour before Derek had to get back on the X-ray table. By this time, the barium had moved partly into his esophagus. Several more pictures were taken. Once again, we waited for an hour before the test could be completed. Derek was bored. I was bored. I became impatient. I wanted to go home and be with the other boys. At last, Derek was called back for the remainder of the test which showed the barium had finally reached his stomach. What should have taken about an hour took more than four hours for Derek. He fell asleep from exhaustion before I even finished dressing him.

The nasopharyngoscopy showed that Derek had bilateral vocal cord paralysis. I knew one vocal cord was partially paralyzed in infancy, but now both were. This meant that the vocal cords did not open and close properly. Derek's were paralyzed in an open position which allowed food and liquids to slip into the trachea and lungs. There was also a problem with the epiglottis at the base of the tongue which also allowed food and liquids to enter the trachea. As a result of these disorders much of his nutrition ended up in his lungs, not in his stomach, causing one aspirated pneumonia after another.

The results of the barium swallow reinforced this information. It showed that things moved more slowly than they should have through Derek's system. For example, once food did enter the esophagus (the tube connecting the back of the mouth to the stomach), the food moved exceedingly slowly before reaching his stomach. There didn't seem to be any reflux of food or stomach secretions back into the esophagus which was good news.

Derek continued to lose weight and became malnourished. After much debate and resistance, he finally agreed to have a feeding tube surgically implanted in his stomach for supplemental feedings when he was just too congested or uptight to eat orally, and to allow

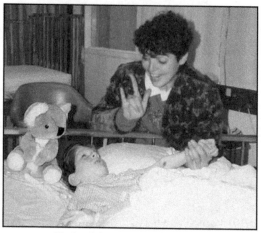
Cindy visits Derek at the hospital

for more fluid intake during travel and hot weather. He accepted the tube well for a couple of days while still in the hospital. However, I was not prepared for the emotional issues that soon developed. I'd had plenty of experience using a feeding tube with Rusty who needed one after he was so ill one winter. Most recently was Ilan, who had a feeding tube as an infant and had not developed a taste for foods or a desire to eat orally. Raymond came with a feeding tube and that was just a part of who Raymond was. With Derek it was a different situation because one of his few pleasures had been eating.

When he saw TV commercials for various foods he liked, especially things related to ice cream, he became upset. The odor of foods cooking in our kitchen just about drove him nuts. To complicate matters, many classroom activities and vocabulary building were centered on cooking and foods. What was the best way to handle this situation? *Do I or don't I make a birthday cake? How would I feel if it were my birthday and I just had this surgery performed?* I tried to put myself in Derek's place. I decided not to bake a cake, since he was recovering from surgery at the time of his birthday.

The original plan was to use the feeding tube for supplemental feedings, but the school nurse had different ideas. She felt once a child had a feeding tube, the child was to no longer be fed orally. I disagreed, but Derek wanted to return to school and I wanted him to be happy. At the insistence of the school, I went back to the doctor for a long, detailed written procedure for school staff to follow. Once again, I could not believe how complicated things became. Feeding Derek through his tube struck me as simple.

After Cindy was trained, Derek could return to school. He was excited as I dressed him and put him in his wheelchair to catch the bus. But I felt I had let him down because tube feeding at school was definitely not part of the original plan. I tried to hide my disappointment when I showed him his lunch.

"Derek, Cindy will give you this (pointing to container with the formula and to the tube) for your lunch," I signed.

Derek did not hide his disappointment. He cried.

Cindy remarks: **I remember when Derek returned to school after his surgery that he clearly was not happy when I had to begin tube feeding him. He relaxed as time went on, but I was actually very stupid about some things, especially cooking. I never thought of how he felt or about things that he might be real sensitive to until Marian brought them to my attention. I didn't think about saying things like, "Oh, I'm mixing this and I'm helping you to cook." When I realized what I was doing, I felt like I was torturing him since he could not eat this stuff! I would secretly sneak him a taste. I feel that he took everything with a grain of salt, eventually. I could just sense him communicating, "I don't like this Cindy, but this is me." I also remember taking him for a walk or finding a book to read while the other students were eating snacks.**

I didn't use canned formulas. I thought since Derek's system was accustomed to digesting regular foods, I would mix his formula as I had done previously with Rusty. When mixed correctly, a balanced diet could be prepared. For example, I put in yogurt, vegetable oil, baby foods (meat, vegetables), bananas, milk, etc. It took some time for his system to begin moving again after the surgery, but he began to regain weight, his coloring improved, and he seemed stronger in all respects. We even stopped the orders for the suctioning machine at school! (He'd been using that for about a year.) I continued to feed him as much orally as I could and used the feeding tube for supplemental needs at home.

With the use of the feeding tube, Derek was receiving more liquids than previously. This was good news because it kept him hydrated, but it definitely increased the pile in his dirty laundry basket. We had worked on toilet training and at one time were fairly successful, but we couldn't find a toilet seat that would allow him to maintain a position to continue it. Also, because of frequent hospitalizations, and without a way to communicate the need to use the bathroom, Derek just continued to use diapers, and there was nothing wrong with that. In many ways, having a child in diapers lessens the stress of parenting a child with special needs because you don't need to be "right there" when a child has the urge to go. It also allows more time to focus on goals the child has a better chance of reaching.

With all that was happening, Derek also brought me a new and dear friend that year.

Diane thinks back: Derek was going to Chandler Tripp School when I was a volunteer there. I didn't realize Derek was deaf until I saw his aide signing to him. I knew a little bit of sign language, so I started signing with him in class. I noticed that, every time I arrived, as soon as he saw me he would get excited and all of his energy would go into his smile. You could just tell by his body he knew who was there. I started reading these simple books like *Mary Had A Little Lamb* or *Baa Baa Black Sheep*. I wondered how much he understood about what I was signing and showing him. Then I saw Cindy, and she was signing with him and I realized by his responses he really understood what was going on. As time went on, even though I wasn't certain how much Derek understood, I just assumed he knew everything! I would treat him and talk to him like he was completely cognizant and I worked to reach him through touching things as well as through signs and visual activities. Later, I met Derek's mom and began attending her sign class and visiting in Derek's home. We became—and remain—very close friends.

Cindy continued to work with Derek and sign everything that happened in the classroom. I made a different Plexiglas communication system to attach to his wheelchair tray. This eye gaze board was now focused on pictures and words, not objects as we previously had used. Cindy, Derek's teacher, Alma, and I added to his collection of icons and words. We selected vocabulary from many different parts of speech and things related to a specific time of year or events taking place.

Derek became more consistent with his eye gaze to answer questions by looking at the words **YES** and **NO** taped on the Plexiglas. I still felt that his eyebrows raised for "yes" and a pout for "no" were clear, but others thought differently. Cindy and I could sign stories that included a variety of topics to Derek, which he delighted in. We asked him questions that he could answer by looking at **YES** or **NO**. He impressed me with his consistent answers and level of comprehension. Witnessing this cognitive growth encouraged me to continue to provide him with exposure to the written word.

My goal for Derek to be able to activate a switch that would allow him to use higher technology for communication had to be put on the back burner. He had fair control over the switch with his left foot in his old wheelchair. When he got his new wheelchair, we never found a position that allowed him to activate the switch.

The highlight of summer school was when Cindy brought her son, who was deaf, to school to interact with Derek. This was his only contact with a deaf peer. I imagine that Derek greatly valued these times. I still grieved that he was not in a program where there were other deaf children with whom he could interact.

Even with all the activity going on in the family, I continued to teach ASL classes one night a week. This became "Mom's night out." Although I was bored at times because of the basic level of the class, teaching allowed me to develop many genuine and lasting friendships.

You can't imagine how difficult it was to find someone I could trust to care for my children, especially Derek with his ongoing medical problems, when Jim wasn't available. Fortunately, I found Linda, a classroom aide in Rusty's class, to come and take over while I was out. I was even able to go on a few short trips with Linda's help at home.

Linda states: **Derek was really cute, but he always cried when he first saw me because that meant Mom was going away and that bothered him more than anything. However, as time went on, he accepted me and allowed me to care for him. I knew Derek from working at a school he had attended, but I had focused on his brother Rusty, who was in my class. Still, I remember one day when his mom came to the school** for a meeting. The teachers had sat Derek facing the walls, with his back to the bus. I remember his Mom getting very angry because all he has is his vision and he was being made to look at a wall. When Marian turned him around he was just so excited to be able to see everything around him rather than the stupid wall! I felt the staff never really looked at him, did not take into account everything he needed. They would deal with his physical limitations, his deaf limitations, or even his sight limitations, but they never dealt with everything at the same time. I always wondered if he was lacking because of that. Being in Derek's home and having Marian as a mentor taught me to look at the whole being which helped me better understand the children in the various special day classes where I worked as an aide.

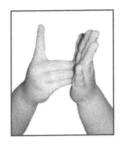

Chapter Eighteen

10 years 8 months - 11 years 8 months old

*D*erek's new teacher, Alma, was trained to work with children with special needs, but she had never worked with deaf children. In the first couple of weeks she had learned several signs from Cindy.

Cindy shared this story: **You know how we do these preschool songs. Well, Alma was learning sign language and she is very good about language and can pick up the signs quickly. She has a gift. So, we did "Twinkle, Twinkle, Little Star" and Derek would begin to laugh and then would start choking. Well, one day I thought I was going to have to suction the poor kid and get him out of his chair to clear his airway, all because he was laughing so hard when we were doing this song! What happened was Alma started signing "like a diamond" and I thought** *No way, Derek's not going to know these signs!* **Derek started laughing and choking, laughing and choking, and all the time I was trying to get him to stop laughing. Finally, I stopped Alma and told her that the sign she was using was not diamond, but the sign for vagina— you know, the female organ! She said, "Oh my gosh!" She turned red and she was so embarrassed. Derek was cracking up, bursting with laughter! It became a joke from that day on. He just loved it when people learned a little sign language to communicate with him. He did not care if they did it right or not. He would just accept whatever people attempted to sign.**

That fall Derek attended a public school day program for deaf children for two hours each day. Even though the program meant another hour on a bus during the school day, he enjoyed being in a place where everyone used sign language. He was especially fond of group story time and language lessons. Then new health concerns surfaced, and Derek's physical needs prevented him from going to class consistently. The staff decided his sporadic attendance was too disruptive for the other students, so his social interaction with children who were deaf stopped, and he stayed in his class with other students who had orthopedic challenges. As I write this, I wish I had pushed harder for him to be part of a class with deaf children when he was healthier. I still can't figure out why he wasn't given that opportunity.

After the feeding tube was put in, we had been able to increase Derek's calorie intake. By age eleven, he weighed about forty-eight pounds. We were also able to administer the muscle relaxants through his G-tube ('G-tube' and 'feeding tube' are interchangeable terms), which decreased his spasticity. Suctioning had stopped and respiratory infections were infrequent. My hopes and spirits had reached an all-time high. Then suddenly for reasons that I just could not comprehend, Derek's health started to spiral downward. I was not emotionally prepared for what was about to happen.

I had to suction Derek every two or three minutes. His secretions were so thick and massive that they blocked his airway and even the suctioning catheters became clogged. Previously, I only needed to suction the back of his throat and his mouth. Now, I had to learn deep suctioning, which meant going down the back of the nasal passages and bypassing the oropharynx (the front of the mouth) to reach the secretions in the trachea. I despised doing this to my son. Again, I felt like I was torturing him. Derek hated the suctioning as well, but always expressed his gratitude that he could breathe again when we finished. I always thanked him by explaining, "Thank you Derek for expressing your appreciation for these things I hate doing but that make you more comfortable."

Again, further medical intervention was needed. Another barium swallow was scheduled to determine what physical changes were taking place. Again, it took forever for the barium to travel through Derek's digestive tract. The test showed Derek now had Gastroesophageal Reflux. Reflux is when the gastric acid, food, and stomach secretions flow back up out of the stomach into the esophagus (the tube connecting the back of the mouth to the stomach). The esophagus can't withstand the acid of stomach secretions. If the reflux causes reddening and swelling of the esophagus, it is called "esophagitis." Esophagitis is extremely painful and can lead to respiratory infections from the stomach contents entering the nose, windpipe, or lungs. It can also lead to bleeding from the inflamed part of the esophagus. In Derek, the ring of muscles, called the lower esophageal sphincter, where the stomach and esophagus join, were not functioning properly. If this sphincter remains relaxed, the food and stomach acid can escape back into the esophagus. That is what was happening with Derek. He was on medications to help eliminate reflux, but they weren't effective.

I tried everything the doctors recommended. I tried to feed him more frequently and in smaller amounts. I tried to position him so his upper body was raised to let gravity help keep his food down. I diluted his formula, hoping it would be easier for him to digest. No matter what I did, he still needed to be deep suctioned frequently. His nasal passages and the back of his throat were inflamed and sore not only from the stomach acid but also from the continuous deep suctioning. There weren't many choices other than another risky surgery. Without it, he could die from internal bleeding of the esophagus or from malnourishment.

A team of doctors believed Derek should have Nissen fundoplication surgery as soon as possible to tighten the sphincter muscles of his stomach. During this surgery the top of the stomach is wrapped around the base of the esophagus to help lessen the acid flow back up into the esophagus. There were problems. Derek's surgeon was at a conference on the East Coast. Normally, I regarded the doctors who cared for Derek and my other children with great respect, but I found myself feeling differently about the surgeon who was on call. He insisted Derek be transferred to the main hospital at Stanford. I didn't want to move him. Derek was receiving exceptional care where he was with nurses who knew him. Also, he was in an environment where he felt comfortable, the old Children's Hospital. The surgery had to be done immediately. After it was finished the surgeon demanded that Derek be transferred to unfamiliar surroundings at Stanford and come under the care of medical staff that did not have a clue about how to communicate with him, or me, for that matter.

I had seen this physician interact with children who were physically able-bodied. I wondered why he acted differently with Ilan when he needed surgery as an infant and again now with Derek. *Is it because my sons are adopted? Is it because they both are not your 'typical, physically normal' child? Why is he negative about doing surgeries that would improve the quality of life for these children? Did his medical school teach him that such children should be hidden and institutionalized?* I never questioned his medical expertise, but he didn't see value in the sons I had adopted and cared for when they had not been accepted or raised by their birth families. *I cherish these boys. Why can't he at least respect them for the individuals they were born to be?*

Derek stayed too long in that hospital environment. His bed could not be angled to allow him to see the TV or the people entering or leaving the room. All he could do was stare at a blank wall. He became deeply depressed for the first time. No matter how often I requested his bed be moved so he could at least see the TV (remember his head was normally turned to the right), my request was denied. I was torn between staying with Derek at the hospital and fulfilling my responsibilities at home with my other sons. My heart ached to be in both places.

While Derek was in the hospital recovering from surgery, Ben was trying to master his new Epson computer/communication device. Ben wore a red light on his head, held on by a black elastic band I had sewn for him. This computer had what is called a "light board," the equivalent of a keyboard for able-bodied people. It was terribly slow for Ben, pointing the light on one letter at a time, holding his head still long enough to activate the computer. The Epson had a monotone computerized voice, as well as a printer to print out his writing on a roll of paper similar to one used in an adding machine. Sometimes it took him more than fifteen minutes to write one sentence, but for once he could communicate much of what had been trapped in his mind all those years.

It was the Christmas season and Ben, a fifth grader, had been assigned to dedicate his writing project to someone. I thought he would select a close friend from church, but that was not what Ben was thinking. He had chosen Derek. Each day, his teacher assigned the students to write about something different. I had not seen everything Ben had written until Christmas morning when Ben and I went to the hospital to share his project with Derek. I sat on the edge of Derek's bed helping Ben show Derek the most unique and meaningful Christmas gift Derek had ever received. As I signed what Ben had written, Derek's eyes would briefly leave my hands to glance at Ben and acknowledge him. I felt real joy that my sons had built such a close relationship. My heart was ready to burst as I recalled how these two boys had entered my life, developing such a strong bond and love for each other.

Here are some excerpts from Ben's writing.

Dedicated to: **Derek Aiken, my brother, who has had to fight many illnesses, but never complains. His example is one that I am thankful for.**

Some presents for Derek: **I'd give you good health forever because I love you and I want you to be healthy. I could buy Derek a video tape and something funny for him to enjoy. I could give him one of my lungs so he could breathe better. I'd like to give him a big hug.**

Recipe for Derek:

> **5 gallons of chocolate ice cream**
> **3 cups of Mom's yucky squash**
> **1 banana**
> **4 cups chocolate milk**
> **1 cup cherry yogurt**

Mix in blender and store in refrig. Warm in microwave. Pour through feeding tube. Don't tell the docs what you eat!

Memories: **Derek, we've had many fun times together. Remember the fun times that Mom, you and I had out in the snow? That was exciting and enjoyable.**

Derek, remember the fun we had together with Grandma and Granddad? Grandma would play cards and games with us and we rode cross-country with them all alone! That was fun and exciting. I was so glad she didn't make us eat ham. Instead, Grandma let us eat ice cream every day.

Hey brother, remember when Mom would take us on hot trips and I was whining, "Let's go swimming"? Later you'd kick around in that old swimming pool while I cooled off in the boat.

Derek, remember those times that Rusty would pat us on the head? I tried to put his hand back on his body, but he is stronger than me.

Derek, remember when you and I lay on the floor and watched cartoons together? I really like being close to you.

Derek, I'm glad that I thought of these great ideas so I can remember you in my heart. - Love, Ben

How could I not be proud of what my boys had accomplished under my care? Derek and Ben were two spectacular sons whom I could hold in my heart as I went about my daily chores and through some not-so-pleasant times.

After two weeks, Derek was finally transferred back to the old Children's Hospital that he knew so well. His recovery picked up speed immediately.

While Derek was in the hospital, I had contact with other families who had children hospitalized for various reasons. Some were there only occasionally, while others more frequently, like Derek. One day a little girl's father approached me. "Marian, the nurses have suggested I talk with you about a power wheelchair that belongs to my daughter." He spoke slowly with a sad expression, saying, "She's a near-drowning victim and is now blind and brain damaged. The wheelchair was donated to us, but she can't use it any more. Could your son, Derek, use it?"

His daughter had been born with *osteogenesis imperfecta*, brittle bones. She was left unsupervised in the bathtub on a weekend visit with her mother and lost her balance while the mother was on the phone in another room. What happened to his daughter was tragic.

"Derek doesn't have enough control over his body to use the chair," I explained. "But I have another child who can definitely make use of a power wheelchair."

"Great! I'll bring the chair in tomorrow and leave it beside Derek's bed," he replied.

It had already arrived when I got there the next morning—a

brand new child's size Quickie power wheelchair perfect for Kyle. Thanks to Derek, Kyle was able to begin driving his first power wheelchair at the very young age of nine months old! Derek was thrilled to watch Kyle experiment and begin to zip around. I think he especially enjoyed Kyle's long period of trial and error, driving the chair with his chin.

Kyle had joined the family as an infant who had been born with severe *arthrogryposis*. Basically, he was paralyzed from the neck down with no muscles in his limbs, a severely curved spine, and limited muscle movement in his intestine. He was a bright child with an outgoing personality at home, but he was extremely quiet and shy in public. Kyle picked up all the facial expressions and body language of the boys who were nonverbal. He quickly learned that he didn't need to speak when communicating with me and just moved his eyes like his siblings did to let me know what he wanted. Derek adored Kyle and would relax when I placed Kyle near him on the hospital bed or on the floor at home. They seemed to communicate through osmosis.

Then one day, while Derek was in the hospital, Mary, one of our favorite nurses, came to me.

"Marian, there's a deaf teenage girl in Room 105. I think she may be mentally slow but I know she's lonely. Can you stop in to visit her for a few minutes?"

"Sure, I'll stop by," I told Mary. "But I have to ask Derek first. He's my priority, you know."

"Derek, is it okay for me to go see a deaf girl (point door and down hall) in the next room?" I signed in ASL. "I think she is lonely," I signed.

Derek looked toward the door with a smile and eyebrows raised, giving me his approval. Then he gazed at the clock on the wall with a questioning expression.

"How long will I stay?" I signed. "Maybe fifteen minutes. I'll come back fast. I will chat with her for a short time." Derek's eyes followed me as I turned to leave his hospital room. "I will hurry. I love you," I signed.

The young girl opened up to me almost immediately, as we communicated through ASL. She really was lonely. Her family lived more than two hours from the hospital and she had no friends in the area. She was a bright youth—not mentally slow at all—and she was concerned and confused about her medical condition. She had many unanswered questions because no interpreter had been provided for her. After our visit, I asked Mary to put in a request for an interpreter so the girl could communicate with her doctor before she was discharged. Individuals who are deaf need clear and accurate communication in regard to their medical care. Thankfully, deaf people's needs are being better respected these days, but there is still room for improvement.

It was spring. Derek's, Sean's, and Raymond's class was going on a field trip near our home. Since their destination was so close, I drove the boys to meet their class at Hidden Villa, an educational working farm in Los Altos Hills, and stayed with them as a helper. Although I had been in and out of their classroom, I had never paid much attention to the other students. This day, I met a child named Coco. He was a beautiful child with sparkling, dark eyes; a deep, olive complexion; raven-black hair; and a smile that spread from ear to ear. I learned that Coco and Derek were frequently paired to do classroom activities and were great pals. A couple of months after I met Coco, I learned that he was going to have to move soon from his foster home. The school staff didn't want him placed in a state institution and asked if they could suggest to his social workers that he be placed in our family. I arranged a weekend visit to see how things might work out and to learn more about Coco.

Like Derek, Coco had cerebral palsy, was tube-fed, communicated through facial expressions and body language, and needed to have all his physical care met by others. Coco could hear, though, and this allowed much more communication with others, not limited to people who only knew sign language. Coco also could vocalize to get people's attention. Before long, Jim and I communicated with Coco's birth father. He was reluctant to allow us to adopt Coco, but I reassured him it would be open; he could visit whenever he wanted and take Coco to his home for visits. I didn't want to exclude him from Coco's life, but we were not a foster care home. Two weeks later, Coco's birth father contacted us. He wanted his son to become a permanent member of our family and we proceeded with the adoption. I will never forget the day I asked Coco if he wanted to live with us. We were in the living room with Derek.

"Coco, what do you think about moving here?" I spoke and signed to include Derek in the conversation.

Immediately, they both became excited and overjoyed with this news! I finally had to warn them that I only had one suctioning machine handy and I could not suction them both at the same time.

"Please stop laughing, you two," I signed big and loud. "STOP LAUGHING!"

Once again, Derek was able to share his love with another sibling.

About this same time we received another call about a child, José, who needed a home. Would we consider taking him in? Again, like Derek, José had cerebral palsy, was nonverbal and non-ambulatory. He also had a feeding tube for supplemental feedings. Physically, he was much like Sean and could use one hand to point to icons to communicate. He needed a power wheelchair, so I fixed him up using an old wheelchair with someone's old insert and parts from other old chairs until he learned to drive fairly well. Once he learned to drive, it was easier to obtain a chair of his own. José always seemed to have a smile on his face and loved being social. Fortunately, he didn't have the respiratory problems that Derek had and he didn't really need a lot of medical attention. He learned several modified signs that allowed him to communicate with Derek.

The house construction was almost complete. With four new boys joining the family within two and a half years, we had to rearrange sleeping areas. Rusty moved to a small room off the kitchen. Sometimes his nighttime seizures woke the other boys who shared a room with him. Derek got to move across the hall to share a room with his favorite brother, Ben, along with Sean and Coco. I asked a man from church, Fred, if he would be interested in building bookshelves for this room, and he was happy to help. When he finished the project, Derek had his own little corner with his fish tank at the head of his bed. He also had space for his collection of lights and kinetic art. Fred would not accept any payment for his work, but was rewarded with Derek's precious smile when we placed his aquarium at the head of his bed.

Thank you, Derek, for being generous, appreciative, and sharing your home and me with so many others. I continue to cherish these qualities you convey through your actions. Love ~ Mom

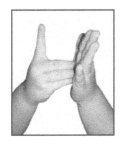

Chapter Nineteen

11 years 9 months - 12 years 6 months old

*T*he Dream: *The dream is crystal clear when I wake about 3 a.m., but I'm very puzzled. Was something wrong in California? I hadn't talked to Marian in months, but I hesitated to call her and tell her about the dream. I saw Derek walking toward the gates of Heaven. He was a teenager, about fourteen years old. He was tall and slim. He turned his head toward me with a big smile. His hair was light reddish-blonde and he still had a freckled face. His smile conveyed his thoughts, "I am going to be okay here, I am happy."*

Fall arrived and although Derek had reached middle school age, he still wore size 4T clothes and weighed less than forty pounds. His new teacher Mary knew sign language, which was exciting for everyone, especially Derek. He now had two adults who could communicate directly with him at school.

Mary recalls: **I ran into Derek in the halls at Chandler Tripp during summer school about a year before coming to Rogers. I remember noticing how responsive he was. Having Derek in my class made me feel like I was one of the honored few who really understood him and could communicate with him. It seemed like there weren't very many of us in the world who really could understand Derek. It did take time to understand him, though. For example, he had this one facial expression that looked like he was very afraid of something, but actually it meant he was very excited about something. In the beginning, I thought it was a bad face, that there was something he did** not want, when actually it was something that he really, really wanted.

Derek was thrilled when he left home each morning because he had become an active participant in his mainstream class. He'd be tired but content when he came home in the afternoon, and would almost immediately take a nap. He was receiving all his nutrition via his feeding tube and was not involved in family meals, but he had plenty of company from siblings who also had feeding tubes: Raymond, Coco, Ilan, José, and a new family member, Dustin. They all shared the living room floor or couches during mealtime. (Eventually Ilan, José and Dustin had their feeding tubes removed as they learned to eat orally.)

Dustin had been born without physical challenges but was left severely disabled from a brain injury when he was strangled at a young age. When Dustin came to us all of his physical needs had to be provided by others. It was difficult to know what he understood or if he even understood anything. As time went on, with hard work and determination Dustin was able to regain some skills, such as eating and feeding himself, speaking, using facial expressions, and interacting socially. Over the years, he also learned some modified signs which he used to communicate with Derek. Although Derek didn't participate in after school activities or dances, he was at last mainstreamed for some of his classes with the regular education students. He enjoyed this immensely. He came home with homework, but he had trouble staying awake to complete the assignments.

Cindy recalls: **Derek loved to do science experiments where he could see something happening. We also were in a California History class. I thought, *'Why are we in this class? Is it too complicated for him? Am I going to be able to interpret enough for him? Are my skills good enough?'* It would bother me that I wasn't a trained interpreter for Derek (and for my own son). I worried I was not giving Derek all the information that was available. As time went on, I came to believe that our communication was sufficient and he was appreciative of what I was giving him. He really did pay attention in the classroom. He truly enjoyed the stories of California's history about settlements and learning about the Indians. It surprised me what he remembered from these lectures. He made my job** exciting and worthwhile. Also, it was gratifying that I didn't need to defend his intelligence any longer!

After twelve years of caring for Derek, I finally felt he was understood by the educational staff, accepted by his classmates, both the hearing and the physically challenged, and included as much as he could be. Not only did Derek have a teacher and aide who could communicate with him, but the students in the mainstream classes also showed a desire to have a connection with Derek.

Mary says: **I started a sign language class with the regular sixth-grade students so they could at least do some basic communication with Derek. I would have kids lined up outside my classroom at break time waiting for Derek to come out of the room so they could talk to him in sign language. Of course, they were just learning and really wanted to get to know Derek. I would interpret for them. I always asked permission from Derek to share about him before answering their numerous questions. It never seemed to bother him when others were curious about him. I should mention the sign language class is still going at school and is in high demand.**

Inclusion was no insignificant matter for a family such as ours and certainly for a child like Derek. Of course, not everyone with mental, emotional, or physical challenges benefits in the regular educational setting. When mainstreaming takes place, there is always a need to balance the amount of time a student can handle in a regular education classroom versus needing specialized instruction. Some of the factors that need to be considered when making decisions about educational placements for students with special needs are:

• Does the student's behavior become disruptive during class time?

• How long can the student focus on material being presented?

• If the child is medically fragile, how long can he or she physically tolerate being in a regular classroom setting?

• What are the academic and social benefits of being included in the mainstream?

• How much will materials in the classroom need to be adapted? For example, they might need shorter written assignments, extended time for testing, enlarged print, desk adjustments, physical room/space for wheelchair users, note takers or interpreters.

• How will the child's physical needs be met without disrupting the regular classroom-learning atmosphere?

Each student who has a special need is required by law to have an Individual Education Plan (IEP), which is designed to assure that each student's needs are met in the educational setting. A plan doesn't mean that all goals and needs are always met. Parents must constantly be in communication with staff to encourage follow-through or determine if the goals must be modified. The composition of the IEP team varies. Any or all of the following people may be included: school administrators, teachers, parents, behavior specialists, therapists, medical personnel, educational advocates, and the student. As mentioned earlier, I now felt Derek was actually receiving support and follow-through with his goals and classes that would stimulate his mind.

Nonetheless there always seemed to be new challenges. For example, by this time Derek was on oxygen all day. At home we needed to find a place to put his large oxygen tank where it wouldn't get knocked over or obstruct the paths of the wheelchairs. Keeping the nasal cannula in place could be a challenge for someone who was spastic and whose skin was sensitive to tape. We also had seventy-five feet of tubing that allowed me to move Derek from the living room to the bathroom, bedroom, or computer room without having to disconnect the tubing each time. Once I was accustomed to carrying him around without tripping, the tubing didn't present much of a problem. That was the case until one of his brothers would enter the living room to be with Derek, watch TV, and park a 300+ pound wheelchair on top of the tubing. We had a lot of laughs about this.

In addition to the large tank, he had a smaller tank that he used at school or church. I learned to refill it before leaving home, but it took me some time to accomplish this without the fear of blowing something up. It was also difficult to find a way to transport the portable tank with Derek's wheelchair. If we hung the tank on the back of his chair, its weight caused the chair to tip backward. Carrying the tank on my shoulder with a shoulder strap was uncomfortable while pushing the chair. Finally, I secured a fifteen-pound barbell weight to the wheelchair's front crossbar under his feet to balance the tank on the back. This worked great and cost only a couple of dollars.

As the 1991-1992 school year went on Derek's health became progressively worse. Constipation had been a minor problem until the previous year. Now, Derek began having trouble passing stools because of frequent episodes of *ileus*, an obstruction of the intestine. These were extremely painful and when they happened, it was not possible to provide nourishment. Once again his weight dipped. There was absolutely no comfortable way to deal with these obstructions.

Marcia, a gastrointestinal nurse at Children's Hospital At Stanford, describes this medical situation: **The definition of an ileus is basically that there is nothing moving through the intestine, so it comes to a standstill and the bowel either goes into spasm of strictures or it just stops. Therefore, anything that would be coming down from above would be causing pressure on an area that was not allowing something to go through. There are a lot of other physiological things that happen as a result of that. If feeding is continued, and even bodily secretions like saliva and gastric secretions try to pass through, pain builds and eventually the person will go into shock. Electrolytes can go out of whack and a lot of physiological responses flow through them.**

Basically an ileus is a blockage. It's just as if somebody takes a hose and bends it as water tries to go through. The liquid can't get through until the bent part of the hose is released. With Derek, in order to release the pressure, we would open up his gastrostomy tube and just let it all flow out and then we would just have to wait for that gut to open up. It took forever for his gut to open up. Once it did, then we would be able to start feeding him again, slowly so that things would go through. But he also had such a terrible motility (movement through the digestive system) that even when he did not have an ileus, he was plagued with spasticity in his GI tract. His motility was so poor that contents in his intestine would move downward a little bit and then come back with a sort of ebb

and flow. Nothing is ever supposed to come back; contents are always supposed to go in one direction in the intestine.

When Derek had an ileus, he either needed to be hospitalized or I would attempt to solve the problem at home, providing I caught it in time. If I could catch an ileus developing, I would administer a go-lightly treatment through his feeding tube for a couple of days. This was extremely messy to clean up, and it was risky because of the danger of causing dehydration and unbalancing electrolytes. Derek wanted to stay at home rather than go to the hospital. If the ileus progressed further, his feeding tube proved to be a real advantage. I could open the tube and allow the built-up stomach fluids or gas to drain via gravity into a zip lock bag or, better yet, a feeding pump bag that had measurements on it. This would help to drain the ileus and relieve the cramping and pressure. I'd contact the nurses and doctors to let them know Derek was having trouble and they'd prepare to admit him. The nurses always asked how much had drained from his feeding tube. When it was 300 to 400 ccs the nurses would *panic* and urge me to bring him to the hospital as soon as I could. I now know they were worried about him going into shock, but at the time I was too naive to understand. I was focused on relieving his pain and making him as comfortable as possible.

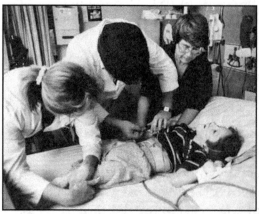
Trying to insert an IV

Being able to drain the ileus through the feeding tube eliminated the need to insert a nasal tube for drainage. Still, while the feeding tube was draining, Derek couldn't receive nourishment. Once we were in the hospital, we needed to start IVs. Sometimes it could take hours to find a vein that would not collapse or blow, especially if Derek was dehydrated. Nurses who were "experts" would be called from different units of the hospital to help. During one admission, it took over four hours of poking and prodding before they managed to insert the IV. Meanwhile, Derek would sweat excessively and become even more spastic and rigid than usual, and his oxygen levels would drop as he struggled to breathe. Once the IV was started, blood samples would be taken and then fluids and nutrition could be administered while the obstruction would continue to drain through his feeding tube.

The medical staff was always concerned about his electrolyte levels. Initially, I didn't understand what "electrolytes" meant. I now understand that they are the minerals and salts in our bodies that are essential for the normal functioning of our organs, fluid absorption and excretion, and nerve function.

The Dream: *The dream had continued to bother me over several months. Yet I had not mentioned it to anyone. I later learned that Derek started having more difficult problems at about the same time as I had my dream.*

Every parent knows how important it is to have good communication with medical staff when a child is ill. So I was thrilled when one of Derek's doctors offered to help make communication easier for us. She thought it would be easier, more reliable, and quicker to connect me with Derek's medical and support personnel through the hospital computer system since I needed to type using the relay operator with my TTY anyway. This was before the time of everyday use of email, and I was greatly intimidated by technology. I gradually warmed up to my computer and was most thankful for this new system. (That doctor was amazing. She even gave me her cell phone number to use in case of an emergency.) The use of the computer allowed me to be home to care for the other children, and saved us many time-consuming trips to the hospital which were extremely draining for Derek. The use of email for communication between families and medical specialists has become the norm today, but at the time I felt like a pioneer in the field.

Derek was once again missing a lot of school. I was concerned about Cindy, his one-on-one interpreter/aide, having to deal with Derek's absences. After all, she needed an income to help support her own family. Eventually, Cindy moved into another position because we just didn't know if Derek would be returning to school.

Carol, Derek's physical therapist, shares her memories: I met Derek for the first time in the fall of 1992. At that point, he was on oxygen and was fed through a gastrostomy tube. He looked very fragile and small. My initial reaction was one of fear for Derek's well-being and fear that I would not be able to help him in any way.

I've heard that the eyes are the windows to the soul. That was definitely true in Derek's case. He appeared frail and delicate but when he looked into your eyes, you felt a strong and beautiful spirit, and all his pain and physical disability disappeared. In his eyes you saw the kind, compassionate, and fun-loving person who was Derek. He had a smile that lit up a room, and he was generous in sharing this gift with others. There were days when he didn't feel great or seemed like he was tired, but I never saw him complain or whine. I admired the grace with which he faced a life that seemed filled with adversity. He substantiated for me that our physical beings are not who we really are.

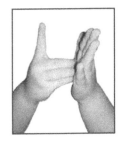

Chapter Twenty

12 years 7 months - 13 years 4 months old

I tried to continue to do regular activities with the family as much as possible. One adventure was an overnight trip to the Monterey Aquarium and the Boardwalk in Santa Cruz. This was enough of a challenge with all the boys who were healthy, but with Derek it meant taking the suctioning machine, feeding supplies, medications, and the large oxygen tank so I could refill the smaller tank as needed. I put the large tank on the wheelchair lift, placed it in the back of the van, and secured it to the floor with the wheelchair tie downs. This worked great. I put a NO SMOKING sign in the window so people would know there was oxygen near. Off we went, squeezed snuggly in two vans, with Jim driving one, me driving the other, all the boys and two able-bodied friends to help push the manual wheelchairs.

Derek loved to watch his fish tank at the head of his bed so the Monterey Aquarium was certainly a special place for him to visit. He could sit contentedly for hours watching the fish swim and feed. To make the trip a bit more special, I took him into the gift shop where he selected a mobile to hang in his room and a T-shirt with a picture of a whale. After our day at the Aquarium, we spent the night at a hotel where we divided everybody into two rooms. Some boys camped out on the floor with sleeping bags while others shared beds. Unlike earlier years when we traveled and Derek would kick around on the bed wanting to play, that night he fell asleep quickly from exhaustion. He appeared to be content and happy in the presence of his family.

The next morning Jim, our friend Diane, and I got all the boys toileted, dressed, fed, into their wheelchairs, and loaded into the vans for our trip to the Boardwalk in Santa Cruz. Derek passively took in the views and watched his brothers gobble down hot dogs, soft pretzels, and cotton candy. He was extremely listless until we walked past the Ferris wheel. Suddenly, I noticed his arms stiffen and his head turn a bit. I moved so I could see his face; his eyes were focused on the large Ferris wheel. He looked at me and back toward the Ferris wheel.

"You want to ride the Ferris wheel?" I signed to him.

"Yes," he indicated by raising his eyebrows and grinning slightly.

Diane was beside me pushing Ilan and following pint-sized Kyle, who wore shades and was stealing the show by zipping around people as he drove his power wheelchair with his chin.

"Diane, Derek wants to ride the Ferris wheel. What do you think? Should I try it?" I asked.

"Sure, go ahead," she cheerfully responded. "I'll stay with Ilan and make sure Kyle doesn't drive away."

I wasn't sure that was the response I wanted to hear, but Derek wanted to ride. What a challenge to carry him up to this ride and hold him while keeping my balance! Derek was not heavy but continued to be either rigid and spastic or totally floppy. I didn't even try to take the oxygen tank on the ride. The ride operator looked at me as if I were totally crazy.

"Lady, are you sure you know what you're doing with that boy?" he asked with a concerned expression on his face.

"Yes, I certainly know what I'm doing," I replied, staggering up the incline to slide into the hard, slippery seat. Derek squirmed a bit on my lap trying to find a comfortable position. He was so thin that his tailbone poked my leg. He couldn't hold up his head, so I held him snugly as the ride slowly rose, stopped, rose and stopped again while other people boarded. Finally, all the seats were taken, and we rode round and round. Derek would stiffen when he saw Diane, Kyle, and Ilan below us. Then he would relax and his hair would tickle my face in the breeze. Eventually it was our turn to get off, which was not a graceful moment for me. My left arm was numb and I had trouble finding my footing, but I finally made my way down the incline without losing my balance. I was feeling light-headed, probably from being afraid I'd fall with Derek in my arms, but Derek beamed with pride when he saw Diane waving to him. As I placed him in his wheelchair and fastened his seatbelt, our eyes made contact. He was thin, pale, and tired, but his eyes spoke, "Thank you, Mom, for taking me on that ride." Diane and I decided to load the younger boys into the van and head home. We stayed close to home the rest of the summer.

It was hard to make decisions about school. Somewhere along the way, miscommunication with the school's nursing supervisor led me to think Cindy didn't want to return to work with Derek. That was not actually the case, but I didn't learn that until much later. Meanwhile, our friend Linda, who worked as an aide for the county, easily passed the training needed for Derek's care. She helped at home when I needed to be away from the house. Her assistance at school was mostly related to his physical and health care needs and not as an interpreter.

Linda recalls: **I was strictly Derek's health aide at Rogers. I worked with him, stayed by his side, tried to sign to him when I could and what I could. He laughed more at me than he did at the books because of my mistakes! I basically was there in case he needed anything medically. I wasn't worried about being around him. I was really glad that he was able to go to school. Because of his oxygen, suctioning, tube feeding, and all of his other medical needs, it seemed like everybody was so worried about what he could not do that they didn't realize what he *could* do or what he *needed* to do. He needed to be in school, to be around the other students. The kids adored him, and they missed him like crazy when he wasn't there. It was nice to be his aide because it made our friendship deepen.**

That fall, Jim left to go to Siberia to bring home Sergei and Kolya to join the family. This was the first international adoption for us. He planned to be gone for two weeks, but things changed once he was there. He stayed much longer while we went into crisis mode at home. Shortly after Jim left, Kyle needed to go to the emergency room because of nonstop vomiting. He had emergency surgery the next day. The following night, Raymond had somehow gone up over the railing of his bed. He seemed to be fine the next morning, however, other than a bruise on his leg where it had gotten stuck between José's feeding pump stand and a chest of drawers. It was not until a day or so later that we realized Raymond was in pain. I could not understand his communication well enough to figure out where the pain was and even asked his teacher to come to the house to try and help resolve the problem. We discovered that his knee was quite swollen. I rushed him to Children's Hospital, where we got an X-ray of his leg, found a break, and put a cast on him. I brought him home with medications to help relieve the pain.

Raymond was extremely spastic and constantly moving, and he rubbed open pressure sores on his shoulder blades, elbows, and lower back. I had never seen sores like those in my life, and I simply could not make him comfortable. Finally, I had to have him admitted to the hospital so that he could be sedated to prevent him from rubbing more sores. Back at home I focused on caring for Kyle as he recovered from his emergency surgery, and of course, Derek and the other children.

When word reached us that Jim's flight schedule had changed, his parents were upset and wanted to help, but they weren't in any condition to physically take care of the boys. Fortunately, friends and people from church helped prepare some meals, or stayed with Derek and Kyle so I could visit Raymond in the hospital. If anything positive developed during this trying time, it was that I finally felt a bond with Raymond and knew he understood that I cared.

When Jim did finally arrive home, he came with three new sons. None of these boys were from the same orphanages and did not know each other. Sergei was the oldest at five years. He had been born with a deformed right leg and arm and had lived in an orphanage his whole life. He clung to Jim when they arrived at the house and was petrified of the dog. Naturally, he spoke Russian but no English, and I didn't know a word of his language. He didn't have much to do with me at first. Sergei's method of mobility was to crawl on his left knee and walk on his right unflexible foot since his right leg was much shorter than his left. He was not able to walk upright. Eventually, his right foot would be amputated so that an artificial leg could be fitted and allow him to walk.

Victor was two weeks younger than Sergei. He hadn't been one of the boys Jim planned to bring home, but when Jim took a walker to him at the orphanage the staff told the boy, "Here is your new Papa." So Jim's trip was extended while he completed paperwork for Victor's adoption and waited for it to be approved in Moscow. Victor was born with moderate cerebral palsy but was able to manage a hop-crawl on the floor to get around. His speech was not nearly as clear as Sergei's because of his cerebral palsy, but he warmed up quickly to people at home. Fortunately, he and Sergei were able to feed themselves, though they needed help with dressing and bathing.

Then there was Nikolai, "Kolya" as we called him. We were told he was deaf; essentially, this was our reason for adopting him. However, fifteen minutes after his arrival, I said, "Jim, this child is NOT deaf!"

"How do you know?" Jim asked with a puzzled look.

"I just turned on Derek's suctioning machine and Kolya turned immediately to see what made the sound," I answered.

Kolya was twenty-one months old when he arrived. At first, he didn't appear to respond to human voices, not even the boys who were speaking Russian, but he did respond to mechanical sounds in the environment. He made almost no eye contact, had poor trunk control, and had never eaten solid foods. He had been born without arms, a deformed left ear and jaw, and a clubfoot. He had been deprived of human contact and stimulation and could barely sit when he arrived.

I really had mixed feelings about so many added challenges. Shortly after they returned, Jim got very sick, which put more on my plate for quite awhile. Within the next several months, Raymond's health continued to decline, Kolya had surgery on his left foot, Sergei had his right foot amputated, and Kyle was vomiting frequently, becoming extremely thin and having lots of trouble. Coco needed to have surgery to replace his G-tube with a J-tube (implanted into the intestine and not the stomach as a G-tube is) and was then put on a feeding pump. All the while, I still tried to make time for my precious Derek. Brothers occasionally shared hospital rooms, but that would confuse some of the medical staff, so they were usually separated. I ran back and forth between the rooms to spend time with each son. I tried to schedule my visits during school hours and would return to the hospital late at night after the boys at home had been put to bed. There was a lot of driving between home and hospital. After a couple of doctor's visits and some medication, Jim eventually began to feel better and was able to get up and about once again.

Life with our three new sons was very different. The boys were active and had no experience of living with a family. My biggest challenge was explaining to them the need to be less active when they were near Derek. He spent most of his time at home in the living room, either on the couch, or on a stack of sheepskins on the floor that kept him free of pressure sores. The language barrier with Sergei, Victor, and Kolya made it really difficult to make them understand why Derek could not move or tolerate much activity around him, but as the boys adjusted to being part of the family, Sergei and Victor gradually understood that Derek was not well. I certainly appreciated them trying their best to cooperate. There were funny moments too, like the time Kolya used his foot to pull the pump line from Derek's feeding tube and spin it like a lasso, splattering formula around the room. Even Derek could laugh about this (once he got my attention and indicated something was happening). Sergei quickly learned how to change videotapes and took the responsibility to find a video that Derek enjoyed and had something to watch. Other times he'd lie on the floor beside Derek sharing his pillow and gently holding Derek's hand.

I wasn't comfortable sending Derek to school because of the nurse's attitude, but he became weaker and could have only attended sporadically anyway.

Linda recalls: **The nurse worried about what being in school and being in his chair would do to Derek's body with him being tired out, rather than understanding that he needed school just to keep his mind going and his spirits up. He would arrive at school and he would light up and be excited. It seems like nobody looked at that part of his life. If he needed to go home, I would try and brace him for that, but you could just see the disappointment in his face that he was not able to stay all day. It was not like some of the kids to whom you would say, "Oh, you're going home because you're not doing well," and then they would just act indifferent. Although Derek knew the reason for going home was because he was not doing well, it was kind of like punishment to him. He would much rather**

remain at school and endure his physical problems than to go home.

Derek's doctors completed numerous forms to get permission to administer a new medication, cisapride. Everyone thought it was going to be the miracle drug for Derek because it was supposed to completely modulate how the gut works, relax the spasm, and increase the peristolic wave. It was not supposed to allow things to ebb and flow as Derek's system had been doing, and if movement got a little slow, it would help speed it up a little bit. The medication had not yet been approved in the United States by the FDA, but it was on the market in other countries. Derek had used some samples of the drug from the clinic and there appeared to be some improvement in the motility of his gut. Also, he never had a massive ileus after using the medication. At the same time we had to seriously consider the side effects: abdominal cramps, diarrhea, headaches, dizziness, convulsions, chest tightness, wheezing, and fatigue. We experimented with the dosage and considered how the cisapride might affect the absorption of his other medications. His system began to slow again, and he eventually had to use a feeding pump which slowly dripped formula through his feeding tube. The "miracle drug" did not seem to be so miraculous after all.

The Dream: *The dream continued to bother me but I had not discussed this with Marian when we talked by phone. I thought the dream was meant for me to be aware that Marian was facing tough decisions and tough consequences in her life, and that I was meant to be there for her as much as possible even though we lived 3,000 miles apart.*

Decisions, decisions, decisions, and more decisions. Many days I felt tremendous anxiety over what to do about Derek's medical procedures. We had reached a point where we had to choose between further medical intervention—specifically, a tracheostomy—or simply continuing with the minimum to help keep Derek as comfortable as possible. We scheduled a meeting that would include Derek's primary doctors at Children's Hospital, our pastor, Derek, Jim, and me so we could discuss a plan. I had had a discussion with Derek about the agenda of the meeting. Derek made it clear in the presence of others that he was strictly against having a tracheostomy.

But how could Derek make such a decision? I'm sure his experience played an enormous part. He had spent much time in the hospital with various children in his room. One child he shared a room with for an extended period had a tracheostomy. We had also cared for an infant with a tracheostomy in our home for a short time. Derek was well aware of what I was communicating to him. As hard as it was to attend to and respect his decision, he was probably right in the end. Would this have improved the quality of his life? Probably not. It would have made positioning his head more difficult, and increased his risk for infections therefore increasing his need for hospitalization.

By this time, Derek was no longer able to attend school. Mary came to the house to try home schooling with Derek. I could not see the point of this but he was always happy to see her when she arrived (if he was awake). I put him in his wheelchair and they would try to find a place where there were few distractions. I would occasionally take him into school for an hour or so, but I worried about how that affected the other students in the classroom.

Mary recalls: **We would talk about Derek's health with the class but I didn't want to dwell on it because they would start worrying about themselves too. I know at one point they wanted to add, "no dying in class," to our list of class rules. Still, I don't think it was a problem to have Derek visit. I think they were just concerned about him. I *know* it was beneficial to Derek to be in school for as much time as he could handle. He loved being with his peers and having the stimulation of school and the school setting.**

It wasn't long before Derek was not able to tolerate the twenty-minute ride to San Jose even for brief school visits, and he had trouble staying awake when Mary came to the house to work with him. His home schooling was discontinued, and he made no more visits to the classroom.

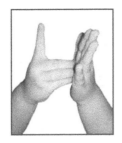

Chapter Twenty-One

13 years 5 months - 14 years old

$\mathcal{A}$lthough Derek's schooling needed to stop, he continued to educate me about the important things in life and how to care for a terminally ill child. We made several trips to and from the hospital for clinics, sometimes just to try to hydrate him and make sure he got some calories. I continued to feel confused about what was happening with his life, and the medical community continued to further confuse and frustrate us.

An example of this occurred one day when we went to the pediatric GI clinic and took seats in the waiting room. In a matter of minutes, parents moved their children as far away from us as possible. They were visibly upset by Derek's thick and raspy breathing. Although I knew he wasn't contagious, they were concerned about their children. It hurt to see others avoid my son. After we sat, isolated, for over half an hour, we were shown to an examination room where we waited for another extended period. Derek became extremely agitated and began sweating and breathing heavily until he was so exhausted he could barely move. About every ten minutes, I walked to the nurses' desk to remind them Derek was there. "Please," I urged the staff.

We had been assigned a resident who had never seen Derek. The resident casually walked into the room with Derek's medical files in two binders, each about three inches thick. He sat down and began slowly to thumb through the pages while muttering to himself.

"Sir, we are both deaf. If you could please at least look up when speaking so I could understand what you are saying, it would certainly help with communication," I explained.

He just nodded and continued to read slowly. I was getting more and more angry. Finally I said that if he needed time to read the files, it would have been more appropriate to have reviewed them before entering our examining room. I pointed out that Derek was a medically fragile child who shouldn't have to wait so long. He looked up, briefly glanced at Derek, and wrote NONRESPONSIVE on a form that he left on the examining table before he left the room, closing the door after him.

That action underscored how insensitive this doctor was. It has always annoyed me that doctors and nurses close the door to the examination room while you're waiting. I guess they expect you to just sit there and stare at the blank walls. I would prop the door open to allow Derek to have a view of the activity in the halls and read to him from books or magazines I brought with us. I also prodded the nurses to please tell the doctors that Derek was there, so they wouldn't keep him waiting forever.

Anyway, after what seemed like hours, the resident re-entered the room to begin the exam. He checked Derek's ears, felt his neck, and then asked Derek to try and open his mouth (while I tried to interpret everything). I stood behind the doctor and signed to Derek, "Open your mouth and vomit." Sure enough, as soon as the doctor put the tongue depressor in Derek's mouth, he gagged. The resident jumped back and knocked over the stool he was sitting on. I smiled, winked, and gave Derek a thumbs-up.

Without much emotion in my voice, I asked, "Did you say he was nonresponsive?"

Derek sat in his wheelchair laughing his head off. I understood that we were in a teaching hospital, but Derek was in no condition to have new residents making decisions about his medical care. They were welcome to watch, but his primary doctor would do the examination in the future.

With each hospital admission, more questions arose. *Is my son going to improve or will he just keep getting worse? Is there an end to admissions and discharges? Which medical staff should I listen to and believe? Am I in total denial about what is taking place before my eyes?* Living with Derek, I didn't see as many changes taking place as did others who saw him less frequently. No one seemed to be able to predict what would come next or to provide information that could satisfy my questions.

Derek continued to be extremely uncomfortable. If I tried to feed him his Ensure formula slowly with the feeding pump, he could only tolerate small amounts (about 2 ounces, equivalent to three gulps of water) before he would begin cramping. His hands would be fisted, his limbs stiffened, his teeth clenched, and his face pale and distressed. I wanted to make the pain go away. There's just nothing more horrible than having a child in constant pain. There was no medication we could give him that wouldn't interfere with his other medications or further upset his stomach and digestive system. It seemed like all efforts to nourish and comfort Derek were defeated. *Please pain, go away,* I begged over and over in my mind.

Marcia states: **It was hard. I think taking care of him or being involved in the decision-making in his care was just an unrewarding and frustrating situation in which we all wanted to be caring, giving, and healing. We were used to being able to at least alleviate pain but here was a child whose quality of life we couldn't improve. It was hard not knowing how to give him comfort, not knowing how to make him better.**

Transporting Derek to the hospital had also become a problem. He could no longer tolerate sitting in his wheelchair or holding his head up while I drove. I finally just stacked layers of sheepskins on the van floor for him to lie on whenever he rode with me. Sometimes a friend would offer to drive us and I would hold him on my lap. By this time, the portable oxygen tank seemed to be heavier than Derek.

During one hospital admission, I questioned myself about why we were there. *What is the point?* I couldn't answer the question; I was in total denial about what was going on. One day a different GI doctor was seeing us because Derek's regular doctor was out of town. I described to him the foul, jelly-like stool that Derek would pass when given suppositories. He told me this appeared to be starvation-type stool. He was the first person who didn't give me hope that Derek would improve. He spoke calmly and gently but the information was harsh and difficult to process emotionally. I was confused as to why the other doctors didn't say anything like that. *Are they trying to* cover something up? Why don't they talk about the outcome? What sort of answers are they hiding from me? Do they have answers to Derek's problems that they are not sharing with me? Are they just too emotionally involved in his care to actually tell me what to expect? I had many, many questions, but I was afraid to ask them.

Then, one afternoon as I lay on a hospital bed with Derek asleep in my arms, Dr. Fisher entered the room with a concerned but peaceful look. I'm sure someone had told her that Derek's heart rate had started to drop and had become irregular. She walked across the room and stood beside us. She said, "Marian, you know he's going to die, don't you? Not this very moment, but it is going to happen before too long."

I was stunned that someone had actually said that Derek was going to die. Had she really said the word? I looked at Derek's content expression as he slept. Yes, it was obvious he wasn't doing any better, but I was not at all prepared to hear the doctor say that death was knocking at our door. I felt denial, anger, despair, loss of faith, and hopelessness; I could not utter a single word.

"I'll be in ICU if you have any questions or need to discuss anything later," Dr. Fisher said. She gave my hand a squeeze, managed a caring smile, and left the room.

I was in a daze. Tears trickled down my cheeks as I continued to cradle Derek who remained asleep. *My first son, who has taught me more than any one person in my entire life, who has shared experience after experience of what acceptance and unconditional love actually means, is going to die?* The doctor must have told the nurses what she had said to me because they came in to inquire about my well-being more frequently than usual. After I gathered myself, I went to ICU to tell Dr. Fisher that I would be in touch with her soon.

Leaving Derek behind in the hospital was frightening. I'm sure I was a very dangerous driver on the road that day. It was impossible to focus after being informed my son was going to die. Of course, I still had all the other boys at the house who needed my attention and care. All the chores had to be done, including grocery shopping, cooking, laundry, homework, toileting, bathing, and yard work. I had to remain composed for the sake of my other sons. I would put on a brave front for everyone and refuse to let my guard down, even with most of my best friends. Yet my heart was in my stomach, and I felt like a zombie. I had some more tough decisions to make. *What is the purpose of leaving Derek in the hospital if they can't comfort him any better than I can at home? Should I bring him home and care for him the best I can? How will his brothers handle having him at home and needing to share my attention and care on a twenty-four-hour basis?* My mind jumped from one thought to another. My ears rang with tinnitus from the stress. My life felt like it was coming to an end, just as Derek's was. That night, after all the boys were in bed, I decided to call my close friend in West Virginia. At least she wouldn't know if I were crying as I typed on the TTY. On the other hand, I felt comfortable letting my guard down with her.

The Dream: *During one late-night conversation using the phone relay operator, I felt Marian was emotionally torn between helping prolong Derek's life and letting Derek go. She was hurting very much. I decided to share the dream. I thought maybe it would help her to know I had seen Derek happy and pain free on his way to the Lord. The dream is still vivid in my mind as if it happened yesterday. I pray it gave Marian comfort in time of need. ~ Maureen Wysopal*

After getting all the boys up and out the door for school the next day, I went to the hospital to share with Derek what Dr. Fisher had told me. Then we discussed what he wanted. His answer was that he wanted to be brought home as soon as possible and for me to care for him without any more hospital visits. I asked one of the nurses to find Dr. Fisher and let her know we wanted to discuss discharge procedures. She released us with instructions to call her whenever we needed to. Within a couple hours, I carried Derek from his hospital bed to the van and gently laid him on the pile of sheepskins so we could go home.

Over the years, Derek had several different doctors who were all sub-specialists. He didn't have a regular pediatrician who could follow through with what was happening. Dr. Fisher agreed to be that doctor. I had continued to wonder why Dr. Fisher could give me the dismal news of Derek's prognosis when she really wasn't Derek's GI doctor who had worked with us for years. Whatever the reason, I ended up feeling confident and trusting in her. Therefore, although she didn't directly care for Derek, she helped coordinate various aspects of his care for the rest of his life and was there to offer support when I needed it most. When I asked her why the GI staff didn't mention to me Derek's irreversible problems, she explained.

Dr. Fisher states: **It is common for sub-specialists to just look at their little area and forget the big picture and I think just by the nature of being a pediatrician, you tend to look at the whole picture. Generally speaking, when kids are seen in the GI clinic, they only take care of that little part and it sounds reasonable from their point of view that he would just keep coming back until he outgrew the problem or they would just continue to cleanse his gut and feed him again.**

I definitely saw things from a different vantage point. I know what it looks like when a child dies slowly, and with Derek, I would get snapshots of him since I did not see him daily. Every time I saw him, there were physical changes in his body and when one thing falls apart it leads to the next thing, and the next thing, and slowly the process continues. There wasn't anything we could fix and it was clear to me that Derek's time was kind of running out. I had the big picture in the back of my mind, and you had Derek in your arms. Those are very different vantage points.

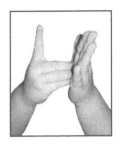

Chapter Twenty-Two

14 years -
14 years 4 months old

I felt better that we had decided not to take Derek to the hospital anymore. It just seemed to make much more sense that he be at home where he was comfortable, with people he loved and who loved him, and where communication could take place between us without being distanced from each other. However, just because he was home didn't mean that I was able to focus solely on him. Jim and I had pretty much divided the responsibilities for caring for various children living with us. Although I was not totally responsible for all the boys, I still had my share to care for and all of them needed to have their physical needs met by me or others we hired to work in our home part-time on weekday evenings. We tried to have respite nurse care for Derek for a couple of hours. But when I returned home from an evening out, he was so stressed, as was the nurse,

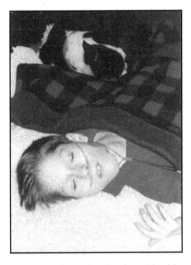

Derek resting with Snuja at his side

that we never tried it again. I continued to teach my Monday evening sign class as frequently as I could, and Linda cared for Derek while I was out. Truthfully, my heart was not there. It was at home with Derek.

Keeping Derek's mind occupied during the day while the other boys were in school was tough. There were plenty of books on tape for the blind, but there was little on the market for Deaf people where sign language was used in the videos. I spent a lot of time writing letters and making phone calls trying to find videos with stories or science lessons in sign language for him. I welcomed anything that would help make his day more pleasant.

There were days when all I wanted to do was to hold him and comfort both of us. Fear was starting to take over. Nights were consumed by fear. Derek grew afraid of being alone in bed. I had been sleeping only a couple of hours a night for months. I would wake up about every two hours to check on Derek. He had become so weak that he couldn't set off the cry signal light that normally let me know he needed attention during the night. Every time I entered his room I would take a deep breath as I tiptoed in. *Will he still be breathing?* If Derek was asleep when I checked on him, I would leave him in his bed, tiptoe out, and try to go back to sleep. He would often be awake, so I'd take him to the living room to avoid bothering the boys who shared the room with him. Sometimes, I simply wanted to hold him or lay beside him on the floor and sleep.

Pain was an ongoing concern. Derek appeared to have cramps even from the diluted formula that was slowly administered through the feeding pump. I sensed he was also feeling hunger pains because of his extremely low calorie intake. However, the hunger pains appeared to subside, probably because his stomach had actually shrunk. There was a new pain I became aware of. It was the pain when being moved or held for long periods of time without sheepskins or pillows to protect the pressure on his bones. As much as I wanted to hold and comfort him, sometimes the pain he appeared to experience from my touch prevented me from having my emotional needs met. I often had to be satisfied with simply being close and holding his hand.

I couldn't lift or transfer him the way I used to. It had been normal to be a little rough with Derek because he liked rough-and-tumble play, especially when I'd move him up in bed.

Chris, a nurse at Children's Hospital, recalls: **As Derek got more fragile and frail, Marian couldn't play with him as she used to. I remember she would just hoist him up in the bed with a sort of rapid swing up onto his pillow. But as he got more ill, he couldn't tolerate that sort of thing any more.**

The conversation with Dr. Fisher in the hospital the previous month made me finally begin to see what I had been ignoring for some time. There were lots of signs of his illness. For example, one day when I was gently brushing his teeth, a permanent tooth fell out. I had not noticed that a tooth was loose! On top of everything else, he was probably suffering from malnutrition. Tears welled up in my eyes, and I turned to hide them from Derek.

His weight continued to drop. He weighed a mere twenty-eight pounds at fourteen years of age. It was hard to know what was left for him to live for. He had once loved to be in the bathtub where he kicked and splashed, but now he couldn't tolerate being in the tub even when laid on several layers of egg crate foam to cushion his bare bones.

Raymond had also been in and out of the hospital during this period. Since Derek had decided he was not going back to the hospital, we arranged to have an Open House and invited the nurses and doctors to come and see the family, especially Raymond and Derek. We didn't have an enormous turnout, but those who came left with a different perspective of the boys and how they lived.

Dr. Fisher comments: **It was pretty nice to see Derek at home because as a resident in the hospital, you never get to see kids at home, let alone kids who are disabled. Sometimes doctors never really know what life is like for them outside the hospital. The thing that struck me the most was how much interaction the siblings in Derek's family had at home. You have this sense that kids are isolated when they can't communicate directly with you, as I felt with my experience of Derek's communication with me since I couldn't sign and he couldn't speak. My bias was that he must be isolated at home, even though Derek had so many brothers. I kind of felt like it would be a big circus and it wasn't that way at all.**

I was happy to see how the boys interacted with each other and clearly loved each other and looked out for each

other. Derek was so lucky to be in that environment because he was not the odd man out, he was just one of the guys. Most children who are different because of a physical challenge are set apart even within their own family, but that's not how it was with Derek. That was the beauty of the family; all the kids had some differences they were dealing with, yet they were all okay. It really was great to see.

Marcia remembers her visit to our home: I remember being so impressed that he had to be on the pump all day, but he was right out in the living room so he could watch the other kids while laying on the floor on an enormous pile of sheepskins. It seemed that small amount of pleasure, being able to be out there in the midst of his brothers, was all he had. I think his love for his family came across to all of us.

Soon, school was out for the summer and most of the boys were home on vacation. Derek remained the focal point of my life even as I cared for the others. I tried to encourage them to assist with his care where possible or to interact in some way that would leave them with positive memories of their brother. Sergei, being one of the most physically and mentally capable of the group, would lend a hand with some of the feedings. He would help hook up the feeding pump to Derek's tube, tell me when the formula bag was empty, or let me know when he thought Derek was cramping too much.

I think Ilan, as intellectually limited as he was, sensed something was not right with Derek. No one could explain to Ilan what was happening. He just didn't have the ability to understand words at that level at all. He would frequently ride his trike over to where Derek would be on the couch, and lean close to Derek's face to check him out. Sometimes he would gently touch his face. For anyone who knew Ilan, this was not a normal gesture for him because he was rough and usually plowed his trike through whatever was in his path. It moved me to witness the love these guys had for each other. Their actions spoke much louder than words.

Although Kyle was only three years old, he understood that he had the ability to cheer Derek up a bit. He would drive his chair into Derek's line of vision and make silly faces. As I was working in the kitchen one day, I was puzzled about why Kyle was driving his wheelchair back and forth between the living room and his bedroom. After he made several trips back and forth, up and down the ramp, in and out of the living room, I was beginning to get aggravated and turned to ask him to stop. As I turned to say something I was the one who stopped. Kyle carried a stuffed toy in his mouth and gently dropped it at Derek's side. Derek smiled with appreciation. As I turned back to my work, Kyle drove his chair over to me and blew on my arm to get my attention. (I could not hear his voice and he could not reach out to tap my shoulder for attention, so at two years old he devised his own way to get my attention.) Bursting with pride, he explained what he had done.

"Mom," he exclaimed, "I have been driving my chair back and forth and showing Derek different stuffed toys. I would shake my head "yes" or "no" and wait for Derek to decide if he wanted what I had in my mouth. Then, if he didn't want that one, I would go get a different one. Finally, I think he said he wanted the small puppy. Mom, he smiled when I dropped it beside him. I think he likes it when I give him something like that."

Then he spun around and zoomed off. That a toddler paralyzed from the neck down would work so diligently to communicate and share with his deaf, terminally ill brother was amazing to witness. I felt a lump in my throat and thought, *I don't need to worry about the other boys finding ways to interact positively with their brother. The ones who are capable and understand will find a way.*

I was concerned about how the other boys would handle Derek's death. At this point, I didn't feel the church was being supportive enough. I wondered if I was becoming self-centered. I felt like we were being ignored while everyone else just went on about their cheerful lives. *Would people be more willing to interact with my sons if they were "normal?"* Were they assuming that the boys could handle whatever happened because so many of them had been in and out of hospitals? I was afraid I wouldn't be of much support to them at all when the time actually came. I asked for a Stephen Minister to visit us and offer support to the children. Stephen Ministers are lay people who visit the ill and shut-ins, or those who need some extra emotional or spiritual support, maybe because of a divorce, loss of a job, or loss of a family member. No one could come to us because they were not trained to work with children in a situation like this. A church staff member finally came to talk informally with the boys. She let them feel comfortable with her first then encouraged them to talk, ask questions, or share their feelings. But it wasn't easy.

Linda L. explains: **Marian had expressed a need to have a pastor or lay person talk with the boys about their feelings about Derek dying. I happened to be filling in for a pastor who was on disability and handling pastoral care. I had never met the family or Derek, for that matter. So I go to their house, and I'm trying to learn all the kids' names and all their own ways of communication. I got all the kids confused because Coco would look up one way for "no" and Ben peered right into your eyes, and Raymond, Alan, and Derek did something different. Sean and José signed a little bit. Sergei and Victor were just learning to speak English. I just kept getting everyone confused! But I continued to go and visit as much as I could and became a good friend to many of the boys.**

I was pleased that we finally had someone coming to the house to speak with the other boys. After Linda L. got to know them, I could see they felt free to talk with her about many things. She also supported me. Still I had mixed feelings about a person coming into the house and being so cheerful while I was so distraught. There was no easy way to maintain a balance between my emotional state and dealing with people outside the family. How could I be cheerful while Derek was slipping from my life? Loneliness set in for both Derek and me. I wanted people to come and visit him, especially Cindy, Mary, and Diane who could communicate with him. I hesitated to call because they knew he was there and if they wanted to come, they would come. Maybe they didn't want to see him like this. Sometimes I would dial one of their numbers, but if I got an answering machine I wouldn't leave a message. Other times, I would begin to dial and then hang up before I completed the number. It was an ongoing struggle knowing what I wanted but not wanting to force myself on others. I just didn't know what to do.

Cindy comments: **Sometimes we don't do things we mean to do or we think there is so much time in this world to do them, and then we turn around and the time is gone. It bothers**

me that I didn't make the time to see Derek because I know he enjoyed my company and I certainly liked sitting with him even if we didn't say anything because he was comfortable with me.

I was also feeling more and more isolated. I was pretty much homebound and unable to come and go as I pleased. Sometimes I saw events I wanted to attend, such as a meeting or retreat with other deaf women. My friends would call and tell me how much fun they had going on a hike or to an event. I would be happy for them but deep inside feel sorry for myself because I didn't feel I could safely leave Derek in the care of others. I was torn between wanting to do things outside and wanting to remain beside Derek and be involved in his care. Of course, there were Ilan, Kolya, Kyle, Coco, Rusty, Ben, Sean and the others for whom I was primary caregiver too, but they were not terminally ill. Most of my trips out of the house were extremely short and only for necessary errands.

With Derek no longer going to the hospital or to clinics, I was constantly around kids. I didn't even have the doctors and nurses to talk with. My thoughts were confused, contradictory, and negative: *Derek, let's get this over with so that I might be able to get on with life.* These thoughts would leave me feeling so guilty, like I was betraying my son. *How can I have such ideas?* My beloved Derek…no, this is not at all what I wanted to happen. I wanted to love and provide and continue on indefinitely, regardless of the loneliness in my life. I wasn't getting what I needed at home, and I couldn't figure out how to get it from outside. I just had to make more of an effort to keep myself occupied with different things around the house and try to use the phone for conversations with adults. People did stop by the house, but not frequently enough to satisfy my emotional needs. I kept these feelings pretty much to myself.

Derek remained fairly alert most of the day regardless of how little nutrition he received, and he continued to want to be involved with family activities. He spent most of his time where he could see what was going on around him, in the living room either on the couch or on the floor on a stack of sheepskins. As usual, there were new challenges with Derek. Instead of sweating and being overheated, he began to experience the opposite. Regardless of a summertime temperature of ninety degrees or above, Derek's limbs would be cold, his fingertips blue, and his lips almost colorless. I would borrow Ben's tube socks, which made Ben feel important and helpful, and put them on Derek's hands and arms to try to warm him up. Because Derek could not move much or communicate verbally, it was too dangerous to use a heating pad or electric blanket because they could burn him. In fact, just the weight of a blanket made it more difficult for him to breathe because he was so weak. I was overwhelmed with feelings of failure because I could not keep my son warm. Slowly I began to understand that his perpetual state of coldness was due to his poor circulation and general deterioration of health, but I just couldn't do anything about that. At the time, I questioned my ability to keep Derek home and meet his needs. When he was asleep, I constantly checked his chest to see if he was still breathing. *How much longer can I continue like this? Am I doing the correct thing here or should I give in and take him back to the hospital? Would he receive better care with trained medical staff?* These questions repeated like a broken record in my mind.

Dr. Fisher shared with me: **How do you make a decision whether to keep a child at home or in the hospital when they are terminally ill? There's the process of dying and there is death, and they are two different things. Unless something very sudden happens, dying usually happens over a period of time, days to weeks to months to years, depending on the situation. The process of dying can be very stressful, more so than people outside the immediate family realize. Families need a lot of support and they need to be taken care of because when you are under a huge stress you don't think straight, you are forgetful, things happen and the whole family goes haywire. It is not just one child. It's other children and spouses who don't communicate well under stress when life is in turmoil. This goes on for days and weeks, and there is always that uncertainty when you go to bed at night: Is my child going to die in the night and I won't even be there?**

I think every family is different and you have to take into account what resources the family has. Do they have support in the home to get them through? When a child has spent a lot of time in the hospital, many times they feel safer in the hospital than they do at home and the parents feel safer as well. So it

is a real individual decision as to what happens when a child actually dies. In Derek's case, he never was comfortable in the hospital because he could not communicate with people well. When he was at home, he was just one of the guys and that was where he was comfortable, in his usual surroundings, and he felt safe. I felt that was where he should die because he was more comfortable at home.

The other thing that was in the family's favor was the incredible support, even though sometimes it did not feel like it. You had a community in the church that knows that you are struggling with this issue. You had people who helped you through it and I know your pastor was involved. Not only did you have this support, but also you were well equipped to take care of his medical needs, more so than in the hospital. Derek was where he should have been: surrounded by loving, caring, and communicating family members.

Here are others' views on their experiences of working with families who have a terminally ill child.

Marcia explains: **I think all of the medical staff knew what Derek's thoughts were. I think this was even more dramatically illustrated when we were provided that letter, which was placed right there in the front of his chart so that anybody who came and opened up the chart, the first thing they saw was this letter from Derek. It stayed with his chart each admission. The letter specifically described to us what he wanted and what he did not want. It was clear that he did NOT want to be in the hospital and go through more painful procedures. I don't think anybody felt uncomfortable about his decision.**

I also feel that when a child is terminally ill, unless the family prefers to keep the child in the hospital, it is the medical staff's wish to get the child home at all costs. These days more and more things are being provided that allow the child to remain at home: VNA (visiting nurses), home infusion services, and critical care therapeutic procedures such as special antibiotics, TPN (total parental nutrition), and even continuous drips of morphine for children dying of cancer. About the only thing that cannot be provided at home now is the need for blood products. Once a decision is made that a child is DNR (do not resuscitate), then that child is no longer a candidate to be admitted to ICU.

There are some families who cannot handle having a child die at home. Sometimes problems come up where one parent

wants one procedure followed and the other parent is unsure of what they want or thinks differently. There is an Ethics Committee in the hospital that meets to discuss the issues at hand. They talk about all the issues, especially the prognosis, then meet with the parents, the child if the child is old enough to help make decisions, and the clergy, and assist in developing a plan that is best for everyone involved. Then, hopefully everyone can follow through with the plan and focus on just being there for the child as much as possible.

Chris shares her thoughts: I believe that if a terminal child knows he is terminal and the family has a strong support system and community resources, such as their church or respite care, then the home can be a calmer and more fulfilling experience for everyone involved. However, the medical staff must make certain the support services are available for the family. Unfortunately, in the hospital we tend to poke and prod and monitor and interrupt. Bells and whistles are ringing and people are coming in and out and this can be a more harried environment for a family who is in the grieving process. A lot of these people, unless it is a primary nurse or a primary doctor who the family knows quite well, are almost strangers to the family.

If the child is at home, the family may have their own personal chaplain or priest, a very close neighbor, a friend, relatives, or respite care workers who have been coming for some period of time to the home and can provide a more positive form of support or a better structure for support for a family. Once again, I cannot emphasize enough that when a family is sent home there needs to be follow up to know that they are receiving adequate support. There have been times when it gets very close to the time of the child's passing, and they are afraid and they actually choose instead to admit the child to the hospital because of fear.

Mary counsels: I think the biggest advice I would give is to develop a relationship of loyalty so the child knows the parent will be there when they are sick and that they are never going to go through this alone. The child will know the parent will be representing them, and I think Derek felt that. I think Derek felt alone when procedures had to be done if Marian could not be there at the hospital but when she was there, I felt he could go through about anything. So I would advise parents of all children to establish a relationship with your child that has a

trust in it and a loyalty and a devotion so that when your child all of a sudden is faced with some really hard, scary times they know they can grab hold of your hand and feel safe.

My support system included some terrific and caring medical staff with whom I was able to communicate through phone, email, or home visits. They encouraged and supported me when I felt inadequate and unsure. Derek could remain at home where he sensed peace and comfort in his everyday family environment.

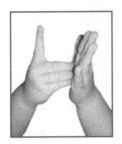

Chapter Twenty-Three

14 years 4 months - 14 years 6 months old

Some of the older boys were attending summer school for part of each weekday. Derek was home with the younger ones and Raymond, who required a lot of attention. The inability to comfort Raymond was taking a toll on the family. Derek and I, not being able to hear Raymond's continuous moans and groans of discomfort, were able to tolerate him more than others in the house. We were both still disturbed by his facial expressions and thrashing, which signaled his immeasurable distress.

Jim, who was the primary caregiver for Raymond, had finally made contact with his social worker in New Mexico and planned to return him there to a facility that might be able to provide continuous care. Meanwhile, since I was already up with Derek, I frequently carried Raymond's long, spastic body to the living room in the early morning before Jim awoke, and began his feedings. Raymond required six tube feedings a day to maintain his weight. As mentioned previously, he was in constant motion and burned off calories steadily. It had come to the point where he needed to be sedated most of the day to keep him from developing open and deep pressure sores on his limbs and back as well as to quiet his unpleasant groans and moans. Although we tried as hard as we could, none of us could determine what was wrong. When he was awake, all anyone could do was to look into his pleading eyes and try to offer some verbal comfort. I still feel he understood that he was going to be taken away from the family and that thought made him tremendously sad.

Raymond was not an easy child for me to bond with or accept. During the preceding year we had connected, and I felt guilty about my earlier feelings toward him. I had finally recognized that, on his better days, Raymond was happy in my presence and could accept my efforts to provide care for him. I felt strongly that it was wrong to return him to New Mexico but didn't know what else we could do. It was obvious that his remaining with the family was not healthy for most of the people involved.

Early in the morning of July 3, 1993, I walked into Raymond's room to bring him to the living room for his feeding. As I lifted his limp, warm body I realized he wasn't breathing. Shocked and quivering, I carried him to the living room, put him on the floor, and began CPR. I worked on him until I became breathless. Finally I collected my thoughts enough to run to Derek's room to get the manual resuscitator which I kept near Derek's bed in case of an emergency. Shaking, I worked as hard as I could to get Raymond breathing again. My whole body was trembling. Everyone in the house was sound asleep and didn't know what was taking place. Derek was on the couch and watched my every move with an expression of fear. I ran back to the bedroom to awaken Jim and ask him to please call 911. He followed the ambulance to the hospital while I remained behind to take care of all the other boys.

As I got the boys up and dressed, they wanted to know what was going on. I couldn't explain because I didn't even know what hospital Raymond was taken to. I didn't know if the paramedics were able to get a pulse or not. Cell phones were rare in those days. I just had no way to contact Jim, no way to find out what was going on. Hours passed with no news of Raymond. I paced back and forth in between caring for the boys. Finally Jim retuned home about dinnertime to let us know that Raymond was in ICU at Children's Hospital at Stanford connected to life support. He was brain-dead. I felt numb hearing this but was also extremely confused and worried about the decisions we would have to make.

We had not legally adopted Raymond. He was still under the supervision of the Department of Social Services in New Mexico. The idea of reaching a social worker on the Fourth of

July weekend, explaining the situation, and having them agree with decisions we needed to make in California made me terribly anxious. I had great misgivings about the actions I had taken that morning. Once again, my deafness had interfered with my ability to communicate with people. I needed interpreters to alleviate the slowness and awkwardness of the phone. I continued to function in a state of shock at home, dressing, feeding, toileting, and caring for the fifteen or however many guys we had at the time, while Jim made arrangements with New Mexico and the hospital.

We had been preparing the siblings for Derek's death, not Raymond's. This was a shock to the boys. It was the first death that many of them had ever experienced. Fortunately, they had all been asleep when the medics arrived and took Raymond to the hospital. Aside from Derek, they hadn't witnessed what had happened to their brother.

The following morning I brought Derek to the living room as I normally did. I was not prepared for what his response would be. In fact, I never gave a thought to my actions. I just did what came naturally. When I placed him on the couch where he had been the previous morning, he became extremely rigid, focusing his eyes on the spot where he had last seen Raymond. I could see panic fill his body. His eyes were focused on the spot where I performed CPR and where the paramedics had taken Raymond away just twenty-four hours earlier. Tears began to well up in Derek's eyes and my heart sank because I suddenly realized how insensitive it was to put him in the same position.

I scooped Derek up and moved him to a different position. I rearranged some of the furniture, thinking that might help. Then I sat in the rocking chair holding him and we both relaxed a bit as we comforted each other.

I finally managed to line up some help so that I could go to the hospital and say my good-byes to Raymond. We had been given permission from New Mexico to allow him to be an organ donor. He would be kept on the respirator until recipients could be located and his organs harvested. I leaned against the side of his hospital bed, holding his hand, smoothing back his beautiful coal-black hair, watching his chest rise and fall with the rhythm of the ventilator. I shed tears for this youth who had recently spent too many months in the hospital and several of those weeks in the ICU. I watched the monitors as some showed flat lines and others registered very little. It was hard to comprehend that Raymond would never return to the family. I didn't say a word to the nurses. They stood nearby taking care of the monitors with cold expressions. *How many times have these nurses been through this process? Do they have feelings while caring for patients like this? How can they do such depressing work and also be capable of going about a typical life once they leave this hospital?* My visit was not long. Within the next several hours seven people would receive organs from Raymond. His life ended on July the Fourth, 1993, on Independence Day. It was a day of freedom for his nation, a day of release from his spastic body, and a day to join his birthparents and siblings who had gone on before him. I had just lost a child.

My responsibilities for the other boys continued, and we needed to plan a memorial service. I was completely drained from the demands of speechreading people who came in and out, trying to focus mentally, arranging for an interpreter, and trying to accept graciously that Raymond's foster mother from New Mexico would be staying in our home.

We held the memorial service at the church, and the entire family went. I got everyone ready to go, but I was in no shape to drive. As it was, we didn't all fit into our two vans, so several of the boys who were not in wheelchairs rode with friends and I climbed into a friend's car with Derek cradled in my arms and his oxygen tank over my shoulder. At church I sat down in the front pew holding Derek. I explained to him that when he died (since we had been discussing that), people would come to the church to remember him just like they were that day for Raymond. He gave me a slight smile and then an expression that said, "But I'm not ready yet, Mom." The service included lots of music and the sharing of memories. There was a reception, but I couldn't eat. I stayed for as long as I felt Derek could tolerate it and then asked to be brought home with some of the younger children. I vomited that night, and night after night for the next couple of weeks, as my body dealt with the sadness in my gut.

Then it was my birthday. I received cards of sympathy

mingled with birthday cards of cheer. I felt so many emotions. The birthday card that moved me the most was from Raymond's foster mother. I had never understood the reason he was placed with us because she loved him and seemed capable of taking care of his needs. However, in her card she explained her reasons for his placement in our home and thanked me for keeping in touch and allowing her to come to the service. I was grateful to finally understand what her reasoning had been. I am told she cried her heart out at the memorial service.

There wasn't much time during the day to grieve the loss of Raymond. In many ways, life just continued as it had before with toileting, dressing, cooking, cleaning, feeding, and shopping. Most of the family went about their lives as if nothing had happened. I tried to remain focused and upbeat for the benefit of the boys, especially Derek, who was becoming more aware of his limited time. I also had another overwhelming decision before me.

I had been nominated by the Los Altos chapter of the Quota Club as International Deaf Woman of the Year for 1993, one of 800 nominees worldwide. The Quota Club is an international service organization that supports and serves hard of hearing and deaf persons, and disadvantaged women and children. I should have been excited about receiving this award, but the ceremony was in Singapore; I'd never been there and didn't want to be away from home for a long time. The Club had already made my travel plans and reservations, but it just wasn't in my heart to go. I considered canceling the trip or asking a member of the Los Altos group to receive the award on my behalf for two main reasons. First, Raymond's death had affected me deeply, and out of respect to him I felt I should not go. Secondly, Derek was getting weaker each day; he just wasn't getting much nutrition. I could barely justify the time it took to go to the bathroom or take a shower. How could I even consider leaving home for several days? I still shudder at the thought. Family and friends felt differently, however, and assured me that things would be handled adequately at home. I had no doubt that Linda could care responsibly for Derek and the other boys. I was afraid that he would be upset that I had left him. Worst of all was the possibility that he would pass away while

I was gone. One of the hardest requests I ever made to Derek was, "Please do not die while I am gone." Then I walked out the front door and headed for the airport.

Linda states: **Before when Marian needed to leave town, Derek wanted to sleep in his bed. Sometimes I would go into his room to check on him and see if he had knocked off his oxygen tube or had his arm caught in the rails. On this trip of Marian's, Derek was willing to sleep in the living room, where I could be more aware of him during the night.**

Caring for Derek at home was different than at school where, for instance, I was obligated to initiate CPR until appropriate medical attention arrived. I was also limited in how deeply and how frequently I could suction Derek at school. The schools call a person like myself a "health aide," but they tie your hands as to what you can do for a child. I felt very uncomfortable and sometimes angry with this attitude, and I didn't trust a lot of people with Derek. I hated leaving him, even during my lunch break, and all I could think of was, Derek, if you need to choke, please wait until I come back. I was afraid that others would not do enough for him. At home, I could use deep suction if needed to help Derek.

I felt honored that Marian trusted me enough to have left him with me, because it couldn't have been easy for her to leave when he was so medically fragile. I made sure Derek was comfortable at all times. All Marian's decisions were based on Derek's wants and needs. I understood the agreement that if he should stop breathing, I was not to bring him back. That was hard for me to deal with, but I understood their wishes. That was the hardest part for me in caring for Derek. Fortunately, my CPR training never needed to be utilized.

I arrived safely in Singapore and made the most of my trip by scheduling a visit to the School for the Deaf, but Derek and my family were constantly in my thoughts. Deaf people in Singapore used fax machines, and not TTY phones to communicate with others. Although the members of Quota Club served the deaf and hard of hearing, they didn't sign and I didn't have an interpreter. So it was extremely difficult to learn what was happening with my family. I gave my speech, received my award, and got to the airport as soon as I could. I was consumed by anxiety during the long flight home. I was impatient while waiting to change planes. I didn't communicate with others on my flights. I just wanted to arrive home as quickly as possible.

I don't even recall who picked me up at the airport, but I do remember where my eyes focused as soon as I walked past the window of our living room: on the couch where Derek lay. Sure enough, there he was with his eyes fixed on the window. A smile of recognition lit his thin, pale face. My body quivered as I exhaled deeply, quickened my steps, and set down my baggage. I gave a silent prayer of thanks. My son was still waiting for me, and he would need to continue to wait for me to pick him up, because Ilan was clinging to me, the dog was jumping around, Kolya had scooted over to seek my attention, and other boys also wanted their share. Without even the slightest hint of jealousy, Derek took it all in with his usual air of contentment. I was where my heart longed to be: home with my beloved family.

Chapter Twenty-Four

14 years 6 months -
14 years 7 months old

*J*et lag overtook me and memories of Raymond's death consumed my thoughts. I also was inspired that Derek was alive and still mentally alert. He had kept his promise and did NOT die while I was in Singapore. After being away from him for several days, it was absolutely shocking to see how frail, gaunt, and pale he was. I wondered how much longer he could continue.

Still, even with his precarious health, Derek continued to take note of positive things happening around him with his siblings. His attitude made me open my eyes to take notice as well, even though my heart was full of grief. He was proud of his brothers' accomplishments. One could see the pride through his facial expressions, smiles, and the limited body movement he had left. One achievement that made him happy was Ben's and Alan's ability to drive their power wheelchairs with head controls in the driveway. I would hold Derek in front of the windows in the living room so he could witness their progress firsthand. He enjoyed the show even more on nice days when I would carry him outside, sit on the bench, and hold him on my lap as Ben and Alan practiced their driving. We just had to be careful that his oxygen tubing wasn't smashed in the front door. Derek even took pride when Ilan learned to stand independently smack in front of the TV, making it impossible for Derek to see his show. Kolya had begun to take his first steps, pulling himself up with his chin along the edge of the couch where Derek lay. More exciting, and sometimes scary, was when Derek was not on the couch, but on the floor on his stack of sheepskins. Kolya would push all the cushions off the couch and sometimes they'd land on top of Derek. Then Kolya would bounce back and forth on the couch springs on his behind. He continued this activity for hours while Derek lay nearby. By then Sergei was not only walking on his artificial leg but could run in his own way. He could also compete with Tim shooting hoops in the living room near Derek's head. Victor was up and walking with a walker to the beat of his Walkman. He had also learned to use a manual wheelchair and could get himself up the ramp into the living room. Given the slope of the ramp, that was not an easy undertaking. Seeing Derek take pride in his brothers' activities allowed me to turn my attention enough to encourage and praise my other sons for their accomplishments. It took all of the energy Derek could muster to remain alert, but this is where he wanted to be, in the midst of the action, right in the middle of the living room.

And with all that was going on in my life at that point, a new infant came to our home. Chris, at the age of eleven months, joined the family. Since Tim had made such a success of himself, despite his physical limitations, the social workers felt he would be a positive influence on Chris' life. Chris was born missing both arms and with extremely short legs and deformed feet. This made Chris similar to Tim physically. Chris had been placed in a medically licensed foster home before joining us. His foster mother had brought him for some visits before he actually moved in fulltime. Jim was ready for another baby, but I was not. I just wanted to focus on Derek and the others.

Even though I felt pressured by Chris' arrival, Derek found him to be entertaining. Chris soon learned to roll, roll, roll, and roll some more. Rolling was his primary method of mobility. Kolya would join in, and the two of them would roll back and forth on the living room floor, sometimes in a straight line, other times in circles. Even as an infant, speed was important to Chris. The wheelchair ramp offered an exciting thrill. Chris would take a deep breath and zoom down the ramp. Derek had an unobstructed view of the ramp and loved watching his newest brother court danger. Sometimes Tim would get on the floor with Chris and they'd have a "wrestling" match, flip-flopping each other around. Derek continued to be an alert observer. I clearly remember that Chris would make Derek laugh by teething on the oxygen tube strung across the floor. Fortunately, he never left holes in the tubing.

Derek continued to hang in there. I honestly don't know what kept him going because he was not receiving much nutrition at all. He was able to tolerate only small amounts of pedialyte through his feeding tube. Instead of keeping him hooked up to the feeding pump all day, which was not successful anyway, we gave him an ounce or two every hour depending on what his body would tolerate. As he became weaker, I wanted to focus exclusively on the remaining time Derek and I had together.

One hot summer day I decided we should do something fun, something that we had not done for years. While Kolya and Chris were taking naps, I changed into my swimsuit. I grabbed a pair of shorts for Derek and signed, "Let's go swimming!" I was nervous, but words cannot describe the expression on Derek's face as I removed his oxygen tube and carried his frail body outside to the pool. I'm still not sure if he was scared or pleased with the idea, but I believed he'd love it once he was in the pool. Slowly, I stepped into the warm water with my son cradled in my arms. His body was limp, and he could not kick or splash around as he had years before, but soon his pale blue eyes met mine with an expression of satisfaction and gratitude for allowing him to enjoy the warmth of the water. I felt content and peaceful. Memories of better times surfaced. Tears welled up in my eyes as I realized we would never do this again. I turned my head so Derek couldn't see the sadness on my face. I desperately wanted the feeling of peace to remain and sustain both of us. As I wiped the tears away (trying to make it look like I was splashing water on my face), I made eye contact with Derek again. A spiritual calmness engulfed us. I wanted time to stand still and bask in the tranquility. No words were spoken. No signs were signed. Our mutual understanding remained as intense as fourteen years before. Derek's eyes then focused on the house, and I knew it was time to go back inside. I wrapped his feather-light body in a towel and carried him into the house. He desperately needed his oxygen, and he was physically drained from our short time in the pool, but our emotional needs had been temporarily satisfied. Even as I write this, years later, tears well up in my eyes. Yet there is a complete feeling of calmness and satisfaction in my soul knowing that what we did that day gave Derek a few minutes of contentment.

Following this time together, I established a new goal: I would try to do something daily that would bring pleasant memories of happier times into Derek's life. He had always loved being outdoors. Because he was not able to be outside much, we brought the outside in to him. I put a little table in his line of vision near the couch in the living room. Each day I cut fresh flowers from my gardens and brought them to him. He could enjoy the bright colors of the mums and the soft rose petals.

One day as I was working in my roses, I found a ladybug. Memories of Derek's excitement years earlier when a ladybug crawled around the rim of his plate flashed through my mind. I ran into the kitchen, grabbed a jar, and ran back to the rose bush. I easily captured the ladybug and took it inside for Derek. I honestly can't say how much pleasure he experienced from that little insect, but I felt a sense of satisfaction that I was at least trying to bring a few moments of comfort to my son.

The circus was coming to town and I simply couldn't pass up this one last chance to take Derek to the circus. A family friend owned a private viewing box at the arena in San Jose. I asked if I could use the box so that Derek could see the circus, and his answer was instant. "Absolutely. I'll get your tickets and my daughters will help watch your other boys while you're gone." I was overwhelmed; I had only asked if we could use the box, not for tickets and childcare. I began to figure out how I would transport Derek to San Jose and get him into the arena through crowds of people. *Will he even be able to tolerate being among a large crowd? Will he enjoy going on an outing? Am I out of my mind?* I was excited, but I was also apprehensive, nervous, and jittery. These thoughts and feelings were much like those I experienced when I first brought him into my home fourteen years earlier.

I had three days to develop a plan to transport Derek to the circus. I came up with the idea of calling the therapy unit at one of the schools to ask if they had a reclining manual wheelchair that Derek could borrow. Fortunately, the response was yes, there was a reclining chair in the therapy unit and we were welcome to stop by and get it anytime. It was more and more complicated to leave Derek, even for short periods, but there was a solution. Some of my boys took classes at the school, riding on buses that could accommodate wheelchairs. I asked the driver if there would be room on the bus to bring the reclining chair home for us, and the answer once again was yes. For a person who had a history of hesitating to ask for help from others, I felt I was doing exceptionally well with asking for assistance and making this outing happen for Derek. That afternoon, the reclining wheelchair arrived, and I readied it for his use.

It had been months since Derek had actually been in a wheelchair. He was no longer able to use his own. I padded the reclining chair with several layers of sheepskins and pillows, then positioned him in it. In order to keep his long, thin arms from rubbing on the tires, I had to cross them over his stomach and hold them with one hand while maneuvering the chair with my other hand. I had used a chair like this with the other boys who had had hip surgeries but they had worn heavy spica casts that helped balance the chair. So I practiced a bit in the house and let Derek get the feel of being moved around like this. Movement seemed to cause Derek some anxiety, so I pushed the chair more slowly than usual. As short as I am, I needed to stoop to reach the handles on the chair and was all but in his face. This wasn't going to be easy. Next I had to deal with the portable oxygen tank. I flung the strap over my shoulder, bent further to hold Derek's arms in place, and almost tipped him over backward. This was almost exactly what had happened on the ice years ago in West Virginia when the oxygen tank strap slipped off my shoulder and the weight of it pulled me toward the floor. This time, Derek's eyes didn't show much faith in my ability to make this work, and it wasn't funny as it had been years ago. Ultimately, I devised a way to make the chair work and felt confident we were ready to see the Ringling Brothers Circus the next day.

You would think after so many years of raising sons who used wheelchairs I would be an expert at handling them. Nope! When I went to put Derek on the lift and get him into the van, things did not go so smoothly. With the chair reclined about as far as it would go, it was much longer than the length of the van's wheelchair lift. I felt like an octopus trying to reach the brakes, secure the chair on the lift, hold Derek's arms in place so as not to rub the tires, work the lift switches, and maintain the chair's balance, and my own. With a lot of extra effort, I was able to get the chair into the van. Miraculously, Derek was still in it.

Positioning the chair in the van was another challenge. I was covered with sweat once I finally had it secured. Since Derek was having so much trouble staying warm, I couldn't use the air conditioning. I wanted to open all the windows and speed down the highway, but instead I drove extra slowly to eliminate any unnecessary motion that could have caused Derek to become nauseated or dizzy. I had some misgivings when we arrived at the arena in San Jose, and I had to unload Derek from the van. *Why am I doing this? Is this just too much for Derek to cope with physically? What if something goes seriously wrong and I am all alone with him among a crowd of strangers? Am I doing all of this to satisfy my own needs or am I truly doing this for Derek?* I was also praying, *Please let us get through this trip to the circus safely and with enough enjoyment to satisfy both of us.*

Meanwhile, Derek was awake and taking in all the sights around him. I was thankful that he was alert and seemed to be tolerating the outing so far. In fact, there had been a grin or two while I was struggling with the borrowed chair on the van lift, climbing back and forth from the driver's seat, and getting everything situated before we pulled out of the driveway. As was the case during his entire life, he appeared to take pleasure simply in what others were doing for him or in his presence. We made it through the crowds and found the private box that belonged to our friend. I lifted Derek and held him so he could take in the sights below. I remembered our first circus when Derek was entranced with the elephants leading the circus parade, the clowns, the animals doing their amazing tricks, the acrobats, and the dazzling colors. Electricity seemed to flow through him. *Am I mentally prepared for what will happen today?* I'm not sure that I was. Derek's body seemed so limp and lifeless on my lap. I got a lump in my throat, but I swallowed and suppressed my emotions.

After a short time, Derek's tailbone pressing on my leg began to hurt. I put a sheepskin between his body and mine. Even though he weighed less than twenty-eight pounds, and he was no longer stiff and spastic, my back was beginning to tire, my shoulder felt heavy, and my arm and hand were numb from trying to hold his head in a position that would allow him to see. I didn't know how much longer I could sit like that, and I was having a difficult time enjoying the circus. Every once in a while some little movement in Derek's body led me to believe that he was pleased with the action before him. Sometimes, I could detect a slight grin or a sparkle in Derek's eyes that would remind me of why I made the extra effort for this outing.

During intermission, I put Derek back in the chair and rubbed some feeling back into my arm and hands. I saw an expression of pleasure on Derek's face, and I realized our emotional needs had once again been met. After intermission, I went to lift Derek so he could watch more of the circus, but his expression said "No." His eyes focused on the door, signaling it was time to leave. *Thank you, Derek, for allowing me to experience this time with you once more.*

As we began to slowly make our way to the van, I asked Derek if he wanted me to buy him a shirt with the picture of a lion on it. His face lit up, and he raised his eyebrows to indicate "Yes." Fourteen years earlier, the sign "lion" was one of the first he had consistently recognized when reading, so it was only fitting to get the shirt. After I paid for it, I laid it on his chest. His smile spoke volumes. It had also touched the salesperson, who was smiling when I turned to say "Thank you." When we got home, I sighed with relief that we were back in the living room where Derek felt more comfortable. He was clearly exhausted, but I hoped he had more pleasant memories to sleep on. I, too, was drained of energy yet grateful I had carried out my plan.

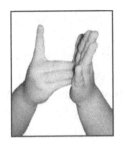

Chapter Twenty-Five

14 years 8 months - 14 years 10 months old

*T*he circus was my last big outing with Derek but he continued to want to go to church on Sunday mornings. I honestly don't know why because he couldn't stay awake for much of the service. For me, it was very hard to get him there while taking the other boys, pushing their wheelchairs and getting them to the correct classrooms, while carrying Derek and the oxygen tank at the same time. I was emotionally and spiritually confused as to why such an innocent child must endure so much pain and suffering. *Why would the great Creator weigh us down with such immense sadness?* But if Derek had the desire to go to church and found peace there, I could muster the physical strength to take him. I sensed some friction with some of the church members who just didn't understand why I would bring a limp, pale, and deathly thin child to church. I knew that if they'd had a child who desired to be a part of church services, they would also have made an effort to have their child attend.

I was at an emotional low as I continued caring for Derek while seeing him waste away. Finally, I called Dr. Fisher. She came to the house to speak with me and check Derek to make certain I wasn't overlooking something in his care. During the visit, she mentioned that she would notify the county coroner's office of our situation. My heart sank right to my gut. I silently begged, *Please stop this conversation. I don't want to hear this. Please STOP!*

I didn't say a word, and Dr. Fisher continued, "I talked with some oncology doctors who suggested I call the coroner. That way, everything will go smoothly when the death occurs. They won't ask any questions as long as they're notified ahead of time. All you'll need to do is call this number and give them Derek's name," she said. She handed me a slip of paper with the phone number of the mortuary we had planned to use. (I later learned that if a person is under the care of a physician and has been seen within a specific time before death, there is no need for an investigation, autopsy, or even to have the county coroner come to the home. This was why Dr. Fisher was discussing these issues with me.)

I could no longer cover up my pain. For months, I'd been guarded and in control around other people, but now my shield fell away. My tears flowed freely. Tons of stress released as I sat with Derek in my arms. Dr. Fisher waited quietly. Eventually I was able to speak between my sobs, and our conversation turned to organ donations. Would it be possible for Derek to donate?

No, his organs would not be acceptable but he could become a tissue donor if he wanted to help others in that way. At least there was something positive to think about. He could still help someone through tissue donation and research.

One day after all the other boys had left for school, I decided I needed to leave the house for a short time with Derek just to be in a place with few distractions and a pleasant atmosphere. I made arrangements for our friend Linda L. to come by and pick us up so I could hold Derek as she drove. We went to the Garden Room at the church. This room has a full view of the gardens and comfortable furniture where we could sit or stretch out. We would not need to turn on lights, which seemed to be stressful for Derek by that time, because we could still see well enough from the natural light coming through the large, glass walls. I had asked Linda to help me carry Derek's large photo albums. Linda held the books so Derek could see the pictures, and I signed with him about the pictures. They showed memory after memory of his life from the moment we first met. Picture after picture of his friends, his dogs, his family, and his schools. Once again, the feeling of being surrounded and enveloped with peace filled me. Even Derek, whose lips were normally blue and his limbs ice cold, was warm and had color in his face and lips during those two hours of relaxation and calm. Too soon we needed to return home. Derek was drained and slept contentedly. I was able to go about my responsibilities with my other sons with my stress level lowered a bit after our hours in the Garden Room.

It was soon time for all the other boys to come through the door from school. Of course, Chris was home all the time and Kyle and Kolya were only in preschool class for a couple hours a day, but by late afternoon the house was buzzing again with activity. I would do the norm, making several trips to push the guys in manual wheelchairs into the house from their school buses, taking them to the bathroom, giving a drink, tube feeding, and giving medications to those who needed them. I lifted them out of their wheelchairs to allow them some physical freedom on the floor or helped them find relaxing positions on a couch or comfortable chair. Some would be positioned in standing equipment. Others would want help with setting up a computer game. Ilan and Rusty would decide they both wanted the same musical toy at the same time. Someone would accidentally park his wheelchair on the oxygen tubing and would need to be reminded to "Please move!" once again.

Dinner needed to be prepared for eighteen or nineteen people every day. It was not just a matter of cooking but also entailed grinding food for those boys who could not chew: Ilan, Alan, Ben, and José. All the plates (making sure they were the correct one for each boy) needed to be filled, placed on the table in the correct place, spoon to the left or right, cup with handle to left or right, or cup with a straw. The guys had to be put back into their wheelchairs. Ilan had to go into his high chair. Bend and lift. Bend and LIFT. BEND and LIFT! Put on belts, straps, wheelchair trays, and bibs. Then, we fed those who couldn't feed themselves.

After dinner, it was the reverse. I had to remove the boys from the table or their wheelchairs, clear the table of all the dishes, put away the food, and wash the dishes. My life as a mom, cook, dishwasher, laundry lady, homework helper, bath giver, and bathroom attendant continued each evening. In between all of this activity, I kept a close eye on Derek to make certain he was doing the best that could be expected. He still needed to be turned periodically to prevent pressure sores from developing. I tried to keep him warm and give him what nutrition he could tolerate. Fortunately, the other boys were close by to provide entertainment and companionship.

As I sorted the mail one day, there was a card and letter for Derek from his Grandma Aiken. I sat on the edge of the sofa while opening his mail and a few tears trickled down his gaunt cheeks. I could only guess what might be going through his mind. *Is this why he continues to hang in there?* I wondered, after reading the letter Grandma had written to him. *Dare I sign to Derek what I am thinking?* My parents were older and traveling wasn't easy for them. I didn't want to give him any false hope. I put the card with its picture of a soft, fluffy puppy and the words "We love you" on the table near the sofa and signed to Derek, "You want Grandma and Granddad to come visit?" Even today, years later, I can clearly recall Derek's response. There was hardly time for him to catch his breath before he started sobbing silently, Derek-style. His body stiffened and so much stuff accumulated in the back of his throat, I had to suction him.

By this time, I was sobbing too. Tears flowed down my cheeks as I lifted Derek onto my lap and snuggled him close. This fragile son of mine was toughing it out because he wanted to see his grandparents, two incredible and wonderful people who cherished Derek as their grandson and accepted him unconditionally. I was torn between satisfying Derek's need to have his grandparents' visit and their need to limit their stress. It was becoming almost impossible for them to travel since my father's stroke that had left him very weak. My mother was doing well, but Dad's care was more difficult when he was not at home. After some time, I decided I could at least make a phone call and share with them Derek's desire. The decision whether or not to make the trip would be totally up to them. After Derek had calmed down I laid him on his sheepskins. As I stood up, I signed, "I will go TTY Grandma and inform her you want Grandma and Granddad to come."

Derek's response was a smile of appreciation to say, "Thank you, Mom."

By this time, all my family members had TTY machines, which made communication more direct for me. It was still problematic because they answered their phone as if it were a regular phone call. I needed to watch the signal light on my TTY after dialing their number to follow the rings and know when someone picked up the phone. When I was certain someone had answered, I would identify myself and ask that they please go to the TTY. Mom would then have to walk back into the room where the TTY was, turn it on, hang up the phone in the living room and then return to the bedroom to type. The sad part was that Dad could no longer get to their TTY himself or see enough to read the TTY screen. So, if he answered the phone and Mom was not there, I would wait and wait but eventually hang up and try again later. Luckily, Mom answered the call that day. She read everything to Dad and I waited for her response while they discussed things. As tears blurred the words and numbers on the screen of my TTY, we began the conversation as usual.

"Hello, Mom here. GA" (Go Ahead).

"Hello, this is Marian. GA."

"Hello Marian, wait until I try and get Dad back here near the phone," Mom responded.

As I waited for them to get situated which felt like forever, I walked back into the living room and signed to Derek, "Grandma answered the TTY. I will let her know what you want." Derek gave a pout, but then his grin appeared.

Finally, Mom typed, "Okay we are ready now. GA."

"Mom, your letter and card came today for Derek. He was greatly moved by his mail from you. Death seems to be 'knocking at his door' and he has one more request of you. Are you reading me okay? GA." (Sometimes the machines were not compatible or the connection was bad and the codes were not readable. It was better to check this out before going into a long conversation.)

"Yes Marian, we are able to read the TTY. I am telling Dad what you are typing so he knows too. GA." Mom typed back.

"Okay, here is Derek's wish. He wants you two to come and visit him. I know this kind of trip would be a great strain on you but I told Derek I would make the call and the decision would be up to you. GA." My tears were making it harder and harder to read the screen.

"Well, we will discuss this and let you know," Mom typed. "Yes, it would be a grueling trip, but we will let you know. In the meantime, please let Derek know we love him, and he is such a precious grandson to us. GA."

I took a few minutes to collect myself after we hung up, wiping my tears away and splashing cool water on my face to help cover up my crying from Derek, as if he didn't know. When I returned to the living room, his eyes showed how he was longing for an answer to his request.

"Grandma and Granddad will tell me later if they can come," I signed. "Grandma and Granddad want me to tell you they love you Derek precious grandson (pause) Grandma and Granddad love you much." He gave a slight sigh of relief, followed by a glance at the card he had just received before he closed his eyes to sleep.

Linda L. from church began encouraging me to start planning for Derek's Celebration of Life service while he was still able to have input. It had only been two months since I had helped arrange Raymond's service, and the thought of doing the same for Derek was nauseating. He was still ALIVE. However, we continued to talk. During our discussion about what hymns might be sung in the service, Linda suggested "Precious Lord, Take Me Home." That about did me in. No way was I going to use that hymn. I just didn't have the heart to ask that Derek be "taken home" when I ached for him to remain in my life. Over the next couple of weeks we managed to put together a basic service for Derek.

Three days after I had phoned my parents about Derek's desire for them to visit, my phone lights flashed.

"Hello, Marian here. GA," I typed.

"Hello Marian. This is Mom and we have arranged to come and spend three days with Derek. Will you please meet us at the airport?"

As soon as we finished our conversation, I rushed into the living room to share the exciting news with Derek.

"That was Grandma TTY type. Grandma and Granddad will come tomorrow to visit you," I signed, my hands shaking. Derek's first reaction was that of excitement as well, but his body and facial expressions soon expressed relief. I could tell that he was thinking *Grandma and Granddad are coming to see me! I have waited so long for them to come and they will be here tomorrow!* I think he was filled with gratitude and peace.

Grandparents play a very important role in the lives of children like Derek. My parents had welcomed him and my other sons into the family with open minds and hearts, and it was touching to witness the bonds that developed between them. My sons were equally cherished by my parents, as were all my gifted nieces and nephews.

Mom and Dad were very at ease as they spent precious moments with Derek. Dad was impaired physically and could no longer communicate with Derek through his limited use of signs. No signs were necessary for them to share moments of solace. A touch of the hand, strong eye contact, a smile, and each other's presence were all they needed.

During their visit Mom set her knitting aside and asked me to carry Derek to her. I placed him on her lap and she opened her photo albums with many pictures of Derek. She signed detailed stories to Derek of the memories she had from the pictures. What a beautiful way to spend time together. She also went to Ilan's room and brought back the blanket she had knitted for Derek that Ilan was using at the time. She shared how she knit this blanket, sweater, and booties especially for him fourteen years before. She went through my bookshelves and found books she and Dad had given to Derek when he was a baby and shared those stories with him once again. For three days he relaxed in these special moments with Grandma and Granddad. They all made the most of their time together.

I was proud that my parents would make this trip not knowing what to expect when they arrived. It was touching, and during their visit I would get choked up and need to leave the room. It was just so difficult for me to accept that this would be their last visit with Derek. While they were there, I constantly tried to find things to occupy my mind and did chores that didn't necessarily need to be done just to keep myself busy. I didn't know how to express my admiration for how my parents remained calm and involved during their visit. I will cherish those memories forever. Watching them say good-bye to Derek tore me apart, but they remained tranquil. Their deep faith must have played an immense role in how they were able to handle the situation. My heart went out to them and the unconditional love they showered on my son. Their involvement was essential and critical in my sons' lives, especially Derek's.

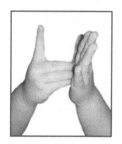

Chapter Twenty-Six

14 years 11 months old ...

On November 1, 1993, Derek slipped into a semi-coma. Not everything had been explained to me, and I was at a loss as to what to expect. I was more or less in a state of shock and consumed by fear. My greatest frustration was the lack of communication with Derek. How could I reassure my son that he had been the greatest gift of my life, that his immeasurable love for life was inspiring, and that my love for him was infinite and unlimited? All I could do was to touch Derek and pray that he knew I was close by. My heart was filled with anguish.

The next day Derek slipped deeper into the coma. I tried to take care of the other boys as best as I could, but I was numb and moving mechanically. Finally, they all left for school. I spent the majority of the day holding Derek close to my heart and hoping he would feel the rhythm of my breathing and know he was in my arms. I could not fathom what was happening. There was just not enough time to be alone with Derek. I so much wanted to hold him because, if he was aware at all, that was the only possible way he would know I was with him. But the day went by too quickly, and the boys began to return from school. I once again needed to meet their needs.

About dinnertime, I realized that Derek had not urinated at all that day. His abdomen had become distended and was extremely hard to the touch. I didn't know what to do or who to call. Fortunately, Linda L. was at the house and could help some with the other boys. She also helped me make some reasonable decisions. I finally called Dr. Fisher, but I couldn't reach her. I panicked. My hands trembled as I tried to type on the TTY.

Anger and fear were getting the best of me. Finally I reached another doctor who had given me her phone number to use in case of emergency.

I tried to explain the situation to the doctor through the relay operator, but I wasn't concentrating. Over and over I hit the wrong keys, backspaced, and then started again. I felt weak and faint. I was perspiring. My hands were clammy. My mouth was dry. My ears were ringing. I finally got through to the doctor. She told me that Derek's bladder had shut down. She suggested that if I had a catheter in the house I could try and insert it. Maybe that would empty his bladder and relieve the pressure in his abdomen. *Why hadn't someone warned me this sort of thing could happen?* I felt incapable of doing what was needed. I searched the bathroom and found a very tiny catheter that had never been used. It was dinnertime, the worst time of the day to deal with all of this.

My legs felt heavy as I returned to the living room to get Derek. *Do I have the guts to do this? Can I stomach this without getting sick myself? Please give me the strength and courage to go through with this*, I begged. Someone must have been listening to my pleading. My hands shook, but somehow my first attempt to insert that catheter was successful. Derek squirmed a little, and as his bladder began to empty, his eyes briefly opened and made contact with mine. "Thank you, Mom," his expression seemed to say. Tears welled up in my eyes as I gently lifted him into my arms, kissed his forehead, gave him a hug, and carried him back to the living room.

After dinner several of the family gathered in the living room. Some were watching TV while others were gathered around Derek. There was no question I longed for peace and time to be alone with Derek. On the other hand, it was necessary to care for the younger boys and give them some attention as I prepared them for bed.

Linda L. looks back at this time: **Probably one of the most special times for me was the night before Derek died. We were sitting on the couch and I had a couple of the kids on my lap with me, sharing memories. Derek didn't have much energy. He was really wasting away. It was just such an intimate moment to be able to share together. The kids would ask questions: "What do you think Derek is thinking right now?" "Where is**

**he going to go?" "What's it going to be like without him here?"
I would simply respond with, "What do you think?"**

After Linda and our friend Diane left and all the other boys were in bed, I struggled to decide what to do with Ben that evening. He was the closest to Derek; they had shared a bedroom since Ben had joined our family. Ben didn't have his computer on his wheelchair since it needed to be charged for the night, so he couldn't directly communicate what he would want to do. I had no idea how much longer Derek would live. His breathing was becoming more and more shallow. My heart ached for Ben as much as it did for myself. Finally, I invited Ben to sit on the couch with Derek and me before he went to bed. He nodded, so I lifted him out of his wheelchair and sat him on the couch with Derek's feet in his lap. I sat on the other side of Ben to help prop him up. No words were spoken. Tears flowed from both Ben and me. My thirteen-year-old son was about to lose his fourteen-year-old brother. Not one word had ever passed between these two boys, but they had developed communication and a bond between them as strong as any brothers would ever develop. They had shared each other's joys and pains. Unlimited love and respect had passed between them, unique only to them. Ben reached out to touch Derek's chest, as gently as a spastic person with cerebral palsy could do. I know that Derek was aware of the different touch. He briefly opened his eyes and saw Ben. Communication through touch. Awareness through feeling.

This was a tremendous relief. If Derek realized that Ben's touch was different than mine, he must have been aware of my presence during the past hours as well. How does one communicate with a deaf person who appears to be in a coma? By touch. I will always believe Derek knew I was with him in his final hours.

Eventually, Ben said his good-byes to his precious brother and was ready to go to bed. I tried to remain strong for him. Instead of putting him back in his wheelchair, I carried him to the bathroom and then tucked him into bed. No matter how many more brothers would join our family, no one would ever take Derek's place in Ben's heart.

I did my regular rounds, checked on the younger ones in

their room to make sure they were all safe and sound, then returned to the living room and found a comfortable position with Derek in my arms. He only stirred a bit and his limbs were frigid, his lips blue, and his cheeks without color. He was still breathing. I dozed off for short periods but woke often to monitor Derek. His time had come. He took his last breath as he lay in my arms with his dog at his feet, my son who had generously and abundantly changed my life. His desire to die at home, in the presence of those who loved him, had come true.

His influence on me was greater than any other person in my life, maybe even more so than my parents. Derek may not have been born into my arms, but that is where he died. He was accepted, loved, valued, and forever cherished in my heart.

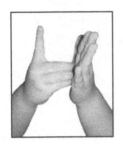

Chapter Twenty-Seven
November 1993

*T*he first year after Derek's death was one of the toughest periods in my life. I had almost no time to mourn because of the ongoing responsibilities of the family and the fact that Jim left less than twenty-four hours after Derek's memorial service to go back to Moscow to bring another child into the family. Several days after Derek's memorial service, I walked into the bedroom to retrieve something. When I saw the lights and mobiles that I'd put in his bed after his church service I thought, *I better get the bed cleaned out so it will be ready when he comes home from the hospital. What? No, he is not in the hospital again. He died and will not be coming home.* The tears came. I was confused and I was tired. I stood looking at his bed feeling empty and useless, but I soon had to move on because one of the boys needed something.

Not only was I trying to deal with my loss, but also the loss Derek's brothers felt. There was really no way I could prepare myself for reactions and questions from some of the boys. What might have seemed like silly ideas to me as an adult made a lot of sense to a child. I would just have to stay focused and do my best to meet their needs.

Meanwhile, even the dog was in mourning. Snuja had slept by Derek's feet day in and day out for the last two plus years of his life. Now that he was gone, she looked everywhere for him and was completely lost because he wasn't there. She would whimper and follow me around in the house, getting under my feet and wanting to be in my lap whenever I sat down. I don't know if it helped, but I put a couple of Derek's shirts in her bedding thinking the scent of his clothes might ease her loneliness.

A few weeks after Derek's death, Ben relayed to me on his computer that he was ready to go to his bedroom for the night. I was puzzled by his request since he didn't have homework that night and it wasn't his bedtime. I asked why he wanted to just go into his room and sit. With tears in his eyes, he typed, "I just want to think about 'you know who.'" Ben could not even bring himself to type "Derek" for a long time because it hurt him so much. After a while, I went back into the room to check on Ben. He immediately started asking questions about what we would do with the aquarium, *his* clothes, *his* lights, and *his* bed. I wanted to leave Derek's things where they were for the time being, but I offered to sort through his clothes and find things that would fit Ben so he could wear them if he wanted to. Ben nodded. He liked that idea. But his primary concern was really about Derek's bed. Ben wanted me to take it down. It bothered him to leave the bed there without Derek. I concluded he was afraid that someone was going to use the bed and try to replace Derek even though no one could ever replace Derek in our lives. I told him I would take the bed down the next day when everyone was in school. I was in for a surprise. I had no idea of what an emotionally draining task I was about to undertake. I sobbed with every twist of the screwdriver as I dismantled Derek's bed. After a few minutes, there was a vacant space where Derek's bed had stood for years. It finally registered that his death was permanent. I felt overwhelmed with grief and sorrow. Thankfully, I was alone and didn't need to cover up my grief. I was grateful for a short time to grieve in private.

The first Thanksgiving after Derek's death, I was so occupied with all the boys and preparing dinner that I really didn't have time to dwell on Derek's not being physically present with us that day. Christmas was a different experience. It had become a tradition that my sign language class come to our home for a holiday party with treats and singing and signing Christmas carols. That year one of the choirs from church was also coming to carol with us. Everyone seemed to be having a wonderful time at the party but I was suddenly overwhelmed by extreme sadness. I desperately missed Derek's presence at the party.

I thought about how much Derek would have enjoyed our friends in our home, with people signing so he could understand everything that was going on. As my friend Diane was leaving, I told her how I felt. She said she had felt Derek's closeness during the party, which made her calm. Where I felt sadness, another person felt calmness. What a contrast. Still it was a comfort knowing another person was thinking of my son and had not pushed his memory aside or forgotten him.

I got through Christmas that first year with support of friends from church and with many candles. This was the first Christmas in three years when I could place candles around the house. We hadn't been able to have open flames near Derek's oxygen tanks. The candles were a constant reminder of Derek's and my earlier Christmases when we would sit peacefully together for hours as the candles flickered.

Two of the boys had made it known that they wanted to have gifts for Derek and be given gifts from him. I searched for things that Derek would have liked to give or receive and wrapped them up. On Christmas morning we gathered in the living room with my sons

Derek's gift for Ben

cheerfully passing out and opening presents. I was doing fine until the first box from Derek appeared. Oh, I just wanted to leave, be alone, and find a few moments of peace. I wanted to hold Derek again, to experience the feeling of his closeness. Instead, I talked to him: *Derek, thank you for being my son. Derek, I feel empty without your physical presence. Derek, look at all these happy boys who surround me and know how thankful I am that you were the child who helped me begin this incredible experience.*

January 3, 1994, which would have been Derek's fifteenth birthday, was another day I was unprepared for. Ben's birthday was December 25, and he and Derek had celebrated their birthdays together between Christmas and New Years for several years. This year Ben asked what we should do for his birthday, and I told him we'd do whatever he wanted. With a sad but determined look on his face, he typed, "Nothing." I respected his decision, and we did not celebrate for him, but some of the younger boys had a different idea for Derek's birthday. They wanted to have a party. This is a perfect example of when children and adults do not think the same and handle grief differently. I was startled by the idea and felt uncertain about it. *How can I have a party for my son who had recently died?* I questioned myself. *Should I respect Ben's decision to do nothing or satisfy the request of the younger boys?* Eventually I realized that having a party meant a great deal to the boys. It was also a way for them to get some closure on issues they needed to resolve. I agreed to have the party.

It was our tradition to fix the birthday boy's favorite dinner so I asked Jim if he would make the delicious chicken crepes that Derek had indulged in for several years before his feeding tube was inserted. Then I went to the store to buy a cake with Derek's name on it. When the lady asked if it was okay to write the price on the box, I almost replied, "Why not? He's dead."

Sergei put candles on the birthday cake. We used it as a language lesson of how to count to fifteen in English. I absolutely could not sing "Happy Birthday," but we did talk a little about Derek before we cut the cake. I had bought a blue and silver dolphin mobile and hung it in his room. He would have loved it. As difficult as it was for me to get through this party for Derek, the boys thoroughly enjoyed themselves. I'm so thankful I allowed that party and gave them the chance to remember their brother.

There were so many incidents when one of the boys would show their love for Derek and their sadness that he was gone. One day José found a toy that my mother had made for Derek when he was an infant. José brought the toy to me and wanted to know about it. I swallowed hard, took a deep breath, and said, "Oh, Grandma Aiken made that for Derek when he was a baby." José looked at me for a minute, then turned toward Derek's old room. He gently placed the toy where Derek's bed had been, gave a satisfied smile, and proudly left the room.

Sergei was the best at catching me off guard during the first year after Derek's death. One evening we were eating dinner and he asked, "When is Derek coming back and where is he?"

After dinner I invited Sergei to come with me to sit on the deck. I brought along a children's book about dying. After reading the book with Sergei, I pointed out two trees that had been given to me in memory of Derek, which I had planted nearby. "Sergei," I spoke in a trembling voice, "when I become sad and lonely, I come here to think about Derek. It helps me to see the trees grow and bloom." We sat close for a time and I noticed he was looking up to the sky. My eyes followed his gaze where an airplane flew overhead followed by jet streams. The plane reflected the evening sun. It was a beautiful sight. In a quiet voice, Sergei commented, "Oh, Mom, look at that plane. It is so pretty and looks almost like a rainbow. I hope Derek is on that plane." *Yes Sergei, it is almost like a rainbow, and perhaps Derek is flying by.*

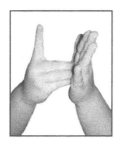

Chapter Twenty-Eight

*A*fter Derek's death I felt alone in the house, even with so many people around. I was overwhelmed by all the work: helping with homework, shopping, cooking, laundry, keeping track of who was where, and all the care my sons required. Also, I was still trying to keep my grief to myself. I didn't want my other sons to see me crying because I knew that would upset them very much. So everyone's lives went along as usual. Except mine.

For a long time communication had been strained between Jim and me. Actually, we had communicated more clearly when we were living on opposite sides of the country. In those days letters flew between us and I didn't have to worry about visual distractions when I was reading what Jim wrote. Also, I have to admit that, during Derek's last months, I didn't want anyone else helping me make decisions about him. He was *my* son and I knew him best. It was partially my own fault that I felt lonely and unsupported by just about everybody. I was stubborn and defensive.

Sometimes Jim attended medical meetings with me, but I felt overshadowed when he was present, especially if there wasn't an interpreter. People spoke directly to Jim when he asked a question, and I couldn't speechread what they were saying, or more than one person would speak at the same time. There was no way I could follow the conversation. I would interrupt to remind them of my communication needs then get frustrated and give up.

Also, we approached the end of life very differently. Where

I wanted to be close to my son who was dying, Jim appeared to want to distance himself. He went about his day as he usually did, and I preferred to stay home and be close by. I don't recall ever discussing these differences. And as Derek became more ill, my energy to communicate was close to zero.

Nonetheless, keeping my feelings to myself wasn't a good idea.

I had been exhausted for a long time, but I knew that the exhaustion I felt now wasn't due only to lack of sleep or my everyday work. I was filled with a level of anger that I hadn't ever experienced. This anger left me with headaches, pains all over my body, and a constant sunken feeling in the pit of my stomach. I needed to be alone, but I couldn't be alone. I wanted to be with friends, but declined most of their invitations. I was really upset about the rush to have Derek's memorial service so Jim could catch his flight to Russia. Days after the service, sympathy cards began to arrive in the mail with statements such as: "Had I known, I'd have attended his service." There had been no time for friends to make travel arrangements. I was angry with myself for not standing up for what I felt I needed at that time. I was embarrassed by my degree of anger. I was angry with myself for being angry.

I was angry with myself for feeling I'd been unable to focus and bond with some of my sons. Although I loved each one it had been most challenging to be able to spread that love during the past two years. At least that is how I felt at the time, especially one day a couple of months after Derek died when one of the boys asked, "If I die, who will replace me?" Oh, that made me even angrier for allowing more sons to join the family so soon after the deaths of Raymond and Derek. They all needed to be loved and valued. Had I not been able to provide that when I was experiencing such deep sadness?

Today, I realize much of this anger was not so specific as it was the lengthy build up of not expressing my overwhelming sadness as Derek's health declined. Had I been able to express that sadness in an appropriate manner, the level of anger that consumed me might not have happened.

Or maybe that level of anger was part of the grieving process. I had grieved for more than two years as I watched my son's health decline, finally coming out of the stage of denial when I at last accepted there wasn't going to be a medical miracle for him. There was plenty to be angry about.

Possibly my biggest adjustment during this first year after Derek's death was learning to sleep again. I struggled with low energy at times due more to my emotions during the grieving process than to lack of sleep. However, after so many years of awakening every hour or so to check on Derek (and Ilan too) my body and brain seemed to be set to that schedule. At first, I tried to stay in bed in an effort to force myself to break the habit, but that didn't seem to change my sleep pattern. After a time, I would eventually get out of bed and walk around, sit on a couch in the living room, read, and then try to go back to bed and sleep. That didn't work either. I gave up walking and reading and went back to staying in bed, trying my best to relax, and thinking comforting thoughts. It took a long time before I could sleep for longer periods. To this day I have made progress, but I still continue to wake up during the night and get out of bed to check on some of the boys. It seems like Derek lives on in my sleep patterns.

I was very aggravated by people who could only think about Derek's care being a burden on me. "He is much better off now" was a typical statement I heard frequently. "You must be greatly relieved to be free of his care," was another one. I wanted to cry out with anger at the ignorance of these statements and tell people, *"Derek was not a burden but my first son, my companion, and a sibling to my other sons! Can't you see beyond the oxygen tank, the wheelchair, the labored breathing, and the spastic limbs? Why would you feel he is better off? I am not there to hold him, care for him, comfort him, or communicate with him."* Even parts of the piece my mother wrote for his memorial service troubled me. Derek had not been able to do many things, but I focused on the things he could do and the love he received and gave in return.

On the other hand, I was fortunate to have friends who would send me a card or call just to chat, or go out for lunch if I was up to it. These were friends who provided gentle words of encouragement to help me move on with life and friends who would also take one of Derek's siblings on an outing or for a walk around the neighborhood to give me a little time to be alone.

257

These people understood my pain and felt comfortable coming into our home knowing I might not be in the best mood. They understood that Derek was not a burden or an inconvenience in my life. Thank God for people like these friends.

Taking my sons to their medical appointments stirred up many memories since I had met most of these doctors and nurses through Derek. Most families don't have several children with similar medical needs as did my sons, unless they have a genetic disorder. In our case, Derek's doctors were, for the most part, my other sons' as well. At that first appointment after Derek died, I didn't even know how to begin a conversation with some of the medical staff. It was an incredibly awkward situation and challenging to focus on the child with me without having my mind flooded by memories of Derek. The palms of my hands got clammy, and I was overcome with nausea. I greatly missed conversations with the medical staff who had become a support system for me, but I would stay quiet. It was just too difficult to think of simple conversation. Thankfully, I have adjusted over time and now feel less troubled when I take my sons to their appointments. Time helps heal the heart.

About six months after Derek's death and after Greg had arrived from Moscow and joined our family, we flew to Arizona so he could meet his grandparents. I was thrilled to present them with a new grandson who was bright and talkative. Naturally, my parents accepted Greg as they had all my sons and took him to see the sights in their area. He had a wonderful time and connected with them quickly. It was a bittersweet visit for me. It was the first time in fourteen years that I had visited my parents without my first son in my arms. I'm sure their arms felt empty as well and their hearts saddened. Derek continues to live on in our memories and in our hearts as we continue to share the love that he deeply engraved in our souls, an unlimited and genuine love for life.

One fall day I was clearing out a shed filled with wheelchairs my sons were no longer able to use. A man was coming in about fifteen minutes to take them to be donated to children in developing countries. When he arrived I should have been upbeat about getting rid of things to make more room in the shed, but instead I was too strongly attached to the small light blue TranSporter Travel chair that had been Derek's first chair.

He loaded all the chairs except Derek's into his truck. "Marian, am I to take that chair as well?" he asked. I was staring vacantly trying to get words to come out of my mouth. "Marian, are you okay?"

I finally managed to say something about why I was having a hard time parting with this chair, and I told him a little about Derek.

Ever so gently he touched my shoulder and said, "I'm sure a small child who needs this special chair will truly benefit from the freedom to go places never possible without a wheelchair. Consider this a gift from Derek to another child in need."

He was right. I said a silent prayer and gave Derek's chair one last touch before he drove away. I knew Derek's love would continue to be spread.

At times I still have periods of sadness. Sometimes it's triggered by one of the hymns we sang for his memorial service being sung in church or the enormous moon that shone brightly a month ago. One day when I was feeling empty I decided I needed to focus on more positive thoughts about Derek. I had several small magnetic picture frames with my photography supplies. I took two of them and found two cheerful pictures of Derek. Each day for the

next couple of weeks I wrote one positive descriptive word or phrase on the magnetic frames. I carry these in my purse and when feeling a bit sad I take a glance at them. I miss our deep level of communication that many others never witnessed or believed was ever possible. But mostly I reflect on the most precious gift every human is entitled to ~ the gift of love ~ the love Derek was able to receive and the love he was capable of radiating. The love of happiness and life.

More Memories

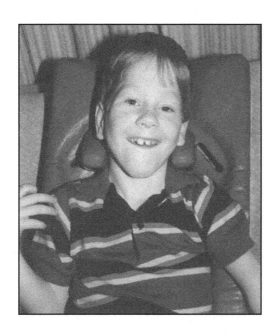

DEREK MICHAEL AIKEN

January 3, 1979 - November 3, 1993

FREE SPIRIT

Free
Free at last
Derek is free at last!

"What is it with this new boy angel with freckles marching across his nose and straw hair and an infectious smile?" a motherly angel asked one of the heavenly host. "He races through the flowering heavenly meadows like a fawn at play; he splashes with wild abandon in heavens woodland streams; he climbs young trees and bends and rides them to the ground; he dives and swims in Paradise Lake like a young dolphin; he shouts along with the heavenly choirs singing praises; and he is always eating -eating--eating! Not satisfied with heaven's manna, he eats ice cream and pizza and hamburgers as if there were no tomorrow"

"Oh, well, you didn't know this boy before he came to be an angel," the elder answered. "This is the boy Derek, who on earth could do none of these things. He was trapped in a body that would not work right. His ears would not hear, his tongue could not speak to tell his thoughts of joy or sorrow. Only his eyes could talk. His arms and legs would not do his bidding. He could only watch other people and animals with delight and smile and laugh with joy at their activity. For the first time since he was born on earth, he is truly free."

"Now I understand his antics," replied the mother angel laughing. "My boys on earth did all these things when they were growing up!"

Yes,

Derek is free at last
Free at last
FREE!

Celebration of Life Service

Derek

Derek you were always such a joy,
Blond-haired and freckled, an always smiling boy.
God made you special, like no other,
You were deeply loved by your father and mother.

I loved to hold you in my arms,
You always won me with your charms.
Fond memories of you are at special games and school,
And watching you find freedom splashing in your pool.

You never were spiteful or hurt anyone,
But dreamed of walking and knowing how to run,
I never heard you cry, although you suffered so,
Brave through many hospitalizations,
I wasn't ready for you to go.

Now you are an angel in heaven above,
Looking down on those you love,
Your parents, friends and many others,
And of course your loving brothers.

~ by Diane

Thoughts from Aunt Lynne: You were a very special boy. I remember when your mother first told me about you. I was afraid—what if he looks so different because of his handicaps that I have trouble seeing past the physical appearance to the person inside the body? What if he demands so much of my sister that she doesn't take care of herself? What if he dies? Derek has taught me much through the years.

Well, he did look different but who couldn't love that grin and those freckles thrown across his nose? He had a strong personality and it shone through. As for his mother, she's strong too. Yes, she has spent lots of time and energy on his care, but I can't think of any better way for her to have spent that time and energy!

And what about dying? Well, he has proven lots of experts wrong there. Derek certainly had a strong spirit to convince his body to hold it just as long as it could. I now realize that dying is part of the life cycle. We will all die when it is our time.

Some people feel it is important to have a mission in life, to accomplish something. I believe that one of Derek's missions was to teach. He has taught me, he taught doctors and nurses. I remember when he visited school with me in Houston. He taught many children and their teachers that it is ok to be deaf and to be in a wheelchair, that he could still learn and laugh and love and be loved.

Now that Derek's spirit has left his body, it is certain that there are many people who admired and loved him, including me. We will miss him and we will always love him.

Love ~ Aunt Lynne

Memories of Derek, Linda Landrith: I have lots of precious memories and some very special relationships because of Derek. Many have shared heartwarming thoughts and words about Derek, but I would like to share a few brief thoughts about how this boy who couldn't hear or speak and who was physically challenged has enriched at least my life.

Derek taught me that there is a universal and creative

language by which we can communicate using smiles, laughter, touch, and pictures. I remember my first meeting with Derek. It was at the old Children's Hospital at Stanford. I didn't know anything about him as a person or much about his family, and frankly I wondered what was I going to do. As soon as I walked in his room, he smiled, and as I smiled back he looked straight into my eyes with that classic Derek look. Derek reminded me that there is always a creative way to communicate: with pictures! I would draw these simple pictures and we could both laugh at them!

I was also reminded by Derek's situation that there is a certain mystery in life for which there are no answers or explanations or solutions. And that's OK, because in the process of living with dying we remain who we are. We are still in relationships with our family and friends, and there becomes an intimate quality to our lives because we know that our existence on this side of eternity is fragile. Last spring Dr. Fisher and I had a conversation about the inevitability of this moment. She had already talked with Marian and we began, at that point, to prepare to let go of Derek. One can never be fully prepared for nor anticipate the overwhelming loss and grief experienced when a child dies, but I commend Dr. Fisher and the medical staff's courage for initiating the letting go process. I see a medical team whose care and concern extend far beyond the role of medical professionals for patients. I see a compassionate group of people who cared for Derek and who had the wisdom and courage to say "There's nothing else that can be done" and support Marian and the family during these final months.

And finally, Derek reminds me that we are never alone; we are in relationship one with another. Derek was blessed to be a part of an incredible web of relationships, as evidenced by each one of you here this morning. The night before Derek died, some of the boys and I were sitting with Derek, sharing memories, telling stories and one of them said, "I don't know where he is going, but we sure are going to miss him." That's being in relationship. That's being loved. Derek knew the love a mother has for her son, parents have for their children, and the love brothers have for brothers.

I thank God for the preciousness of Derek's life and for bringing him into my life. Amen.

Words from Dad: Derek, you have been part of our lives for so long that it is hard to comprehend that you are not with us in body now. Certainly your spirit is with us now as we feel your presence here. We want you to know how much you meant to all of us and how much we appreciated you.

You helped us to understand that there are many ways to communicate and that perhaps the most important one of all is to be able to look one another in the eyes, be sensitive to one another's feelings, and to really notice the small gestures that can mean so much. You understood everything that was going on around you and challenged us to put ourselves in your position in order to make ourselves understood by you and for us to appreciate the world from your perspective.

You were a wonderful older brother to all your little brothers. Always interested in what the other boys were doing and very tolerant of the many annoyances you had to put up with from all the little ones that shared your space. You always had a smile of encouragement to give us all.

Derek, this past year has been very difficult for you and your family. Through all hard times you never lost your ability to smile and to show us that you were still interested in what was going on. Now you are at peace in God's loving care. We can still feel your presence with us and know that you are at last free to express yourself and move about with all the other angels. Your gifts have enriched our lives tremendously and you will remain with us in spirit for the rest of our lives.

Love, Dad

Ben's remembrances:
To Derek Aiken, my brother, who has had to fight many illnesses, but never complains. His example is one that I am thankful for.

******

Derek's smile is as bright as the sun shining on a sandy beach.

When Derek laughs I feel like jumping up and down with
    endless joy.
Derek is sweet as candy.
Derek's eyes are blue as the sky.
Derek's hair is blond as straw.

Memories: Derek, we've had many fun times together.
Remember the fun times that Mom, you and I had in the snow?
That was exciting and enjoyable.

Derek, remember the fun we had together with Grandma
and Grandpa? Grandma would play cards and games with us
and we rode cross-country with them all alone! That was fun
and exciting. I was so glad she didn't make us eat ham. Instead
Grandma let us eat ice cream everyday.

Hey brother, remember when Mom would take us on hot
trips and I was whining, "Let's go swimming?" Later you'd
kick around in that old swimming pool while I cooled off in the
boat.

Derek, remember those times that Rusty would pat us on
the head? I'd tried to put his hand back on his body, but he is
stronger than me.

Derek, remember when you and I lay on the floor and
watched cartoons together? I really liked being close to you.

Derek, I'm glad that I thought of these great ideas so I can
remember you in my heart.

Tim shares: Derek, when we both were little, we were two
boys that were the same in many ways. You were happy and
loved playing with the other guys, Ben and Rusty. You never
seemed to run out of energy, always kicking people and moving
around on the floor. I never went close to you because I knew I
would always get a hit at least once!

As we grew up, I could never look at it as if I was older or if
you were. When you started getting weak and sick, I wondered
if your body was so sick that your heart couldn't take your pain.
You showed everyone that you had the strongest heart and that
you weren't going to die. Just watching you lie on the couch

or on the floor gave some the impression that you didn't really understand or couldn't communicate with anyone, but I knew that that wasn't true. I knew that you saw everyone's face and the way you reacted by the expressions they made to you. Even though you didn't have the hearing, you had your eyes and facial expressions and that was enough.

Until about a month or two ago, you still smiled and showed a little happiness. But then you really didn't after that. No one could blame you either, but the night you passed away, before I went to bed, I went over to you and saw the unhappy look on your face. Once you made eye contact with me, you gave me the same old smile you always did. That was probably the best way to show me how much I meant to you and the rest of the family. You will always be in our hearts and we can never forget your smile that you gave to everyone. We will always love you Derek.

Your brother, Tim

And from me: Derek, you came into my life as a tiny infant with more questions than answers. Now, you've left me with a few questions but lots of answers. One of the questions that you answered was yes, you'd live to see your first birthday and many more after that one. Secondly, you were able to bond and interact with so many people and things in your environment regardless of the severity of your disability. You definitely had a lot of spunk and courage to carry on as you have. You definitely had a mind of your own.

Being my first son, you taught me many things. You've taught me how to deal with medical issues that I had never before experienced. You taught me how to speak up for what I felt was right for you and others like you. You taught me how to enjoy the simple things, such as fireworks, the circus, Christmas tree lights, and candles to the fullest, and that gifts were okay but not necessary. Your excitement for traveling was contagious. You loved the airplane rides cross-country to visit your grandparents and even the long van rides to visit friends and relatives. Your eyes sparkled at the beauty of the sky at dusk and again at sunrise. You could see and appreciate the splendor of the flowers that surrounded you. You enjoyed so many little things, like the ladybug crawling around your plate one day. Forget the food, because the ladybug was more interesting. You taught me how to love and accept individuals who were so different from the majority of the population.

Because of your ability to enjoy life and bond with those in your environment, you led me to expand our family from you and myself to a family with a father and all your fantastic brothers. Although you never spoke a word, your ability to express your appreciation to those around you was very evident when one could understand all your nonverbal ways of communicating. One of the most remarkable things I will always remember is that you were never jealous of having a new brother join in your life. In fact, they brought you so much enjoyment with their various ways of entertaining you. I know that the past couple of years your brothers have been your link for wanting to continue to live. You were always appreciative of them when they would get someone if you needed help, or when they'd hold your hand, or share your pillow and be close to you.

Derek, although you were deaf due to nerve deafness, you have given the gift of hearing to another person by donation of your middle ear bones. You have also given your eyes to be used for medical research. I pray that the lives of people who you may have helped will be full of love and joy as your life has been.

Derek, I will greatly miss your eyes following my every move as they have while I worked in the kitchen or in your line of vision for the past two years when you were not able to go to school. I want to thank you for all that you have given me, for all the moments of pleasure and love, and for all of your smiles and triumphs. Thank you for such a delightful sense of humor, even when things were not going your way. Thank you for that splendid "happy-go-lucky" personality. Thank you for having such a positive relationship to those who have had contact with you. Thank you for your courage. Thank you for being such a tremendous and caring son.

With love ~ Mom

Acknowledgements

I began this project many years ago and it was stored in a box under my bed for way too long, yet always on my mind. One day I decided to pull that box out and finish what I had started. You now have before you the final outcome that could never have been achieved without the support of many individuals. I would personally like to thank everyone who has contributed his or her memories, medical knowledge, and wisdom to my story. However, it's close to impossible to mention each of you by name. You know who you are, and you can brag loud and clear about your input to your family and friends.

First is a special thank you to Sandy Giffin O'Brien, my first social worker, who believed my home was acceptable for adoption and who made me feel I was capable of caring for children with special needs. I would also like to thank my friends and other social workers in Romney, West Virginia who accepted my family as part of the loving community of Romney while we lived there.

I am indebted to Dr. Zinnia Giron and the medical staff at Hampshire County Memorial Hospital in Romney for the incredible care that was provided to my first three sons. I'd also like to express my gratitude to the many doctors, specialists, and nursing staff at Children's Hospital at Stanford where my sons went for treatment after we moved to California. I felt supported emotionally during the many medical challenges my sons faced. The compassion you showed my family was exceptional.

Thank you to Eleanor and Jim Normile for an incredible gift that allowed me to complete my manuscript with up-to-date technology.

I am forever grateful to Derek's educators who believed he was capable of learning more than basic facts and included him in classroom activities. An extra thank you to Cindy and Mary who challenged him academically and to Linda who supported him as a classroom health aide.

Another special thank you goes to Susan Little, my editor, who urged me to keep marching along with my project. She understood when I occasionally needed a break but always invited me back to work with encouraging words.

Thank you to John Dewing for editing my photos and my dear friend Cathi Bouton for her unwavering belief that this project could be completed. Her ability to format my manuscript and design my web site has surpassed anything I had expected.

Thank you to the United Methodist Church of Los Altos for ongoing financial support to my family, locating my editor and for being a place where I found several readers who encouraged me to move forward through constructive suggestions to improve my manuscript.

I must express my immeasurable gratitude to my parents, brother, sister, and my hometown community for instilling in me values that helped me become the person I am today. I didn't understand the impact of such on my life until years after I moved away. The value of acceptance, life, and love remain embedded in my heart.

And lastly, I'd like to share my gratitude with my sons who allowed me to be their mom through the many ups and downs of life. Each of you has a special place in my heart. I know at times things didn't go the way we may have wanted, as I took the responsibility of being your mom seriously, but I love each and every one of you. I continue to be amazed with what you are capable of accomplishing and the courage that you have to face society especially with the many challenges in your lives. Thank you for your love. Thank you for being my sons. ~ Mom

Additional Interview Information

When I started this project, I collected a number of insights that I could not incorporate into my story. However, I believe my readers would enjoy reading these additional thoughts.

Do you have any advice for parenting or educating children who are similar to Derek?

I would tell parents to incorporate their children into their normal everyday life as much as is physically possible with these children, because that is what being a family is about. If you can do that it will benefit both the child dealing with special challenges and the entire family.

As much as possible, and depending on the intellectual ability of the child, (s)he should go to school. The children should be as active as they can, both mentally and physically, and the more they get out the better life will be, because all children need interaction and stimulation. If a child can't move he might be able to see or hear. If not, just being in a different place enhances sensations. It's very important for every child to have the opportunity to interact as much as they can with people and places outside the family.

~ Dr. Joan Fisher, pediatrician

* * *

Parents need to talk, sign, or communicate in any way possible with their children. Children need to be included in all parts of the family life and life outside the home. It's cruel to take care of the strictly physical needs of a child and then sit him or her in front of the TV for the day. That's not good for anyone. Communication and language are key to involving the child in life. Because of his mother, Derek was included in activities and communicated to from infancy. That interaction was everything to him and helped to make him a higher functioning kid than any of those I worked with. He certainly was aware of what was going on and he was fun, loving, sensitive, and simply glowed. Why? Because he had been included in outings, family life, and communicated with. *~ Cindy Wright, interpreter/aide*

You need to learn how to communicate with your child to find out what they want and what they need. Your child is a person who needs to be allowed, as much as possible, to help make decisions about their care and treatment. Even if it is harder for the parent, it is always necessary to do what will be better for the child.

After working with Derek I became more aware of the needs of the other children I was working with. Now I see past their physical and communication limitations and find the person inside who, just like everybody else, wants to be understood and to communicate with others. I also became aware that I could become emotionally attached to medically fragile children and not let worry about how long the child could survive keep me from doing what I could for them to make them comfortable, happy, and secure that day. All I wanted to do was to make their lives better.

~ Linda Hambly, health aide

* * *

Marian helped Derek communicate to express his feelings and his desires and his needs. She was completely there for him. Considering all the other children and duties she had, she was always there when he absolutely needed her. Marian made it clear how especially important it is that parents are with their children during stressful medical procedures.

~ Marcia Kreisl, GI nurse

Discussions on medical care

I learned one day that one of my students, who lived in an institution, was in the hospital. I went to visit her and saw that her food had not been touched. At that moment an orderly came into the room to remove her tray and commented she must not have been hungry. I went to the nurse's desk to ask what the story was and I was told they had forgotten about her. She was a nonverbal and nonambulatory child who needed to be fed, and they forgot about her? How many other unspoken things had she endured in her life? Without a family to stay on top of her needs, she was neglected. I am so thankful Derek and his brothers had Marian as their mom to be an advocate and make sure their needs were met.

~ Maureen McLoughlin, special education teacher

* * *

Making medical decisions for any child, or any older person, has changed with so much available technology. Now medical decisions include the institution of new treatments, another tube, another operation, a ventilator, special nutrition, etc. The decisions feel far more ominous. It's like playing God every step of the way. If I don't do this he is going to die and if I do do this, he might live. But what about his quality of life? Everyone, including the nurse, doctor, parent or caregiver, and child, will be involved in these decisions and they will be very, very, very hard to make. For those of us with deep faith, we can ask God for help and do the best we can at the time to make the right decision. By being true to ourselves, to the child, and to what we think God wants, we don't need to second-guess ourselves, though that's hard not to do sometimes.

~ Mary Fitzgerald, pediatric nurse

* * *

I've heard people, including medical personnel, question why children who are severely disabled deserve our caring, time, and money. After all, people say, their situations are hopeless and they are never going to get better. People question the value of these children's lives and talk about the burden they place on their families. That never ceases to amaze me. What I notice most about the children who have special needs is that they are not a burden to their family. There are difficulties, to be sure, but those kids are taken care of with lots of love and acceptance. The real burden comes when the kids need to be hospitalized and are separated from their family. These children's lives are so precious because their days are very limited. The time available to spend with them far outweighs any of their disabilities. Their lives have tremendous value.

~ Dr. Joan Fisher, pediatrician

Parents are legally responsible to make medical decisions for their child until (s)he reaches the age of eighteen. However, if a child has reached a certain level of maturity, no matter what his age, and his input and ideas are clear and are communicated to the parent, his opinions need to be incorporated in the decision-making process. Marian certainly showed that respect for Derek. They had discussions, he shared his desires, and Marian honored him. There's really no way to predict an age at which it's appropriate to involve the child in health care decisions, but, hopefully, the parent or caregiver will recognize when that time comes.

Legal responsibility for care can be very complicated. For instance, when medical staff believes that the child's chance of survival or quality of life can be improved but the parent prefers not to have suggested therapy given, the courts can get involved and take over responsibility. This can also happen when the parents choose treatment when the medical personnel feel it would be much kinder not to treat the child. Some things are more clear-cut, like giving blood where someone is going to hemorrhage to death, versus whether to intubate a child. But in all cases, we medical staff, although we do have our shortcomings, try our best to honor the wishes of the parents. If the child is younger, we look to the parent to give us input. If it's an older child or teenager we feel it is important to get direct input.

One other thought I'd like to share is that if a patient is capable of any amount of independence and you take that away or don't respect his or her choice, you are taking away the last, most important thing that person has and are removing all his or her humanity. It is very cruel. Giving a patient his choice when he is facing death is the ultimate gift to someone who has any kind of independence.

~ *Marcia Kreisl, GI nurse*

* * *

Discussion on terminally ill children dying at home versus hospital, and the dying process

The time of death can be a very beautiful and peaceful time for families or it can just be sorrowful and frightening. At the very least it is awkward and difficult, but the aftermath can be even worse when families have to go home and face life again without their children. For a terminally ill child, family and medical staff know death is coming and have, hopefully, helped prepare the child. But sometimes they really don't know what to do. Some families have friends or relatives who can help them stay focused and that makes my job a lot easier. If the families are people with faith, then praying or reading from the Bible or various spiritual books can be very comforting and helpful. I also encourage parents to talk to their children about happy times, tell them how much you love them, maybe talk to them about the good things you think happen after death. These things are important even when we've withdrawn life support and there is a very limited amount of time before the child dies. You want the child to be sent away not with grief, but with blessings and love. It's also important for the parents to know that they've had happy times with their child and gave that child as good a life as they had the power to give. This does not take away any of the pain of losing a child, but it is something that parents have to hang on to, to be able to say when my child died (s)he was surrounded by positive feelings and lots of love. We weren't out of control with grief and not knowing what to do. That makes all the difference in the world.

Watching a child die is especially hard because it is so foreign and unnatural. Children should live! But if you can help a family get through the experience, after their acute grief is gone, they can have that last happy memory of love and well-wishing for the child they lost.

~ *Dr. Joan Fisher, pediatrician*

* * *

Different families deal with death differently. But I believe the way Marian dealt with Derek's death was right in that it respected Derek's intelligence. Every parent needs to develop a relationship of trust and of loyalty with their child so he or she knows you are there when they are sick and that they are never going to go through any challenges alone. They know that you will be there for them, representing them. I know Derek felt that.

~ Mary Fitzgerald, pediatric nurse

* * *

How does the medical community meet the emotional and moral needs of children and families as well as its own?

With a dying child in the hospital, the staff work as a team. We can go to the chaplain, we have each other to talk to, and some of us have our own family to go home to and say, "I have had a bad day," and get a big hug. (We never give personal information about our patients or their families.) From my viewpoint, I have always found that support to be enough.

If the child has become a very close part of the hospital environment we sometimes have a service for the child. I remember where balloons were released for a child and there were get-togethers where everybody reminisced something special that they remembered about the child and this provided some closure for the hospital staff. In other cases, staff got together among themselves, the primary nurses, and shared their experiences and memories.

~ Chris Almgren, pediatric nurse

* * *

When we lose children at the hospital, the nursing staff frequently feels a stronger attachment to the parents of the child than to fellow nursing staff. We feel that we're going through the process with the family. When a child dies at home, sometimes it can be a very big shock to those of us who have cared for the child in the hospital. You have built a close relationship with the family because you've taken care of them and their child for long time. Then all of a sudden the end comes and then you are denied being able to say goodbye. Still, if it were my child, I would like him to die at home where I am in familiar surroundings. Also, sometimes at the hospital people are in a hurry and get caught up in procedures that need to be done, and you might have different staff that come in and do not really know the children. At home, everyone knows and cares for the child.

When we have a child die whom we have known for a long time, whether he has had frequent admissions or he has been in for a long time with one admission, we definitely get help and support. If we have a trauma come to the emergency room and a child dies all of a sudden, the policemen, firemen, and everyone who has tried to save that child has support set up by the community to talk through the death and to be with people who also are in the same circumstances.

~ *Mary Fitzgerald, pediatric nurse*

* * *

Support around death, particularly the death of a child, is a real deficit, both for residents and staff physicians, and for nurses. This is something I am trying to improve. I've set up a committee to oversee individual situations. I have a psychiatrist who comes in once a week to meet with the staff, not on a one-to-one basis but as a group, to discuss issues such as how to deal with angry parents, how to deal with a child dying, and how to go on and work for the rest of the day. I don't think we do a good job of supporting each other or even dealing with our own emotions at times. I am hoping the staff will be well cared for regarding issues that have been covered in this book and when taking care of kids whose parents are difficult, who are dying, or who have extensive problems we can find no answers for. We need to help the staff to do the best job they can do, both for the kids and parents, without sacrificing their own emotional well being.

~ *Dr. Joan Fisher, pediatrician*

Discussion on memorial services

I always want to go to the memorial service for a child that I have taken care of and have learned to love through the years. I go because it is a support for the family to know that others love the child as much as they do. It is also respect for the family when you go as you are kind of "amening" their care and their decision making. It's closure for myself also. When I see a loving family and a loving community, even because of the death of a child, it's spiritually uplifting.

~ Mary Fitzgerald, pediatric nurse

Do you feel Derek lived a full life?

I measure a full life by how much we fill the cup we are given. Derek didn't get a very large cup, but Marian helped him fill it to the brim. She respected his intelligence and capabilities through sign language, exposing him to as much as he could handle, and through her love. In doing that, she filled her own cup as well. Lives can't be measured by degrees we hold or races we run. A full life is one that has included being the best we can be and being kind and supportive to others. Marian was there for Derek all the time. Many children have more capabilities than Derek did, but might not live as full a life. In some very important ways, Derek was a very lucky boy.

~ Mary Fitzgerald, pediatric nurse

Last memories

Derek was a very lucky and special child to have been adopted by Marian, who never stopped advocating for his needs and providing him support, and cuddling, and caring, and rough and tumble fun, and silliness, and...overall...everything that he needed. When he became very, very ill he knew he had support, someone to reach out for and a solid basis to help him get through all the scary things that he must have been feeling. He was a very wonderful and special child with a wonderful and special mother.

~ Chris Almgren, pediatric nurse

Marian's Sons

Over the ensuing years, a lot more boys joined Marian's family:

Name	Year	Age	Disability
Rossie	1977	13 yrs	Deaf
Derek	1979	6 mos	Cerebral Palsy, mixed quad-riplegia, deaf
John	1980	13 yrs	Deaf
Rusty	1982	3 yrs	Cerebral Palsy, triplegia, mixed seizure disorder
Ben	1983	3 yrs	Cerebral Palsy, quadriple-gia, non-speaking
Sean	1985	5 yrs	Cerebral Palsy, spastic triplegia, non-speaking
In August 1985 she became step-mom to the next six boys. She had known Jay, Tom and David since 1979, and met the others as they joined Jim before 1985.			
Jay	1985	22 yrs	Dwarf
Tom	1985	16 yrs	Cerebral Palsy, spastic triplegia
David	1985	16 yrs	Cerebral Palsy, spastic quadriplegia
Donald	1985	9 yrs	Cerebral Palsy, athetoid quadriplegia, low vision
Alan	1985	9 yrs	Cerebral Palsy, spastic quadriplegia, non-speaking
Tim	1985	6 yrs	Congenital quad-amputee
These guys filled out the family:			
Alberto	1986	16 yrs	Scoliosis of the Spine
Ilan	1987	1 mo.	Rubenstein-Taybi Syn-drome
Raymond	1989	9 yrs	Cerebral palsy secondary to near drowning, non-speaking
Kyle	1991	9 mos	Arthrogryposis, severe

Name	Year	Age	Disability
José	1991	7 yrs	Cerebral Palsy, spastic triplegia, non-speaking
Coco	1991	10 yrs	Cerebral Palsy, spastic quadriplegia, non-speaking
Chris	1992	11 mos	Congenital quad-amputee
Sergei	1992	5 yrs	Proximal femoral focal deficiency
Victor	1992	5 yrs	Cerebral Palsy, spastic biplegia
Kolya	1992	20 mos	Congenital Upper Limb Amputee, Autism
Dustin	1992	8 yrs	Cerebral Palsy quadriplegia, secondary to strangulation
Greg	1993	3 yrs	Holt-Oram Syndrome
Paul	1995	9 yrs	Bilateral deformed arms and club hands
Peter	1996	9 yrs	Dwarf
Vitya	1996	7 yrs	Deaf

In addition to the above listed disabilities and with respect to privacy, several have secondary challenges which can include one or more of the following: learning disabilities, emotional problems, fetal alcohol syndrome, exposure to drugs as a fetus, seizure disorders, visual impairment, and mild, moderate or profound mental challenges.

To learn more about Marian's sons, please visit her website: www.MarianAiken.com.